Rethinking Tourism and Development

RETHINKING TOURISM

This series offers a forum for innovative scholarly writing that reflects the new and previously unforeseen challenges, competing interests and changing experiences that tourism faces. It showcases authored books that address key themes from a new angle, expose the weaknesses of existing concepts and arguments, or 're-frame' the topic in an innovative way. This might be through the introduction of radical ideas, through the integration of perspectives from other fields or disciplines, through challenging existing paradigms, or simply through a level of analysis that elevates or sharpens our understanding of the subject.

For a full list of Edward Elgar published titles, including the titles in this series, visit our website at www.e-elgar.com.

Rethinking Tourism and Development

Richard Sharpley

Emeritus Professor of Tourism, School of Business, University of Central Lancashire, UK

David J. Telfer

Professor, Department of Geography and Tourism Studies, Brock University, Canada

RETHINKING TOURISM

 Edward Elgar PUBLISHING

Cheltenham, UK • Northampton, MA, USA

Published by
Edward Elgar Publishing Limited
The Lypiatts
15 Lansdown Road
Cheltenham
Glos GL50 2JA
UK

Edward Elgar Publishing, Inc.
William Pratt House
9 Dewey Court
Northampton
Massachusetts 01060
USA

A catalogue record for this book
is available from the British Library

Library of Congress Control Number: 2023941378

This book is available electronically in the **Elgar**online
Geography, Planning and Tourism subject collection
http://dx.doi.org/10.4337/9781802205978

Printed on elemental chlorine free (ECF)
recycled paper containing 30% Post-Consumer Waste

ISBN 978 1 80220 596 1 (cased)
ISBN 978 1 80220 597 8 (eBook)

Printed and bound in the USA

To Rosie, Olivia, Sakura and Kyoko.

Contents

Tables

Acknowledgements

The authors would like to thank Stephanie Hartley and colleagues at Edward Elgar Publishing for all their assistance.

David J. Telfer would like to thank Atsuko Hashimoto for all her support during the writing of this book. Richard Sharpley would like to thank Sarah for being there and for the innumerable cups of coffee.

1. Introduction: the need to rethink tourism and development

That we live in a world increasingly dominated by consumerism – or at least in a world in which some but not all are fortunate enough to live consumerist lifestyles – is generally undisputed. Influenced by a pervasive consumer culture (Arnould & Thompson, 2018), those with sufficient time and financial resources seek meaning in their lives through consumption. More simply stated, we buy and accumulate stuff beyond what we need to fulfil our basic requirements. We buy not only material goods but also experiences of one form or another including, of course, travel and tourism, in the belief that it will make us feel happier and more fulfilled or that it will say something (in the eyes of others) about who we are. In short, in a consumerist world, we are what we consume.

Equally, it has long been recognised that such consumerism is, from an environmental resource perspective, untenable. More than 30 years ago, one report highlighted that 'More affluent groups and countries live unsustainably because of ignorance, lack of concern, or incentives to wasteful consumption' (IUCN/UNEP/WWF, [1991] 2009: 52) and consequently called for the adoption of new attitudes and practices including more sustainable (explicitly, lower) levels of consumption. Since then, however, and in significant contrast to the declining – and in many countries zero or negative – rates of population growth, global consumption has grown enormously and is forecast to continue doing so. For example, it has been claimed that the size of the global middle-class (a proxy for the consumer society) will increase from about 3.5 billion people in 2017 to around 5.3 billion by 2030 and that, commensurately, middle-class spending will increase from around US$37 trillion to US$64 trillion over the same period (European Commission, n.d.). Whether such dramatic growth in consumption (and the necessary increase in the production of goods and services to feed it) will occur remains to be seen, but even current levels of consumption are environmentally unsustainable. As MacKinnon (2021: 6) observes, 'we are using up the planet at a rate 1.7 times faster than it can regenerate'.

There is, then, a pressing need to reduce our exploitation and destruction of the Earth's natural resources. We are, as David Attenborough (2020: 7) powerfully argues, living 'our comfortable lives in the shadow of a disaster

1

of our own making. That disaster is being brought about by the very things that allow us to live our comfortable lives'. And to avoid that disaster we must, he proposes, not only learn to live in balance with the natural world but also allow it, through a process of rewilding, to regenerate and to regain its vitality and diversity. A similar point is made in the UNDP's 2020 Human Development Report which suggests we have entered a new geological epoch: the Anthropocene or the age of humans. 'We are the first people to live in an age defined by human choice, in which the dominant risk to our survival is ourselves' (UNDP, 2020: iii). Therefore, in order to ensure our survival, we must 'do away with the stark distinction between people and planet' (UNDP, 2020: 8). In other words, we must do away with the dualism between nature and humanity that, since it became entrenched in European culture in the seventeenth century, has relegated the natural world to a resource to be exploited for the benefit of people or, more accurately, for capitalistic profit (Hall, 2022; Hickel, 2020).

Such arguments are not, of course, uncommon and nor are they particularly new; in a paper published in *Science* some three decades ago, it was observed that, generally, 'resource problems are not really environmental problems: they are human problems' (Ludwig, Hilborn & Walters, 1993: 36). For instance, climate change, undoubtedly the most pressing existential threat facing humanity, is the outcome of anthropogenic activity (primarily the excessive use of fossil fuels but exacerbated by the destruction of natural carbon 'sinks', such as the rainforests). Moreover, although proposed solutions vary from radical demands for an immediate ban on fossil fuel use to a more gradual transition to so-called net zero carbon emissions, a reduction in the rate of global warming is entirely dependent on appropriate human actions. Similarly, the excessive demands being placed on the Earth's resources more generally can only be alleviated by a transformation in human behaviour – by reducing our levels of consumption.

Importantly, however, although the environmental consequences of excessive consumption are experienced globally, excessive consumption itself is not a global phenomenon – hence the frequent calls from less developed countries, for example, for the wealthier industrialised nations to subsidise the costs of addressing climate change. In other words, per capita levels of consumption, or how much each person consumes, must be taken into account when considering the causes of and potential solutions to the global environmental crisis. According to MacKinnon (2021: 6), 'The average person in a rich country consumes thirteen times as much as the average person in a poor one', pointing to not only those societies that impose the greatest demands on the natural environment but also where the responsibility arguably lies for reducing those demands.

In his book *The Day the World Stops Shopping*, which he describes as a 'thought experiment' that explores what would happen socially, economically and environmentally if people reduced their consumption – in a sense, cutting back on the size of their shopping basket of stuff – by 25 percent, MacKinnon (2021) goes on to suggest that the aim should be for all countries to move towards the adoption of what he refers to as a one-planet lifestyle. To explain this idea, he describes the work of the Global Footprint Network (GFN), a non-profit organisation based in the US that, over the last two decades, has been calculating the ecological footprint of more than 200 countries (and their individual citizens / communities) around the world (see www.footprintnetwork.org). The concept of the ecological footprint originates from a PhD thesis undertaken by Mathis Wackernagel at the University of British Columbia in the 1990s which developed a means of calculating the amount of natural capital required to support a particular individual, community or country's lifestyle. More precisely, 'it measures the ecological assets that a given population or product requires to produce the natural resources it consumes … and to absorb its waste, especially carbon emissions' (GFN, 2021a). If the demand for those ecological assets exceeds the area's biocapacity (the productivity of its ecological assets), then a given population is running a biocapacity deficit. On the global scale, the GFN expresses that deficit as Earth Overshoot Day, the day when humanity will have used up 'nature's resource budget' for the whole of a particular year. In 2019, that day fell on 29 July; reflecting the impact of the coronavirus pandemic, in 2020 Overshoot Day fell three weeks later on 22 August (GFN, 2021b). In 2021, it returned to 29 July (see www.overshootday.org).

The GFN also produces data that reveal the national environmental resource cost of consumption measured in terms of 'Earths', or how many Earths would be required if the world's population as a whole enjoyed lifestyles similar to the average citizen of a particular country (hence the one-planet lifestyle objective). Perhaps unsurprisingly, top of the list is the US with a five-planet lifestyle; second is Australia at 4.6 whilst the average citizen in the UK lives a 2.6 planet lifestyle. Also unsurprisingly, the figure for many (though not all) less developed countries is less than one Earth whilst, for example, the average Indonesian enjoys a one-planet lifestyle. Interestingly, the rankings differ when a particular country's environmental footprint is measured against its own natural resource supply. Japan, for example, requires 7.8 Japans to meet its citizens' demands on nature whereas reflecting its greater resource availability relative to demand, the US requires just 2.3 USs; Bermuda tops the list with a remarkable 57.1 (EOD, 2021).

The most evident implication of the ecological footprint research is that it confirms what is widely acknowledged, that consumption on a global scale is exceeding the Earth's natural resource capacity. More simply stated, we are living not with the Earth but off it. This is perhaps most starkly revealed by the extent and impacts of global warming. According to the International Panel on Climate Change (IPCC), the crucial 1.5°C warming limit will be reached by the early 2030s (IPCC, 2021) but already human-induced climate change is having an indisputable effect on global weather patterns, with many countries experiencing more frequent and damaging extreme weather events. Moreover, a recent report by the IPCC reveals that not only are the impacts of climate change occurring more quickly and intensely than expected, but these will be irreversible if the 1.5°C limit is even just temporarily exceeded, a scenario that is becoming increasingly likely (IPCC, 2022a).

What is also evident, however, is that although all countries in the developed world and many in the developing world exceed the one-planet lifestyle threshold, not only do many others fall well below that threshold but also the responsibility for excessive consumption and resource use (and, implicitly for creating and implementing policies to address the environmental crisis) lies of course primarily with wealthier countries. This in turn points to a second global challenge, though one from which attention has to a great extent been diverted by the dominant climate change rhetoric: inequality.

More than seven decades ago, towards the end of his 1949 Inaugural Address following his re-election as president of the US, Harry Truman proclaimed that more than half the world's population lived 'in conditions approaching misery' (see Hickel, 2017: 8). He went on to argue that the US should take the lead in employing its considerable financial and technical resources to help improve the conditions for those living in what he referred to collectively as 'undeveloped areas'. In so doing, he introduced 'development' as a global project to be led by Western institutions and ideology in the emerging post-colonial world (Rist, 2014). In short, Truman drew attention to global inequality, to the 'divide' (Hickel, 2017) between the then wealthier industrialised nations and those in the rest of the world – many on the cusp of achieving independence from Western colonisers – and the role that the US and other Western countries could or, indeed, should play in facilitating the development of those nations, thereby reducing global inequality.

Since then, the development narrative has become pervasive; as Hickel (2017: 11) puts it, 'development is everywhere'. From the activities of international organisations such as the United Nations Development Programme (UNDP), the development aid and investments provided by the World Bank and other national and international financial institutions and the extensive work undertaken by innumerable NGOs and charities (many staffed by development professionals) to the contribution of individuals who, for example, sponsor a child in a developing country or participate in so-called volunteer tourism (McGehee, 2014), development is a process that many people in the Western world contribute to in one way or another. Yet, despite the billions of dollars invested in development, despite the efforts and contributions of all those either working formally in the development sector or participating individually in other ways, and despite national and international policies such as the UN's ambitious Sustainable Development Goals (SDGs), alarmingly little progress has been made towards reducing inequality. Indeed, it could be argued that President Truman's observation that half the world's population was living in a condition of misery continues to hold true today. In other words, from an equality perspective at least, the development agenda has failed.

To some, this might seem to be a baseless, erroneous claim. After all, between 1960 and 2019 the size of the global economy (world GDP) grew from US$13.5 trillion to US$87.6 trillion, a six- to seven-fold increase, whereas over the same period global average per capita income grew from US$445 to US$11,417 – a more than 25-fold increase (macrotrends, 2021a, b). At face value, such headline figures suggest that not only has the world as a whole become richer but also, at the individual level, people have on average also become significantly richer, implying that the number living in 'misery' has inevitably declined. Indeed, proof would seem to lie in the official narrative that the Millennium Development Goals (MDGs), the 15-year global development campaign superseded in 2015 by the SDGs, met the target of halving the rate of extreme poverty five years ahead of schedule and almost met the target of reducing by half the proportion of undernourished people in developing countries (UN, 2015) – although not only were most of the MDGs not achieved but also in some instances (notably related to the environment) the situation actually worsened (Ritchie & Roser, 2018).

Yet, although the world has become richer both overall and at the average individual level, global wealth inequality has significantly increased. The richest one percent of the world's population (those with more than US$1 million) own 43.4 percent of the world's wealth whilst the 53.6 percent of the world's population with less than US$10,000 collectively hold just 1.4 percent of global wealth (Inequality, 2021). This is more starkly expressed by Oxfam (2021); the world's richest one percent enjoys more than twice the wealth than the total wealth of 6.9 billion people. A similar story emerges when looking at global poverty levels. Hickel (2017: 37–43) explains how MDG data are massaged (what he refers to as the 'great poverty disappearing act') to convey a good news story; from focusing on the proportion as opposed to the absolute number of those living in poverty (with rising populations in many less developed nations, even though the proportion of poor people fell the absolute number increased) to backdating the starting point to 1990, allowing the significant success achieved by China in particular in reducing its levels of poverty during the 1990s (that is, before the official start of the MDG campaign) to be taken into account, it was possible to claim that global poverty had been halved. In reality, today the 'extreme poverty headcount is exactly the same as it was in 1981, at just over 1 billion people' (Hickel, 2017: 43); take China and some south-east Asian countries out of the equation, and poverty has in fact increased in many countries.

It should also be noted that the target of the MDGs was the developing world; the significant incidence of poverty in developed countries was ignored, even though it is widely acknowledged that, despite increases in average per capita GDP, income inequality and relative poverty continues to grow in the developed world (Jackson, 2016; Wilkinson & Pickett, 2010). Moreover, the yardstick for measuring poverty is highly questionable. The current income threshold of extreme poverty is just US\$1.90 a day 'based on the average of the national poverty lines of 15 of the poorest countries' (World Bank, 2021). This threshold is, however, unrealistically low. In many less developed countries, it would not provide for basic nutrition whilst in richer countries where poverty remains a significant challenge – according to the 2020 census in the US, 37.2 million people, or 11.4 percent of the population, were living in poverty (US Census, 2020) – it is simply an unimaginably low level of income. For this reason, an 'ethical' poverty line of US\$5 a day is considered by many to be a more realistic threshold (Hickel, 2017: 50); by that measure, about half the world's population continue to live in poverty.

A similar story emerges when looking at the incidence of hunger around the world. According to Hickel (2017), a significant discrepancy exists between official figures and reality. It is estimated that, based on a minimum intake of up to 1,800 calories a day to support a sedentary lifestyle, between 720 and 811 million people are hungry (FAO et al., 2022). However, when a variety of factors are taken into account, such as broader nutritional measures and people's actual food needs to support required activities, the figure might be two to three times higher. Importantly, though, the problem is one of distribution. The world as a whole produces more than enough food to feed everyone but each year about one third of all food produced globally for human consumption is, for a number of reasons, lost or wasted (with a commensurate waste of resources, particularly water, in producing this food). Reducing this waste by just 25 percent would feed 870 million people (UNEP, n.d.). And as a powerful example of inequality, in contrast to the number globally suffering from hunger, 1.9 billion adults were overweight and 650 million were obese in 2016 (WHO, 2022).

It is not, of course, only poverty and hunger that are pressing developmental issues; a lack of access to health facilities, education and decent work, racial and gender discrimination and the denial of human rights all contribute to the inequality that remains pervasive around the world. Quite rightly, these are highlighted in the SDGs which, as observed above, represent the 'official' response to the twin challenges of inequality and the global environmental crisis. A set of 17 goals embracing 169 developmental and sustainability targets, the SDGs have been widely and enthusiastically adopted, not least by the UN World Tourism Organization which claims that 'tourism has the potential to contribute, directly or indirectly, to all of the goals' (UNWTO, n.d., a.). Others are more circumspect of the potential contribution of tourism to the SDGs (for example, Bianchi & de Man, 2021) whilst a fundamental criticism of the SDGs as a whole is their explicit foundation on neoliberal economic growth-based policies (Adelman, 2017). As Sharpley (2020: 1939) notes, not only is economic growth seen as the principal mechanism for addressing poverty but also, 'Goal 8 ("decent work and economic growth") proposes annual economic growth of at least seven percent per annum in the least developed countries and sustained economic growth elsewhere, contradicting ambitious environmental objectives established elsewhere in the SDGs'. As such, the SDGs lie towards the right-hand pole of what might be described as an environment–development policy continuum (see Figure 1.1); that is, similar to the foundations of preceding sustainable development policies including both the well-known Brundtland Report (WCED, 1987) and the MDGs, economic growth is seen as essential to the achievement of both development and sustainability objectives. The dominant economic growth policies on the right of Figure 1.1 are further discussed in Chapter 3 and are firmly based in neoliberal economics, globalisation, capitalism and the market with success measured by increases in GDP.

Figure 1.1   *Environment–development policy continuum*

For others, sustainable development has long been considered an oxymoron (Redclift, 1987); how is it possible, they ask, to seek resource-hungry growth-based development at the same time as sustaining (that is, avoiding further depletion of) the world's natural resources? Their answer: it is not. For them, environmental sustainability or, as David Attenborough would put it, living in balance with the natural world, is dependent on the implementation of degrowth policies. Overall, these propose an absolute reduction in global production and consumption requiring not only the adoption of post-growth lifestyles (Jackson, 2021) but a fundamental restructuring of the global political economy (Liegey & Nelson, 2020).

For yet others, the solution to balancing development with sustainability lies somewhere between these two extremes on the environment–development policy continuum. For example, the contemporary and politically popular objective of net zero production – essentially relying on technological advances to 'de-couple' production from resource exploitation – falls under the banner of so-called green growth which, proponents argue, would permit continuing (allegedly sustainable) economic growth in the pursuit of development. Inevitably, however, this technocentric position is criticised. Not only does it maintain the untenable dualism between humanity and nature but, more specifically, the reliance on yet to be developed technologies is considered wishful thinking (Dyke, Watson & Knorr, 2021). Hence, the concept of the steady-state economy (stable levels of population, per capita consumption and resource use – see CASSE, 2021), first proposed by Daly (1972), might also be located towards the degrowth pole on the continuum. Whichever policy is favoured, however, the inescapable fact is that, from a development perspective, global inequality must be addressed but, at the same time, so too must the global environmental crisis.

But, what has all this got to do with tourism, the focus of this book? The answer is quite straightforward. Since the 1950s, tourism has evolved into a widespread and popular form of consumption, undoubtedly viewed by many as an essential component of contemporary life. The figures are well known and widely cited. Following exponential growth over seven decades, by 2019 around 1.5 billion international arrivals were recorded; had the Covid-19 pandemic not intervened, the UN World Tourism Organization's (UNWTO) long-standing forecast of 1.6 billion arrivals by 2020 would have almost certainly been realised. To this must be added domestic tourism – accurate data do not exist though it is generally suggested that, annually, the total number of domestic tourism trips worldwide is some six times greater than that of international tourism. Translating this mass annual movement of people into its economic value reveals it to be a significant contributor to the global economy; according to the World Travel and Tourism Council, the direct, indirect and induced economic impact of travel and tourism in 2019 amounted to a staggering US$9.2 trillion or 10.4 percent of global GDP, supporting 10.6 percent of global employment or 334 million jobs (WTTC, 2021a). And it is for this reason that tourism has long been viewed as an effective means of contributing to the development of destination countries (Sharpley & Telfer, 2015).

However, such development is not without cost. A variety of environmental, social and economic costs are associated with tourism to the extent that there exists a 'tourism-development dilemma' (Telfer & Sharpley, 2016). That is, it has been long acknowledged that the potential developmental benefits of tourism must be balanced against its negative consequences. Nevertheless, despite a plethora of policies and initiatives, most notably the idea of sustainable tourism development, that balance has proved increasingly difficult to achieve in recent years. In particular, much publicity has surrounded the increasing occurrence of the emotively termed phenomenon of 'overtourism' (see Milano, Cheer & Novelli, 2019), although this is nothing new, a prime example being Venice which has suffered from excessive numbers of tourists for decades. Moreover, it is also a symptom of a wider problem. Specifically, prior to the pandemic-induced collapse of tourism in 2020, the UNWTO was celebrating the fact that not only were international arrivals continuing to increase, but also that the rate of growth in international tourism (5 percent in 2018) was outstripping that of the global economy as a whole (UNWTO, 2019), in so doing making an increasingly important contribution to global GDP. Yet, this not only implies that the tourism sector's demands and impacts on the world's resources have been growing relatively faster than those of the economy as a whole – for example, one report suggests that tourism now contributes around 8 percent of global carbon emissions (Lenzen et al., 2018) (though it must be acknowledged that pandemic-induced restrictions on travel revealed the potentially significant environmental benefits of reduced levels of tourism). It also means that tourism is becoming ever more responsible for the unsustainable levels of consumption referred to earlier. Hence, tourism in particular cannot be immune from, but must be included in, the reduction in global production and consumption in general necessary to address the environmental crisis. In other words, whilst solutions that tinker with tourism at the destination level might encourage greater local sustainability, its global contribution to climate change and resource exploitation can no longer be ignored. Despite its role in economic growth and development, there is nothing special about tourism to suggest it should be treated differently to any other form of consumption.

The inherent inequitable nature of tourism adds further weight to this argument. Tourism is promoted primarily for its contribution to development, the overall objective of which, as discussed above, must be a reduction in all forms of inequality. It is ironic, then, that tourism essentially exacerbates inequality. For instance, international tourism in particular remains, on the global scale, the preserve of the privileged few; not only is access to tourist experiences limited to the relatively wealthy but also, as with their consumption habits more generally, they make an enormously disproportionate contribution to carbon emissions and resource depletion. For instance, just one percent of the world's population (frequent flyers) account for 50 percent of aircraft emissions (Gössling & Humpe, 2020). At the same time, although the patterns of international tourism are changing with travel within the Asia Pacific region in particular on the increase, it is the wealthier regions of the world (notably Europe) that continue to benefit most from tourism – more simply stated, those regions that least need tourism as an agent of development in fact benefit from it most. And there also remains much truth in the argument that, within destinations, the benefits of tourism are not spread equitably and that its wider developmental contribution remains questionable.

As this book sets out to do, therefore, there is a need to rethink the relationship between tourism and development. In particular, there is a need to abandon the primarily tourism-centric perspective that has dominated much of the tourism-development literature; tourism must be considered not separate from but as part of the global system of production and consumption, a system that, as this introduction has suggested, is making unsustainable demands on the global ecosystem. If, as many now argue, there is a need to reduce our exploitation of the Earth's natural resources or, more precisely, to reduce how much we produce and consume on the global scale, there is absolutely no justification for excluding tourism from that process. In fact, given that tourism, particularly international tourism, is for the most part a form of lifestyle consumption enjoyed by a privileged minority of people who, both individually and collectively, make an excessively disproportionate contribution to carbon emissions, it could be argued that the consumption of tourism should be reduced more than that of other more essential products and services.

At the same time, however, tourism remains a vital and powerful catalyst of economic growth and development. Most if not all countries benefit from a tourism sector; in many, tourism is an integral element of the national economy whilst some countries, notably island states, are highly dependent upon tourism. Yet, not only is that developmental role of tourism driven primarily by (unsustainable) growth policies but also the extent to which tourism contributes to development in general, and to greater equality in particular, is the subject of intense debate. Therefore, reducing tourism's contribution to climate change and resource exploitation must necessarily be balanced with maintaining its role as an agent of development; that role, however, must be guided not by the objective of economic growth but by the principle of equality both within and between societies and countries.

In rethinking tourism and development, then, this book adopts a position on the environment–development continuum that lies towards the 'degrowth policy' pole. This is not to say that the concept of degrowth has been unquestionably adopted as the framework of the book; far from it. As discussed in Chapters 3 and 7, degrowth remains a highly contested and, for many, unpalatable concept whilst for others, it is simply an unrealistic, impractical objective. Nevertheless, degrowth is not only about what the term implies: degrowing, or reducing, overall levels of consumption to address the environmental crisis. It also offers an alternative vision of development, of what constitutes human well-being in a post-growth world (Jackson, 2021) in which economic growth (measured by GDP) is rejected as both the means and objective of development. As such, the idea of degrowth points to ways in which the future trajectory of tourism might be reimagined, on the one hand addressing the urgent need to reverse the incessant growth trend in tourism whilst appropriately maintaining its contribution to development and enhancing global equality and, on the other hand, exploring ways in which the consumption of tourism might be realigned to post-growth lifestyles. It should also be emphasised that it is not the intention of this book to be prescriptive. Rather, it seeks to stimulate debates about how tourism can be enjoyed and better contribute to development within the broader context of transforming – or more precisely, rebalancing – humanity's relationship with the natural world upon which it depends.

2.   Transformations in tourism and development

INTRODUCTION

In 2019, international tourist arrivals totalled 1.46 billion (UNWTO, 2021). This is not to say, of course, that almost one and a half billion people travelled internationally that year; although precise figures do not exist, it is acknowledged that many people make multiple international trips both for pleasure and business. For instance, the average UK resident took 1.9 overseas holidays in 2019 (Statista, 2022a) whilst earlier research in 2014 revealed that the 15 percent of the UK population who were frequent flyers (three or more flights a year) accounted for more than 70 percent of all flights within and out of the country (DoT, 2014). Hence, the actual number of individuals participating in international tourism each year is much lower than the overall arrivals figure – perhaps around half of the total – indicating that only a privileged minority of the world's population, probably around 10 percent, travel internationally. As noted in the introduction to this book, this inequity in international tourism is of particular significance and is returned to in later chapters, whilst it must also be recognised that an undoubtedly much greater proportion of the global population engage in domestic tourism.

Nevertheless, the point here is that since the early 1950s when relevant data were first published on a regular basis, international tourism has grown consistently in scope, scale and value. Indeed, as can be seen from Table 2.1, prior to 2020 when, as a consequence of restrictions on mobility in response to the Covid-19 pandemic, the global travel and tourism sector was obliged to almost completely close down, a decline in annual international arrivals had been experienced on only three occasions: 2001 (after '9/11'); 2003 (the Iraq War and the SARS outbreak); and 2009 (the global financial crisis). Despite these and other external 'shocks', international tourism has demonstrated remarkable resilience; not only have international arrivals increased at an

Table 2.1   International tourist arrivals and receipts, 1950–2020

Year	Arrivals (million)	Receipts (US$bn)	Year	Arrivals (million)	Receipts (US$bn)
1950	25.3	2.1	2002	707.0	488.2
1960	69.3	6.9	2003	694.6	534.6
1965	112.9	11.6	2004	765.1	634.7
1970	165.8	17.9	2005	806.1	682.7
1975	222.3	40.7	2006	847.0	742.0
1980	278.1	104.4	2007	903.0	856.0
1985	320.1	119.1	2008	917.0	939.0
1990	439.5	270.2	2009	882.0	851.0
1991	442.5	283.4	2010	940.0	927.0
1992	479.8	326.6	2011	995.0	1,042.0
1993	495.7	332.6	2012	1,035.0	1,075.0
1994	519.8	362.1	2013	1,087.0	1,159.0
1995	540.6	410.7	2014	1,130.0	1,252.0
1996	575.0	446.0	2015	1,184.0	1,196.0
1997	598.6	450.4	2016	1,235.0	1,220.0
1998	616.7	451.4	2017	1,329.0	1,346.0
1999	639.6	465.5	2018	1,408.0	1,460.0
2000	687.0	481.6	2019	1,460.0	1,481.0
2001	686.7	469.9	2020	409.5	536.0

Source: Adapted from UNWTO data.

average annual rate of almost 5 percent over the last decade alone, but the 2019 total exceeded a long-standing forecast:

> At the projected pace of growth, international tourist arrivals worldwide are to surpass 1 billion by 2012, up from the 940 million of 2010. By 2020 the number is expected to reach close to 1.4 billion. The 1.5 billion mark will be in sight by 2023 and 1.8 billion by 2030. (UNWTO, 2011: 15)

Whether the predicted continuing growth towards 2030 will materialise (or, in the context of this book, is desirable) remains to be seen. However, as impressive as the arrivals figures are, it is the translation of these into the economic contribution of tourism that is more significant.

International tourism receipts (direct tourist expenditure) alone amounted to more than US$1.4 trillion in 2019. If global domestic tourism spending is added to this along with indirect (capital investments, government expenditure and supply chain effects) and induced (spending by those directly or indirectly employed in tourism) contributions then, according to the World Travel and Tourism Council (WTTC, 2020), the global travel and tourism economy in 2019 was worth a remarkable US$8.9 trillion – often alternatively interpreted as tourism contributing over 10 percent of global GDP.

Perhaps equally remarkable is that it is actually possible to collate and analyse these data on a global basis to arrive at this total – though cynics might question the accuracy and scale of the figures, not least because the objective of the WTTC is to promote the travel and tourism sector which it represents worldwide. Nevertheless, there can be no doubting the overall value and economic contribution of the global tourism sector, a contribution that was cruelly exposed during the Covid-19 pandemic. In addition to the 74 percent drop in international arrivals and the commensurate loss of US$1.3 billion in international receipts and US$2.4 trillion overall in 2020 (UNWTO, n.d., b), some 62 million jobs in tourism were also lost that year. However, international arrivals recovered slightly in 2021 (a 4 percent increase on 2020) and more significant growth was recorded in early 2022, suggesting that, as travel restrictions continue to be eased, tourism will in all likelihood rebound and, over time, regain its position in the global economy.

It is because of its economic contribution that tourism is so widely promoted and developed. In more basic terms, tourism destinations do not seek to attract ever-increasing numbers of tourists just to be hospitable; indeed (and as the residents of some destinations realised during the Covid-19 pandemic), life without tourists is in many respects much more preferable. Rather, tourists are generally welcomed simply for the money in their pockets; their spending provides income to businesses, supports jobs, encourages the growth and diversification of the local economy, contributes to government revenues, attracts wider investment in the tourism sector and so on. In other words, tourism is primarily utilised as a catalyst of development or, as Sharpley and Harrison (2019: 1) put it, development is the '*raison d'être* of tourism'.

Recognition of tourism's potential to stimulate the economic and social development of destination areas first emerged in the 1950s, not surprisingly coinciding with both the nascent years of contemporary mass international tourism and also the adoption of development as a global project (Rist, 2014). The subsequent rapid growth in international tourism during the 1960s and 1970s (the 1960s witnessed an average annual increase in international arrivals of over 9 percent), particularly in Europe, was reflected in the rapid development of resorts around the Mediterranean (Segreto, Manera & Pohl, 2009) with many countries such as Spain seeking to build their economies on the foundation of the tourism sector (Towner, Barke & Newton, 1996). It is not surprising, therefore, that by 1980, tourism's developmental role had been officially sanctioned:

> World tourism can contribute to the establishment of a new international economic order that will help eliminate the widening economic gap between developed and developing countries and ensure the steady acceleration of economic and social development and progress, in particular in developing countries. (WTO, 1980: 1)

Since then, tourism has to a lesser or greater extent become firmly embedded in the development policies of countries and regions around the world. Whilst generally seen as an effective vehicle of economic and social development (Sharpley & Telfer, 2015), in some instances where few if any alternatives exist – notably in small island developing states but also in countries with limited economies and resources – tourism has long been employed as an option of 'last resort' (Brown, 1998; Lea, 1988). Elsewhere, it has been fundamental to the regeneration of peripheral rural areas or of post-industrial cities, whilst even oil rich nations such as Saudi Arabia are seeking to diversify their economies through tourism (Abuhjeeleh, 2019). In short, over the last half century or so, tourism has 'become a ubiquitous agent of development in almost every corner of the globe' (Sharpley & Harrison, 2019: 1).

Importantly, however, the relationship between tourism and development is both dynamic and complex. Not only has tourism expanded enormously in scale over time, evolving into the major form of consumption that it is today (with concomitant demands and impacts on the world's natural resources); the nature of both the demand for and supply of tourism also continues to evolve and change in response to wider economic, social and technological transformations. Equally, the world in which tourism exists and with which it interacts is also in a state of constant flux, whilst understandings of what development is or, rather, what the objectives of development policies should be and the processes by which they might be achieved (through tourism and otherwise) have also continued to evolve. In his widely cited though now dated review, Jafari (1989) suggests that knowledge and understanding of the tourism–development relationship has progressed through four identifiable stages: (i) the initial advocacy stage (1960s), when tourism was celebrated and uncritically promoted for its perceived economic contribution; (ii) the subsequent cautionary stage (1970s–1980s), during which increasing concern was expressed with regards to the negative consequences of tourism development; (iii) the consequential adaptancy stage (1980s), manifested in the emergence of the alternative tourism movement; and finally (iv) the knowledge stage (1990s onwards), characterised by a deeper, more nuanced and multi-disciplinary understanding of tourism's role in development. This fourth stage has been notable for a dominant focus on sustainable tourism development which has framed both academic and policy thinking about tourism and development.

We would argue, however, that we have now necessarily entered a fifth stage: the rethinking tourism and development stage. Not only has there been a failure during the knowledge stage to find a solution to what Telfer and Sharpley (2016) refer to as the tourism–development dilemma (essentially, the need to balance the developmental benefits of tourism with its costs) – as argued elsewhere, there is little or no evidence of sustainable tourism development in practice (Sharpley, 2020) – but also that dilemma has become more acute. In other words, it is now widely acknowledged that there is an increasingly pressing need to address the contemporary environmental crisis to which tourism undoubtedly contributes; moreover, underpinning that crisis are the overall excessive levels of all forms of consumption, including tourism. This, in turn, suggests that although tourism fulfils a fundamental role in development, priority must now be given to reducing its impacts and demands on the environment in line with the more general need to reduce consumption at the global level. Hence, as this book sets out to do, there is a need to rethink how we 'do' (or consume) tourism whilst seeking to maintain its essential contribution to development.

As established in the introduction, challenging (and indeed reversing) the objective of continuing economic growth is fundamental to this rethinking of tourism. Putting it another way, in recent years the concept of degrowth, first mooted in the late 1970s, has attracted increasing support. More than simply requiring a reduction in production and consumption or what some see as a move towards lifestyles based on austerity, it in fact proposes a new approach to development and well-being that rejects the focus on economic growth that pervades most contemporary development policies in general, and tourism development in particular. Therefore, whilst not uncritically adopting the tenets of the degrowth thesis, this book draws on many of its ideas and principles as a basis for rethinking the tourism–development nexus.

The purpose of this chapter, then, is to set the scene for the rest of the book. More specifically, in order to justify the emphasis on degrowth or, perhaps more precisely, aligning tourism with post-growth living (Jackson, 2021), it traces the evolution of contemporary tourism in the context of development thinking and processes from the early days of arguably naïve 'advocacy' through to a critique of the worthy, ambitious but ultimately unrealistic concept of sustainable tourism development. First, however, it reviews briefly the well-known reasons why tourism has long been and continues to be viewed as an attractive and effective agent of development, for these are explicitly reflected in many contemporary tourism development policies.

DEVELOPMENT: WHY TOURISM?

As explained above, over the last seven decades tourism has increasingly been adopted as a catalyst of development. By the early 1990s, it had been recognised as 'an important and integral element of ... [the] development strategies' (Jenkins, 1991: 61) of many countries and, since then, the developmental role of tourism has become more widely and firmly established. In fact, it is probably safe to assert that tourism can to a lesser or greater extent be found in the development policies of every country in the world. Nevertheless, international tourism has been in evidence for centuries (Zuelow, 2015); for instance, the Grand Tour from the seventeenth century onwards is considered by many to have been the forerunner of contemporary tourism (Towner, 1985) whilst Thomas Cook arranged his first overseas trip in 1855. However, it was the beginning of the transformation of international tourism from the preserve of the elite into the mass social phenomenon that it is today that spurred interest in its potential to contribute to development. Initially, it was the countries of the Mediterranean that sought to exploit the benefits of early mass package tourism but, as the reach of the so-called 'pleasure periphery' of tourism spread more widely, the less developed countries began to turn to tourism to kick-start their development. Consequently, much of the earlier academic interest in the tourism–development nexus was in the context of the developing world (Harrison, 1992), interestingly (given the World Tourism Organization's claim about tourism contributing to a new international economic order) with much attention focused on the emerging unequal relations within the international tourism sector (for example, Britton, 1982). Indeed, this was seen as one of the early manifestations of the negative consequences of tourism or the 'dilemma' referred to above. Today, both international and domestic tourism's position in development policy is, as already suggested, almost universal.

The principal reason for tourism being adopted as a development strategy has always been, as observed earlier in this chapter, the perceived economic benefits it brings to destinations (Mihalič, 2015; Wall & Mathieson, 2006). There can be no denying the overall economic value of tourism; its contribution to global GDP demarcates it as one of the world's most significant 'industries' whilst international tourism in particular is recognised as one of the world's largest export sectors. However, the precise benefits sought (and the extent to which they are realised) vary from one destination to another. For example, one of the main reasons that governments might seek to promote international tourism is its potential to generate foreign exchange earnings (Baretje, 1982; Oppermann & Chon, 1997). This is particularly so in the case of less developed countries with few if any alternative export sectors, although the need to import goods to meet the needs of tourists (so-called 'leakages')

Table 2.2   Tourism employment in selected European countries (2016)

Country	Employment in tourism (%)	Country	Employment in tourism (%)
Greece	23.9	Italy	10.3
Cyprus	20.3	Netherlands	8.8
Malta	15.3	Denmark	8.6
Ireland	13.3	Sweden	8.5
Austria	12.7	Germany	8.4
Spain	12.3	Bulgaria	8.3
Croatia	12.2	Luxembourg	8.0
United Kingdom	11.6	Belgium	7.9
Portugal	11.3	France	7.3

Source: Adapted from Eurostat (2018).

may result in significantly reduced net foreign exchange earnings. Equally, international tourism contributes positively to the balance of payments of many developed nations and is of particular importance to major generators of international tourism by helping to balance their travel account – for example, in 2019, outbound tourists from the UK spent over £62 billion abroad whilst, in the same year, inbound tourist receipts amounted to about £28 million or less than half the travel deficit. In contrast, during the latter half of the 1980s, Japan sought to double the number of its citizens travelling overseas, from 5 to 10 million annually, in order address the country's then large balance of payments surplus (Sharpley & Kato, 2021).

More generally, tourism is seen as a vital source of both income and employment. Overall, more than 330 million people, or more than 10 percent of the global workforce, were employed in tourism and hospitality in 2019. In countries where tourism is the dominant economic sector, however, that proportion is often significantly greater. For example, in 2019, more than 40 percent of the workforce in the Seychelles was employed in tourism; in Jamaica the figure was 31.5 percent, whilst 36.3 percent of Fijians worked in the sector. In European countries with diverse economies, tourism also accounts for a perhaps surprisingly high proportion of employment (see Table 2.2) although the figure is higher in tourism-intensive regions within some countries. For example, tourism provides for more than 31 percent of jobs in the Spanish Balearic Islands and more than 50 percent in the English Lake District (Sharpley, 2004). Nevertheless, some caution is necessary in claiming the employment contribution of tourism; overall numbers disguise the nature of work in tourism, which is often seasonal, part-time and low grade / low paid (UNWTO, 2014).

An additional important though often less heralded economic benefit of tourism is its contribution to government revenues. Income tax paid by employees in tourism, tourism business taxes, sales taxes on goods and services purchased by tourists, import duties, tourism development fees, visa fees, departure taxes and other forms of taxation, such as the UK's Air Passenger Duty (APD) levied on people flying out of the UK (though not transfer passengers), are amongst the principal – and often significant – sources of government revenue. APD alone contributes around £1 billion (or 0.1 percent of government receipts) in the UK (OBR, 2022); in Zanzibar, the government depends on tourism for up to 80 percent of its revenues (Ussi & Sharpley, 2012). It is not surprising, therefore, that despite its acknowledged environmental and social costs, the fundamental policy objective of most destinations, encouraged in no small measure by the UN World Tourism Organization's rhetoric, is to increase tourism numbers. In simple terms, more tourists mean (in principle) more income, more jobs and more investment or, in other words, economic growth providing more government revenue to (again in principle) finance broader development activities.

Destinations also follow tourism growth policies in order to maintain if not increase their share of what had, prior to the onset of the Covid-19 pandemic, long been a growth market. As noted earlier, since the 1950s international tourism has demonstrated consistent growth, often exceeding the rate of growth of the global economy as a whole and, at the time of writing, all the indications are that, other things being equal, demand for tourism will continue its growth trajectory post-pandemic. This points to another major reason for the ubiquity of tourism in development policies; given its growth record, it is considered a safe development option. In addition, tourism is seen as an effective means of redistributing wealth from richer to poorer countries and regions, whether through direct tourist expenditure on goods and services (with spending in the informal local economy often transferring wealth directly to the poor) or through foreign / external investment. As such, tourism may address one of the most pressing global development challenges: inequality (UNDP, 2019).

A further reason that tourism is utilised as an agent of development (or more precisely, of economic growth, for 'development' is not an inevitable outcome of tourism but is dependent upon how its economic contribution translates into broader development policies) is its potential to create what are often referred to as backward linkages. Tourists inevitably demand a variety of goods and services whilst in the destination, from food and beverages and souvenirs to entertainment, transport and guiding services. The opportunity exists, therefore, for local businesses and individuals to meet these needs by, for example, supplying food to hotels and restaurants (Telfer & Wall, 2000; Torres, 2003) or producing local handicrafts. However, the extent to which such backward linkages occur depends very much on the diversity and maturity of the local economy or the volume and quality of local products; for instance, local small-scale farmers may not be able to meet the demands of hotels or restaurants which are then obliged to import the products they need – hence the leakages referred to earlier (Anderson, 2013).

There are two other characteristics that enhance the attraction of tourism as a development option. First, unlike many other sectors or products, tourism does not face any trade barriers or quotas. Typically, tourism-generating countries do not place limits on where or how many of their citizens may travel overseas, although some have done so in the past for primarily political reasons. Equally, destinations are free to welcome as many tourists as they wish, subject to the capacity of international transport networks and their ability to accommodate them. In short, destinations have free and equal access to international tourism markets and are able to exploit 'an export opportunity free of the usual trade limitations' (Jenkins, 1991: 84). Second, tourism is often considered to benefit from low start-up costs. Some of the resources that attract tourists, whether natural or built heritage, already exist and thus are, in a simplistic sense, 'free'. In reality this is not, of course, the case given that costs are incurred in the upkeep and protection of these resources, whilst significant investment might be required in infrastructure and facilities to enable tourists to travel to and enjoy them. Nevertheless, tourism is often favoured as a development option given the pre-existence of these basic resources. And finally, it should be noted that the provision of tourism facilities and infrastructure along with, for example, environmental protection and enhancement policies, may be of equal benefit to local people as to tourists, whether improved transport systems, the provision of entertainment facilities or recreational opportunities in national parks.

To summarise then, tourism's role in development is primarily founded on both its perceived economic contribution and also, as this book argues, the erroneous assumption that this contribution outweighs the well-known costs incurred in building and maintaining a tourism sector. Of course, these costs or impacts of tourism have long been acknowledged and as discussed earlier in this chapter, the relationship between tourism and development has been commensurately dynamic. More precisely, with greater knowledge and understanding of tourism and its consequences (both positive and negative), the theory and practice of tourism development appears to have evolved over time, the objective being to optimise the economic and social outcomes for destinations whilst minimising its environmental and other costs. Hence, concerns with regards to the initial (over)enthusiastic mass production of tourism in the 1960s and 1970s led to a plethora of alternative (to mass) approaches to the development of tourism from the 1980s onwards (Smith & Eadington, 1992), such as green tourism, responsible tourism, ecotourism, community-based tourism and so on. These subsequently became subsumed under the umbrella of sustainable tourism development which, since the early 1990s, has been – and continues to be – the dominant approach to tourism development, being seen by many in both academic and policy circles as a potentially effective means of fulfilling tourism's developmental role within environmental constraints. Importantly, however, and as suggested in the following section, the theory underpinning the tourism–development nexus has not evolved as much as the evident transformations in tourism policy and practice might imply. That is, although recent decades have witnessed the emergence of a variety of new approaches to tourism development, the development theory that informs them, namely, economic growth-based modernisation, has by and large remained constant. This, in turn, goes some way to explaining the unsustainability of contemporary tourism in general and the failure to achieve sustainable tourism development in particular.

TOURISM AND DEVELOPMENT THEORY: FROM MODERNISATION TO... MODERNISATION?

As intimated above, there are two broad perspectives on the dynamic relationship between tourism and development. First, it can be assessed or described in terms of the emergence of new approaches to the planning and development of tourism that, in principle at least, seek to achieve particular objectives or to enhance tourism's developmental contribution more generally. For example, during the early 2000s, significant attention was paid to the idea of pro-poor tourism which, perhaps reflecting the increasing focus on poverty reduction as the first goal of the then Millennium Development Goals, sought to generate 'net benefits for the poor' (Roe & Urguhart, 2001: 2). Essentially an interventionist policy, pro-poor tourism did not offer an alternative approach to tourism development – as Harrison (2008: 860) points out in his thoughtful critique of the concept, it depended on mainstream tourism and, hence, 'tacitly accepts [the] neoliberal status quo'. Rather, its success depended on projects that manipulated the existing tourism system to provide employment opportunities for those normally excluded from it. Unsurprisingly, perhaps, many such projects lasted only as long as the funding that supported them and, as Spenceley (2022) observes, pro-poor tourism has more recently been subsumed into broader ideas of destination resilience and regeneration.

The important point to make about pro-poor tourism is that it was not a distinctive approach to tourism as a development tool. More specifically, it was 'neither a theory nor a model, and [was] not a niche form of tourism' (Harrison, 2008: 864). It was, rather, a targeted intervention in the neoliberal tourism system with the specific objective of involving some of the poor in some destinations (that is, including some of the excluded) and, as such, might be better thought of as a movement that adopted the moral high ground occupied by other concepts such as responsible (Goodwin, 2016) or 'just' (Jamal, 2019) tourism (see also Butcher, 2003). The same cannot be said about other forms of tourism, such as ecotourism, agritourism or community-based tourism, that are distinctive in both aims and approach and that in some cases are recognised tourism products. That being said, however, they are nevertheless not theories but simply approaches to or models of tourism development that seek to achieve specific outcomes.

In contrast, the second means of exploring or understanding the dynamic tourism–development nexus is from the theoretical perspective. This might be more accurately described as the application of development theory to tourism as a specific agent of development, similar to the way in which other aspects of tourism are necessarily framed within broader established, disciplinary-based theories. In other words, despite the ambitions of some, such as Enzensberger's (1996) essay *A Theory of Tourism*, Graburn's (2001) theorising of tourism as a secular ritual or MacCannell's (1976) seminal *The Tourist: A New Theory of the Leisure Class*, there can logically be no general theory of tourism as a specific social and economic activity. Rather, tourism experiences / consumption and management are typically best studied and understood within the context of existing sociological, cultural, economic and other relevant theory; hence, the study of tourism's role in development should logically be informed by theory emerging from development studies.

Development studies first appeared in the 1950s, opening an academic window on the emerging world of development policy and practice. Initially a branch of development economics, it became established as a distinct, albeit interdisciplinary, field of academic endeavour in the 1960s, going on to address development from a variety of disciplinary and practical perspectives (Desai & Potter, 2013). Subsequently, and reflecting questions over the validity of development as a global objective – the post-development school, for example, argues that the global development project is flawed, unjust, has failed and, hence, should be abandoned (Ziai, 2007) – the contribution of development studies has itself been questioned. It has become 'an uncertain and under-confident discipline' (Payne & Phillips, 2010: 3) that has retreated into the security of the 'intellectual project of political economy and the diverse theoretical traditions associated with it' (Payne & Phillips, 2010: 181; also, Leys, 2009).

Debates surrounding the contribution and future of development studies are beyond the scope of this chapter although they should not be ignored – given the increasing dependence on tourism as a vehicle of development, development itself as both a process and outcome demands critical examination. Nevertheless, the point here is that theories of development have evolved over time, offering a dynamic theoretical framework for considering tourism's developmental role. Typically, this evolution of theory is seen as following a trajectory from top-down economic growth-based approaches to development (essentially, development policy and support devised at the national or international level and 'imposed' on nations and societies) to a broader focus on enhancing human well-being with an emphasis on endogenous, bottom-up development – that is, development driven from the grassroots level. There is consensus that the starting point, or the first development theory, is modernisation theory; there is less consensus, however, with regards to where we are now. For some, sustainable development remains the dominant development paradigm whereas others suggest that it has been superseded by human development and global development. Yet others (Mastini, 2017) argue that degrowth should be considered a newly emerging development paradigm. Given that this book argues for reframing tourism and development within the concept of degrowth, this is embraced in Table 2.3 which provides a chronology of development paradigms and their key theoretical tenets. The time frames are offered as a guide only and indicate when a paradigm gained prominence. The roots of some paradigms appeared earlier than indicated.

Two important points should be noted. First, although there is a clear temporal structure to the evolution of development theory, emerging paradigms have not replaced but merely supplemented existing ones. Hence, in the tourism context, there is an explicit alignment between alternative development and alternative forms of tourism whilst pro-poor tourism, discussed above, might be considered a manifestation of human development. However, as will be argued shortly, much contemporary tourism policy and development continues to closely reflect modernisation theory.

And second, a distinction must be made between development 'theory' and development 'paradigm'. Table 2.3 lists a number of development paradigms that have emerged since the 1950s, but these are not all theories of development; whereas a theory can be defined as 'a plausible or scientifically acceptable general principle or body of principles offered to explain phenomena' (Merriam-Webster, 2022), a paradigm is 'a model or pattern, a set of assumptions, concepts, values and practices that constitutes a way of viewing reality for the community that shares them' (Free Dictionary, n.d.). Hence, a theory might underpin a paradigm, but a paradigm is not a theory. For example, sustainable tourism development is clearly a paradigm – a model of tourism development that reflects various assumptions, values and practices – that, as discussed later, is arguably (and contradictorily) underpinned by modernisation theory. Consequently, despite a proliferation of development paradigms, it is suggested that there are in fact just two development theories: modernisation theory and dependency (or underdevelopment) theory, both of which, according to Harrison (2015: 57), increasingly have come to be considered 'empirically invalid, theoretically inadequate and politically ineffective' (see also Harrison, 1988).

Table 2.3   *The evolution of development theory*

Period	Development paradigm	Theoretical perspectives
1950s– 1960s	*Modernisation*	Stages of growth
		Diffusion: growth impulses/trickle down effect
1950s– 1960s	*Dependency*	Neo-colonialism: underdevelopment caused by exploitation by developed countries
		Dualism: poverty functional to global economic growth
		Structuralism: domestic markets, state involvement
mid- 1970s– 1980s	*Economic neoliberalism*	Free market: free competitive markets / privatisation, globalisation, Washington Consensus
		Structural adjustment: competitive exports / market forces
		One world: new world financial systems, deregulation
1970s –early 1980s	*Alternative development*	Basic needs: focus on food, housing, water, education, health
		Grassroots: people-centred development
		Gender: women in development, gender relations, empowerment
		Sustainable development: environmental management; balance economic, social and environmental considerations.
Late 1980s –early 1990s	*The impasse and post-development*	Rejection of development; postmodern-critique of metanarratives of development discourse; pluralistic approaches that value local knowledge and solutions
1990s– 2000s	*Human development*	Human development: human rights; freedom; democracy; poverty reduction; pro-poor growth; good governance; debt cancellation
		State-led development
		Focus on civil society and social capital
		Transnational social movements: environment, peace, Indigenous Peoples, feminists, etc.
		Culture: different worldviews are accommodated
		Human security; challenging the 'failed state'
2000s and 2010s	*Global development*	Focus on enhancing global international relations and governance through yet to be built supranational political institutions

Period	Development paradigm	Theoretical perspectives
mid-2000s and 2020s+	*Degrowth*	From development to transitional discourses to the pluriverse and degrowth
		Challenge hegemony of economic growth and its ecological consequences
		Redefining prosperity away from infinite economic growth (measured by GDP) as a social objective
		Equity, redistribute wealth
		Downscaling consumption and production to live within ecological limits
		Transition from materialistic to participatory society
		Downshifted lifestyles, value unpaid activity
		Importance of local perspective

Source: Adapted from Telfer (2015: 36–37); see also Telfer and Sharpley (2016: 16), Escobar (2018), Kallis (2018), Demaria & Latouche (2019), Hickel (2020), Jackson (2021), Mastini (2017).

A fuller discussion of this issue falls beyond the scope of this chapter. However, it is nevertheless useful to review transformations in approaches to tourism from the perspective of the emergent development paradigms (and two development theories of modernisation and dependency) as a framework both for exploring the relationship between tourism and development and also for justifying the need for a rethinking of that relationship. It must be pointed out that detailed discussions of tourism and development theory can be found elsewhere (specifically, Telfer, 2015); here, a summary of key themes will suffice. The concept of degrowth in particular is explored in more detail in Chapter 3.

Modernisation Theory

Fundamental to modernisation theory is the idea that all societies follow an inevitable evolutionary path from being traditional (a focus on the past, social and economic structures based on kinship systems, social status by ascription, influenced by superstition and so on) to economically, politically and socially modern. Once a point along that path at which certain economic and social conditions are in place has been reached – referred to by Rostow (1967) as the 'take-off' stage – then development based upon economic growth can occur. Indeed, modernisation theory reflects the early belief that development is synonymous with economic growth (Mabogunje, 1980). In terms of development policy, such economic growth may be stimulated by the introduction of a 'growth pole' (that is, an industry or economic sector) from which 'growth impulses' diffuse throughout the region. There is, then, a direct corollary with tourism; a tourist resort may act as a growth pole, the growth impulses being the backward linkages referred to earlier in this chapter.

Undoubtedly, the initial 'advocacy' stage of tourism development in the 1960s was both influenced by and mirrored modernisation. In particular, the rapid development of large-scale resorts around the Mediterranean, in the Caribbean and elsewhere at that time was undertaken to stimulate economic growth and development and, in many cases, such as in Spain, that objective was achieved. Specific evidence of the application of tourism-related modernisation theory can also been found in the case of Cyprus post-1974 when tourism was explicitly employed as a means of rebuilding the Cypriot economy (Sharpley, 2003) and in the development of Cancun in Mexico from the 1970s onwards (Clancy, 1999, 2001). Perhaps unsurprisingly, and as Telfer (2015: 42) notes, some early academic studies similarly focused on the economic benefits of tourism (for example, Bond & Ladman, 1980; Davis, 1968) although soon many commentators were beginning to draw attention to the negative consequences of tourism against which its economic benefits should be balanced (seminal texts include de Kadt, 1979; Young, 1977). In other words, academics were ushering in what Jafari (1989) labelled the 'cautionary' stage of tourism knowledge although, significantly, this was not reflected in practice. On the one hand, the 1980s witnessed ever-increasing attention paid to the environmental and social costs of tourism, with mass tourism in particular being singled out for criticism in both academic and media circles. By the mid-1990s, such criticism had reached a crescendo; mass tourism was described as a 'spectre... haunting our planet' (Croall, 1995: 1) and there were increasing calls for people to become 'good' tourists (Wood & House, 1991). On the other hand, tourism development continued apace around the world, not only in less developed nations seeking to exploit the economic opportunities it affords but also in the developed world where it was utilised in the regeneration of post-industrial urban centres and peripheral rural economies. And the driving force behind such development continued to be economic growth; tourism was 'promoted as a development strategy to ... increase employment, generate foreign exchange, increase gross domestic product, attract development capital [and] promote a modern way of life with Western values' (Telfer, 2015: 41) – or, intentionally or otherwise, according to the tenets of modernisation theory. Hence, despite the advent of both new development paradigms and, as will be seen shortly, new approaches to tourism that can be aligned with these paradigms, tourism development continued (and continues to be) an explicit manifestation of economic growth-based modernisation.

Table 2.4   Modernisation and dependency compared

Modernisation theory	Dependency theory
Focus on the nation state	Focus on global political-economic systems
Developing countries are on a similar path to development as Western countries	Developing countries remain undeveloped because of the West
Western development was built on capitalism	Unequal exchange within the global capitalist system maintains underdevelopment
Developing countries can develop by adopting Western-style modernisation structures and processes	Tradition does not prevent progress in developing countries; their development is restricted by Western exploitation
Modernisation defines the structures, institutions and character of society	Developing country structures and institutions reflect Western domination
Policy: developing countries should follow the lead of Western countries and become more like them	Policy: developing countries should break ties with the West and follow an independent path

Source: Adapted from Harrison (2015: 56).

Dependency (Underdevelopment) Theory

Dependency theory emerged in the 1960s as a critique of the modernisation paradigm. Indeed, as can be seen in Table 2.4, the key features of the two can be seen as 'polar opposites' (Harrison, 2015: 55). In essence, dependency theory seeks to explain why development does not occur, hence it also being referred to as underdevelopment theory. Its fundamental premise is that a country's lack of development reflects not the assumed constraints of traditional societies but, rather, the internal and external political, economic and institutional structures that keep it in a dependent position relative to developed countries. More specifically, dependency theory argues that global political and economic relations are such that wealthier, more powerful Western nations are able to exploit weaker, peripheral nations (often mirroring earlier colonial ties), thereby limiting developmental opportunities within less developed countries.

Inevitably, dependency theory embraces a variety of theoretical and policy positions (again, see Telfer, 2015 for more detail) although there are two dominant intellectual approaches. First, its roots can be found in Latin America in the 1930s and 1940s where there was increasing concern over the continent's excessive economic dependence on North America. The creation of the Economic Commission for Latin America (ECLA) in the late 1940s – headed by Raul Prebisch, one of the early proponents of dependency theory – led to the implementation of economic development strategies based on domestic industrialisation, import substitution and protectionism and, hence, dependency theory became associated with a set of policy responses comprising a form of economic nationalism (Hettne, 1995) designed to sever economic links with or dependency on the West. During the 1970s, newly independent developing nations in other parts of the world adopted similar policies as a means of enhancing their economic independence from their former colonial rulers. Referred to collectively by Hickel (2017) as developmentalism, these policies proved in many cases to be successful but, being seen as a manifestation of neo-statism as well as impacting on international businesses based in the West, were soon challenged by Western developmental policies and institutions.

The second broad perspective on dependency theory draws very much on neo-Marxist theory. Adapting traditional Marxist theory with regards to the exploitation of labour within the capitalist production system, under development was similarly considered to be the outcome of unequal centre–periphery relations. Consequently, the means of achieving economic growth (modernisation and dependency theory share the ultimate aim of economic growth) was considered by some, such as Celso Furtado (see Mallorquin, 2020), to lie in national-focused economic policy. In contrast, others, notably Frank (1966), argued that it was capitalism itself that propagated to the continuing under development in the periphery, although it has since been observed that dependency theory fails to explain how a number of developing countries, particularly in south-east Asia, have achieved remarkable economic growth within the global capitalist system.

Inevitably, dependency theory has attracted much academic attention in general (Ghosh, 2001), whilst it has been widely applied to the study of tourism development in particular (Telfer, 2015: 46–48). Broadly, the dependency perspective proposes that destinations, particularly those in the developing world, tend to be in a position of dependency in an international tourism system dominated by Western-owned multinational corporations (Britton, 1982; Nash, 1989). More precisely, through their ownership of airlines, tour operators, hotel chains and cruise lines and their foreign direct investment more generally, these multinational corporations are able to control flows of international tourists as well as the nature and directions of tourism development at the destination level. Island tourist destinations in particular have long been singled out as being particularly susceptible to dependency (Bastin, 1984; Macnaught, 1982) whilst it has also been suggested that mass tourism can be a catalyst for cultural dependency (Erisman, 1983).

Interestingly, many dependency theory-informed critiques of tourism development date back to the 'cautionary' period of tourism knowledge during the 1970s and early 1980s, unsurprisingly corresponding with the increasing concerns over the consequences of the then rapid development of international tourism referred to in the previous section. Since then, such critiques have become less common, perhaps reflecting the fact that many (though of course not all) destinations, despite being in a position of dependency, have made significant advances in their development with some now boasting their own successful multinational tourism and hospitality organisations. Southern Sun Hotels, for example, has 80 hotels in South Africa, 8 hotels in the rest of Africa and one each in the Seychelles and the UAE while Chinese hotel chains have made varying degrees of purchases in Western hotel chains (Baker, 2022). Moreover, within an increasingly inter-dependent global economy character-ised by ever-increasing mobility of finance, technology and human resources, the dependency thesis has arguably become of less relevance – although the continuing power and influence of multinational tourism organisations main-tains a form of dependency (see Chapter 5) – whilst it must be acknowledged that, albeit simplistically, tourism is an inherently dependent socio-economic activity. That is, though it is rather stating the obvious, destinations depend on the desire and ability of people to engage in tourism (as revealed during the Covid-19 pandemic) and on some elements of the international tourism system to facilitate this. Therefore, from a sustainable development perspec-tive, the objective should not necessarily be to limit a destination's ties with or dependence on external businesses in the tourism system but to diversify their economy into other sectors (Cronin, 1990) – though this might not always be possible. That said, some 'developmentalism' has been in evidence in the tourism sector in the past, such as government investment in early hotel devel-opment in Tunisia (de Kadt, 1979), but beyond offering a theoretical frame-work for describing power relations within the tourism system, dependency theory has exerted little if any influence on tourism policy and development processes in practice. As Harrison (2015: 63) summarises: 'Dependency or underdevelopment may have been a preferred academic approach, but it has rarely been taken up by policy makers and governments, though popularised versions of it have been adopted by groups and movements opposed, in par-ticular, to mass tourism'.

Economic Neoliberalism

Perhaps as a reaction to the increasing developmentalism (Hickel, 2017) or what was seen as excessive state intervention in Keynesian-informed develop-ment policies, the 1980s witnessed the return of classic economic liberalism (Brohman, 1996). Directly influenced by the conservative politics in the US (Ronald Reagan), the UK (Margaret Thatcher) and other Western nations, the neoliberal revolution promoted the freedom of the markets and was manifested in, for example, deregulation, reduced state intervention, the privatisation of state enterprises and, certainly in the UK, the diminished power and influence of the trade union movement. International development policy in particular followed a similar path. In what transpired to be a misguided attempt to counter existing excessive state intervention, development lending became contingent on market liberalisation, the privatisation of state enterprises and the overall reduction in the role of the state. Such so-called Structural Adjustment Lending Programmes (SALPs) became popular yet soon became widely discredited for enhancing rather than then solving development challenges (Harrigan & Mosley, 1991). In fact, according to Hickel (2017), development lending based on structural adjustment was a deliberate attempt on the part of the West to maintain its advantage in the global economic system. The SALPs were consequently superseded by Poverty Reduction Strategy Papers which encouraged local participation in development strategy; however, these too have proved to be unsuccessful (Lazarus, 2008).

For tourism development, economic neoliberalism served to strengthen the process of economic growth-based modernisation whilst fundamentally influencing the nature and scale of tourist flows. Most notably, the deregulation of international air transport in the late 1980s led to the emergence of low-cost airlines which not only rendered frequent air travel affordable for the masses but also transformed how, when and where people travelled. In so doing, tourism became further entrenched as an economic growth policy in numerous destinations. At the same time, both the European Union and the World Bank provided financial support for tourism development projects around the world, typically in countries where tourism would stimulate wider economic growth (Pryce, 1998). Consequently, by the early 1990s, tourism development in practice continued to be defined by modernisation.

Alternative Development

According to Brohman (1996), dissatisfaction with mainstream top-down, economic growth-based development policies emerged in the 1970s and by the 1980s, whilst the neoliberal agenda was gaining traction, many in the development community were seeking alternatives to mainstream policy and practice – hence the notion of alternative development. In contrast to the established top-down, interventionist approaches to development, the alternative approach, based upon the fundamental tenet that development should be endogenous (or driven by those societies undergoing development), is a resource-based, bottom-up method that focuses primarily on human and environmental concerns. In other words, the development process should start within and be guided by the needs of each society rather than being externally imposed upon them; it therefore emphasises the importance of satisfying basic needs and of encouraging self-reliance (Galtung, 1986).

The alternative development paradigm not only underpinned the subsequent emergence of sustainable development but, with its focus on community-level empowerment in the development process, is also reflected in the political tenets of degrowth. This grassroots perspective has, perhaps inevitably, attracted criticism, with many questioning the extent to which local communities possess the resources, skills, knowledge or, indeed, desire to participate. Nevertheless, the principles of alternative development have been adapted to the specific context of tourism, with 'alternative tourism' becoming, as one early critic expressed it, 'a fashionable idea among those... dissatisfied with the nature of mass tourism' (Cohen, 1987: 13). As such, it is as much about alternative (to mass) tourists seeking more individualistic, non-commoditised experiences as it is about alternative approaches to the planning and management of tourism development.

In essence, then, alternative tourism is an umbrella term that embraces a variety of approaches to both the production and consumption of tourism, the overall objective of which is to optimise the developmental benefits of tourism to destination communities and minimise its negative socio-environmental consequences at the same time as offering tourists more meaningful experiences. Manifestations of alternative tourism include ecotourism, green tourism, nature tourism, responsible tourism, slow tourism, adventure tourism and so on, and all share the characteristics summarised in Table 2.5.

There can be no doubting the extent to which alternative forms of tourism development exist in practice; the number of applications to the WTTC's annual Tourism for Tomorrow Awards are testament to this. Equally, their popularity amongst tourists cannot be underestimated. For example, ecotourism is often claimed (without irony) to be one of the fastest growing segments of the global tourism market although doubts have long been expressed with regards to its sustainability, the degree of benefits that accrue to local communities and, indeed, the environmental credentials of ecotourists themselves (Cohen, 1987; Sharpley, 2006; Wheeller, 1992). More generally, the extent to which local communities are willing or able to participate in tourism (a fundamental tenet of most forms of alternative tourism) has also been questioned by many (Tosun, 2000), whilst proponents tend to conveniently overlook the fact that alternative tourism is not distinct from but a part of the mass tourism sector upon which it depends. It is in essence a niche market within the international tourism system, and one promoted for the same reason as all tourism – its economic benefits. Hence, from a development point of view, alternative tourism is little more than a continuation of the modernist, Western-centric approach to development (Cater, 2006).

Human Development and Global Development

Mention must be made here of both 'human development' and 'global development. Emerging in the early 1990s after a period when 'concern for people had given way to concern for balancing budgets and payments' (Streeten,

Table 2.5   Characteristics of mass vs. alternative tourism

Conventional Mass Tourism	Alternative Forms of Tourism
General features	
Rapid development	Slow development
Maximises	Optimises
Socially/environmentally Inconsiderate	Socially/environmentally Considerate
Uncontrolled	Controlled
Short-term	Long-term
Sectoral	Holistic
Remote control	Local control
Development strategies	
Development without planning	First plan, then develop
Project-led schemes	Concept-led schemes
Tourism development everywhere	Development in suitable places
Concentration on 'honeypots'	Pressures and benefits diffused
New building	Re-use of existing building
Development by outsiders	Local developers
Employees imported	Local employment utilised
Urban architecture	Vernacular architecture
Tourist behaviour	
Large groups	Singles, families, friends
Fixed programme	Spontaneous decisions
Little time	Much time
'Sights'	'Experiences'
Imported lifestyle	Local lifestyle
Comfortable/passive	Demanding/active
Loud	Quiet
Shopping	Bring presents

Source: Telfer and Sharpley (2016: 57), adapted from Lane (1990) and Butler (1990).

n.d.), human development is not strictly a development paradigm. Rather, it is a refocusing of development away from broad objectives such as economic growth towards putting people – their needs, freedoms, capabilities and aspirations – at the centre of development policy. Therefore, whilst measured against tangible indicators such as life expectancy, education and income, it also embraces issues such as human rights, democracy and good governance. Consequently, human development has three broad components: (i) human well-being and the freedom to flourish; (ii) empowerment and agency; and (iii) justice and equity (see UNDP, 2011).

This focus has been evident in some forms of tourism policy and practice. For instance, pro-poor tourism which, as discussed earlier in this chapter, is an interventionist policy with an explicit emphasis on meeting the basic needs and expanding the capabilities of the poor, can be clearly aligned with the principles of human development. Similarly, volunteer tourism, in which individuals pay to travel and engage in development-related voluntary activities (typically in developing countries) for all or part of their trip, may contribute to human-focused development (Wearing and McGehee, 2013). It must be noted, however, that significant controversy surrounds the latter, not least with regards to whether participants are motivated primarily by altruism or self-interest (Daldeniz & Hampton, 2010) and, more significantly, the extent to which positive benefits actually accrue to host communities (Lupoli et al., 2014). More recently, the notion of human development has also become evident in the more general emphasis on promoting justice and human rights in tourism. This is explored in some detail by Jamal (2019) and Hashimoto, Härkönen and Nkyi (2021), the former providing a number of case studies of human-centred development through tourism, such as the social entrepreneurship-based Street Voices project in Copenhagen (see also Dredge, 2017). Nevertheless, these and other forms of tourism with a human development focus remain marginal to tourism and development as a whole. In other words, their developmental contribution is minimal in the context of tourism globally which, as we have suggested, has intentionally or otherwise continued to follow the path of economic growth-based modernisation.

Although human development focuses implicitly on the individual, at the same time it has been recognised that in an increasingly globalised world (at least, prior to the re-emergent nationalism of the last two decades or, perhaps, because of it), the path to global development is dependent upon improved international relations and global governance (Hettne, 2009). As Held (2010: 220) observes:

> Today, there is a newfound recognition that global problems cannot be solved by any one nation-state acting alone, nor by states just fighting their corner in regional blocs. What is required is collective and collaborative action – something the states of the world have not been good at, and which they need to reconsider and advance if the most pressing issues are to be adequately tackled.

In other words, despite the right of individuals and nations to address their developmental needs, the challenges faced by an increasingly connected world, from climate change and economic crises to international political tensions, require the establishment of new supranational political organisations, or global development. Hettne (2009) refers to this as an emerging discourse – the required organisations have yet to be established – and, hence, it cannot be considered a development paradigm. Moreover, the lack of progress in, for example, building a global response to climate change is indicative of the idealism underpinning the concept of global development. Of course, the

UNWTO is one such global body although it is not globally representative (not all countries are members of it) and it is ill-equipped to guide the fragmented, multi-sectoral industry that is tourism (McKercher, 1993).

Thus, whilst development theory and paradigms have evolved over time, tourism in practice – as an agent of development – remains firmly embedded in modernisation theory, leading Harrison (2015) to ask 'what has development theory done for us' in terms of understanding and informing tourism development. Most significantly, perhaps, although sustainable tourism development has been (and remains) the dominant tourism development paradigm, both occupying a dominant position in tourism studies / research and also informing – at least in principle – much real-world tourism development, there is little if any evidence of a major shift away from economic growth-based policies in tourism.

To a great extent, we should not be surprised about this. After all, as we observed in the introduction to this book, we live in a world wedded socially, politically and economically to the idea of acquisition, consumption and growth. Hence, it is both idealistic and illogical to expect tourism, as a specific socio-economic activity, to buck this trend. Yet many in both academic and policy circles continue to adhere to the belief that the concept of sustainable tourism development can resolve the tourism–development dilemma, that if developed according to the principles of sustainable development, tourism will somehow contribute to development in an environmentally sustainable manner.

That this has quite clearly not occurred, that there is little evidence of sustainable tourism development 'on the ground', can in part be explained by the inherent limitations and contradictions of the sustainable development paradigm itself. We return to this in the next chapter but, by way of completing the story of the evolution of tourism and development theory, the next section summarises why it has proved difficult if not impossible to translate the concept of sustainable tourism development into practice and, by extension, why there is a need to move on and rethink tourism and development.

SUSTAINABLE TOURISM DEVELOPMENT: A FAILED PARADIGM

The concept of sustainable tourism development first emerged in 1990. More precisely, perhaps one of the first academic references to it was a 1990 conference specifically focusing on sustainable tourism development; in the introduction to the conference proceedings, it was claimed that 'sustainable tourism is an idea whose time has come' (Howie, 1990: 3). More than three decades later, we would suggest that it is now an idea whose time has passed but, in the intervening period, sustainable tourism development has in all likelihood proved to be one of the most popular and enduring subjects of research in tourism. For example, a review published in 2012 suggested that, by then, the number of related research publications was in excess of 5,000 (Buckley, 2012) whilst more recently, Niñerola, Sánchez-Rebull and Hernández-Lara (2019) identified 4,647 papers published between 1987 and 2018 that focus on sustainability issues in tourism. Undoubtedly, the literature on sustainable tourism development, if books, chapters, policy documents and so on are included, is far more extensive than these reviews suggest and continues to grow – the *Journal of Sustainable Tourism* alone, first published in 1993, continues to thrive, publishing around 120 papers across 12 issues a year.

It is not our intention here to indulge in a lengthy critique of sustainable tourism development. Not only have many others done so but also the arguments are well rehearsed and widely acknowledged. Rather, the purpose of this section is two-fold: first, to provide evidence of the failure to achieve sustainable tourism development in practice and, second, to summarise the reasons for this as a justification for proposing a rethinking of tourism and development. Nevertheless, by way of introduction it is important to return to the roots of the concept of sustainable tourism development, primarily because the driving force behind its adoption and early interpretations of it set it on a path that, ironically, diverged considerably from its parental paradigm of sustainable development.

As noted above, sustainable tourism development first entered the tourism studies lexicon in 1990, not coincidentally just three years after the World Commission on Environment and Development (better known as the Brundtland Commission) published its report, *Our Common Future* (WCED, 1987), that launched sustainable development on the worldwide stage. However, the framing of tourism development within the principles of sustainable development was arguably less to do with a positive attempt to apply those principles to tourism and more about jumping on the sustainable development bandwagon as a convenient solution to the perceived negative consequences of the rapid growth in mass tourism. As already discussed in this chapter, the 1980s had witnessed increasing concerns about the environmental and social consequences of the widespread development of tourism destinations appealing to mass markets and so, building on the work of proponents of alternative tourism, sustainable tourism development almost immediately came to be seen as an alternative to mass tourism. For instance, it was argued that for tourism development to be sustainable it should be based upon 'options or strategies considered preferable to mass tourism' (Pigram, 1990: 3), an approach that was both saturated with implicit elitism and that challenged what many considered (and still consider) to be a manifestation of neoliberal capitalism (Mosedale, 2016).

Subsequently, despite the logical observation that 'those who insert the word "tourism" between "sustainable" and "development" ... [should] ... ensure that, under all circumstances, the resultant principles of sustainable tourism development are also principles of sustainable development' (Hunter, 1995: 163), sustainable tourism development became essentially focused on sustaining tourism's resource base rather than on enhancing tourism's contribution to wider sustainable development. Indeed, the word 'development' was soon dropped and the tourism-centric focus of sustainable tourism became cemented in the definition offered in the very first issue of the *Journal of Sustainable Tourism*:

> [Sustainable tourism is] a positive approach intended to reduce tensions and friction created by the complex interactions between the tourism industry, visitors, the environment and the communities which are host to holiday makers. (Bramwell & Lane, 1993: 2)

In short, sustainable tourism is seen as a means of reducing tourism's negative impacts. Such a perspective does not permit an interrogation of tourism's role in (sustainable) development and avoids more fundamental questions such as whether, in particular contexts, tourism is the most appropriate path to development. Rather, it appears to be assumed that achieving sustainable tourism will inevitably contribute to sustainable development; as Bramwell et al. (2017: 1) argue, 'sustainable tourism is often now seen as a normative orientation... toward sustainable development'. It also does not encourage an holistic, global perspective on tourism, ignoring one of the three fundamental principles of sustainable development (these being: an holistic perspective; futurity or a longer-term perspective; and inter- and intra-generational equity) and resulting primarily in a focus on the (individual) destination with an implicit continuing anti-mass tourism stance. Hence, the concept of sustainable tourism development has evolved not only 'alongside, but separate to, its parent paradigm of sustainable development' (Ruhanen et al., 2015: 518) but also, for the most part, within academic and policy circles, with little consequential influence on practice. In other words, although it must be acknowledged that the supply and consumption of sustainable forms of tourism is on the increase, these constitute only a small proportion of tourism activity worldwide which, as the following section suggests, has continued to follow an unsustainable trajectory.

Unsustainable Tourism: the Evidence

Sustainable tourism development has remained the dominant paradigm in tourism policy for more than three decades, yet there is little evidence of this policy being translated into practice.

- Over this period, international arrivals increased exponentially from almost 440 million in 1990 to 1.46 billion in 2019; in absolute terms, international arrivals more than tripled. At the same time, the number of international air passengers increased more than six-fold, from 0.3 billion to 1.9 billion (IEA, 2022) whilst, interestingly, domestic air passenger numbers increased from 1 billion to 2.7 billion, now accounting for around 60 percent of all air travel. Such growth is environmentally unsustainable. Overall, tourism accounts for between 8 percent and 11 percent of global carbon emissions (WTTC, 2021b: 13); a pre-pandemic report predicted this would rise to 12 percent by 2025 (CarbonBrief, 2018), an utterly disproportionate contribution given the exclusivity of international tourism consumption.
- At the destination level, there has been increasing evidence of carrying capacities being exceeded, or so-called 'overtourism'. This is by no means a new phenomenon – many destinations have long experienced excessive numbers of tourists at particular times. What is new is the emergence of an anti-tourism movement (Clancy, 2019; Hughes, 2018), pointing to the socially unsustainable nature of tourism. Notably, there appears to be a direct correlation between anti-tourist sentiments and the intrusion of peer-to-peer accommodation, such as Airbnb, into urban residential areas (Celata & Romano, 2022).
- To a great extent, the continuing growth in tourism has been accounted for by the emergence of new markets, notably China and other Asian economies. There has also been a greater propensity to travel amongst existing markets. Given that just one sixth of the global population currently engages in international travel, the potential for continuing future growth driven by emerging tourism markets (and hence greater impacts on the global scale) is significant.
- As has always been the case, the increasing consumption of tourism is driven by greater levels of disposable income. However, a significant factor underpinning the growth of tourism has been the liberalisation of markets, the airline sector being a notable beneficiary. As discussed elsewhere (Sharpley, 2020), it was only in the early 1990s that low-cost carriers (LCCs) first emerged as a result of the deregulation of the sector but by 2006 they accounted for 15.7 percent of the global airline market. This share (of a rapidly growing market) grew to 31 percent by 2018. As they predominantly operate short haul routes with relatively high per pas-

senger carbon emissions (Miyoshi & Mason, 2009), the success of LCCs in democratising air travel must be balanced against their contribution to global carbon emissions.

- As tourism has continued to grow in scale and scope, not only have new destinations emerged but also many have competed for and attracted ever-increasing numbers of arrivals. Roughly half of all destinations around the world received more than 1 million tourists in 2017, of which 73 received more than 3 million tourists and 35 more than 10 million. Consequently, many destinations suffer an unsustainable economic dependence on tourism (as noted previously, sadly revealed by the Covid-19 pandemic). Table 2.6 lists the 50 nations most dependent on tourism; as can be seen, tourism contributes 15 percent or more of GDP in 44 countries, directly contradicting the objective of self-reliance in development.

- Despite all the publicity surrounding the environmental impacts of tourism, the increasing popularity of allegedly sustainable tourism experiences, such as ecotourism, and numerous books and codes of conduct exhorting 'good' tourist behaviour, there has arguably been little evidence of the adoption of responsible or sustainable tourist behaviour. This was predicted by McKercher (1993: 7) who observed – in the first issue of the *Journal of Sustainable Tourism* – that one of the fundamental truths of tourism is that 'tourists are consumers, not anthropologists'. This has been supported by more recent research demonstrating that even those with strong environmental values tend to ignore such values when on holiday (Juvan & Dolnicar, 2014a, 2014b). In other words, a basic requirement for the achievement of sustainable tourism development – sustainable tourism consumption – has been notably absent (see Chapter 6).

Unsustainable Tourism: the Reasons

Given the trends in tourism over the last 30 years outlined above, it would be difficult to claim that the tourism sector, on the global scale, has become more sustainable; in fact, it has become less so. Moreover, it would also be difficult to claim that tourism has made a broader contribution to sustainable development. That is, whilst it has undoubtedly come to occupy a more significant role in national and global economic growth, this has not been translated into the achievement of the goals of sustainable development. This is not to say that there has not been some progress; at the local level, there are numerous projects that meet some of the objectives of sustainable development. However, these lie at the margins of mainstream tourism; they are, in a sense, micro success stories within a macro problem.

Table 2.6   *Contribution of travel and tourism to GDP 2017: top 50 countries*

Country	% of GDP	Country	% of GDP	Country	% of GDP
Maldives	76.6	St Kitts & Nevis	26.8	Tonga	18.2
Seychelles	65.3	Albania	26.2	New Zealand	17.9
Macao	61.3	Croatia	25.0	Portugal	17.3
Antigua & Barbuda	51.8	Sao Tome & Principe	24.3	Dominican Republic	17.2
Bahamas	47.8	Mauritius	23.8	Hong Kong (China)	16.7
Vanuatu	46.1	Montenegro	23.7	Madagascar	16.6
Cape Verde	44.9	St Vincent & Grenadines	23.4	Mexico	16.0
St Lucia	41.8	Grenada	23.3	Armenia	15.7
Belize	41.3	Cyprus	22.3	Estonia	15.4
Barbados	40.6	Thailand	21.2	Honduras	15.0
Fiji	40.3	Philippines	21.1	Spain	14.9
Dominica	36.6	Kiribati	20.9	Austria	14.6
Iceland	34.6	Gambia	20.1	Azerbaijan	14.6
Jamaica	32.9	Greece	19.7	Panama	14.5
Cambodia	32.4	Jordan	18.7	Tunisia	14.2
Georgia	31.0	Morocco	18.6	Namibia	13.8
Malta	27.1	Lebanon	18.4		

Source: Adapted from World Data Atlas (2018).

The question then is: why has there been a failure to achieve sustainable tourism development? Some of the answers have been alluded to above, not least the ever-growing consumer demand for tourist experiences spurred on by increases in personal wealth and mobility, technological innovation and transformations in the supply of travel and tourism services. From a more conceptual perspective, however, there are some clear reasons for this failure, in particular the uneasy relationship between tourism and the notion of sustainable development (Berno & Bricker, 2001; Liu, 2003). Putting to one side for the moment the long-debated controversies and ambiguities surrounding sustainable development (for example, Dernbach & Cheever, 2015) and, notably, its inherent contradictions, an immediate problem is that the fundamental principles of sustainable development – an holistic, long-term approach emphasising equality within and between generations – are unworkable in the tourism context (Sharpley, 2000). As a multi-sector, short-term profit-oriented 'industry' bringing benefits to a privileged minority of the global population (those fortunate to engage in its supply and consumption), tourism simply cannot be mapped onto these principles. Moreover, as a resource-hungry activity (McKercher, 1993), tourism inevitably contradicts one of the essential objectives of sustainable development: environmental sustainability. In short, the achievement of sustainable tourism development – logically conceived by some as tourism as a vehicle of sustainable development – fell at the first hurdle; though an admirable ambition in principle, the realities of tourism are such that sustainable tourism development can never be achieved in practice.

Whether because of the early support for sustainable tourism development as an alternative to mass tourism rather than, as the UNWTO later proposed, an approach relevant to all forms of tourism, or because of tacit acceptance of the lack of fit between tourism and sustainable development, it was inevitable that the focus became tourism-centric (Hunter, 1995) with a concern for sustaining tourism's resource base. Not only did this serve to deny the opportunity to consider tourism as a sustainable development option within a wider bundle of development opportunities – a necessary element of sustainable development (Cronin, 1990) – but also academic research and policy statements focused for the most part on the destination. This, in turn, resulted in two failings. First, both the production and consumption of tourism were considered independently from global production and consumption more generally; as argued in the introduction to this book, tourism is just one of many environmentally damaging forms of consumption and so it is illogical not to consider the sustainability of tourism within this broader context. And second, the sustainability of the global tourism system as a whole was overlooked. This not only ignored the 'elephant in the sustainability room', namely, the unsustainable nature of most forms of travel to the destination, particularly air travel (Høyer, 2000) – it is only relatively recently that concerns about air travel's contribution to global warming have come to the fore – but it also established the potential for a tragedy of the (tourism) commons; although some destinations might adopt sustainability policies, the unsustainable activities of others could eventually destroy the overall tourism resource base.

In addition to these issues, much of the discussion of and research into sustainable tourism has remained within academic and policy circles. With some exceptions (for example, Higuchi & Yamanaka, 2017) there has been a failure on the part of academics to engage with an industry to which much of the sustainable tourism rhetoric is either irrelevant or challenges the very basis of the business. Also, the focus on sustainable tourism has long been justified, other than on environmental grounds, on the misguided belief that tourists themselves are not only cognisant of tourism's negative consequences but actively seek out responsible tourist experiences. Originating in the early 1990s, the concept of the 'new' tourist (Poon, 1993) proposed that predictable, organised, passive holidays were no longer attractive; tourists, it was claimed, were now seeking more meaningful, active holidays that respected local cultures and communities. This was extended into the notion of the 'good' tourist (Popescu, 2008), with the popularity of ecotourism and other allegedly responsible forms of tourism being offered as evidence of increasing interest in and demand for sustainable tourism products. Nevertheless, as observed above, tourism continues to be consumed for more egocentric reasons. This issue is considered in more detail in Chapter 6 but, suffice to say, the attitudes and behaviours of tourists themselves tend to militate against sustainable tourism.

Undoubtedly, however, the most significant challenge to the achievement of sustainable tourism (and, as discussed in the next chapter, sustainable development more generally) is the continuing emphasis on growth. Despite all the attention paid to sustainable tourism development, all the research and policy documents, all the accreditation schemes, sectoral initiatives and sets of sustainability indicators, all the various bodies established to promote sustainable tourism, such as the Global Sustainable Tourism Council (GSTC), the development and promotion of tourism worldwide continues to be driven for the most part by the growth imperative. Research has revealed a predominant focus on quantitative growth in national-level tourism policy documents (Torkington, Stanford & Guiver, 2020) whilst global bodies such as the World Tourism Organization and World Travel and Tourism Council, though quick to embrace the concept of sustainable tourism development, have arguably done so in order to 'greenwash' their explicit growth agendas.

This emphasis on growth is unsurprising. Tourism is firmly embedded in a global economic and political system that is, by and large, organised around capitalism within which economic growth is both explicit and necessary (see Chapter 5). For destinations, growth in tourism means remaining competitive in global tourist markets and, more pragmatically, more tourist spending to support local economic growth. Yet, continuing growth is, by definition, unsustainable or, as Daly (1990) puts it, 'sustainable growth is a bad oxymoron'. Similarly, sustainable tourism development based on a growth agenda is a contradiction in terms, an impossibility.

CONCLUSION: TOURISM AND DEVELOPMENT – WHICH WAY NOW?

As this chapter has discussed, the relationship between tourism and development has been, and continues to be, dynamic. The social and economic activity that is tourism has evolved over time, growing remarkably in both scale and scope with a commensurate increase in its environmental consequences. At the same time, tourism policy and planning has also evolved, in part in response to the acknowledged negative impacts of tourism and, in part, reflecting transformations in understandings of and approaches to the objective of tourism, namely, development. Early tourism development policy mirrored modernisation theory based on economic growth which was considered to be synonymous with development. However, as the concept of development came to embrace a wider set of aims and objectives broadly concerned with human well-being, so too did a variety of approaches to tourism development emerge that typically sought to enhance the benefits of tourism to destination communities (or, in the case of pro-poor tourism, specific targeted groups) whilst minimising its negative social and environmental consequences. Since the early 1990s, such planning approaches have fallen under the umbrella of sustainable tourism which nowadays not only remains the dominant tourism development paradigm but also reflects the continuing focus on sustainable development more generally, most recently manifested in the UN's 17 Sustainable Development Goals (SDGs).

The important point to emerge from this chapter, however, is that the great majority of tourism paradigms that have emerged over the last half century or so, including sustainable tourism development, continue to be underpinned by one of only two actual development theories, namely, modernisation theory (the other being dependency theory). Fundamental to modernisation theory is economic growth which, as we have seen, remains explicit in most if not all tourism policies and which goes some way to explaining the lack of progress in practice towards achieving sustainable tourism development. Such a failure should not, however, come as a surprise; not only is economic growth a clearly expressed goal in the SDGs but it is also synonymous with the neoliberal capitalist system prevailing in most, if not all countries. Yet, it is continuing economic growth that, as established in Chapter 1, not only translates into excessive and unsustainable production and consumption (of which tourism is but one manifestation) on the global scale but also acts in opposition to many development objectives, including reducing inequality.

It is for this reason that the notion of degrowth is attracting increasing support as an alternative development paradigm, not least because the restrictions imposed during the Covid-19 pandemic offered a glimpse of the benefits of a 'post-growth' world. And if degrowth represents an alternative vision of development then tourism – as a vehicle of development – should logically be reframed within the degrowth paradigm. The overall purpose of this book is to do just that and, therefore, the next chapter explores why and how development as the objective of tourism might be redefined, in particular introducing and critiquing the degrowth concept presented in Table 2.3 above. Three subsequent chapters focus on, respectively, tourism and the environmental crisis, the supply of tourism and the consumption of tourism to justify degrowth before the final chapter explores the ways in which degrowth might inform a rethinking of the relationship between tourism and development.

3. Redefining development as the objective of tourism

INTRODUCTION

For many individuals, companies, destinations and governments, tourism is the primary source of economic livelihood and, more broadly, a foundation for development noted for generating income, employment, foreign exchange and economic diversification. Indeed, the rapid decline in global tourism due to the Covid-19 pandemic and its resulting devastation emphasised this importance of the tourism industry. Nevertheless, despite its economic value, tourism is inherently interconnected with capitalism and globalisation and, consequently, criticised from a critical political economy perspective for contributing to exploitation and inequality. The income inequality gap between rich and poor in both developing and developed economies is not only at a high level but continues to rise, thereby creating the potential for social unrest (Mdingi & Ho, 2021). Even in major tourism destinations in developed nations with high standards of living measured by Gross Domestic Product (GDP), high rates of unemployment, poverty, exploitation and inequality occur (Telfer, 2019). As such, there is a need to critique the reliance on indicators such as GDP as a measure of development and the expectation that tourism's contributions to GDP will continue to grow given the current environmental crises facing the planet. A central question for this chapter is, then, how should development be defined or measured as the objective of tourism and, in fact, should development even be the objective of tourism?

In considering development and, therefore, tourism's contribution to it, it is possible to distinguish two interrelated dimensions of development (Hettne, 2009). The first is development which draws on social science theories to explain the development process as a whole, focusing on long-term, structural transformations towards improving the functioning of societies. In contrast, the second dimension is a more short-term pragmatic approach concentrating on the instrumental understanding of development through the planned achievement of specific development goals in local contexts as set out in policy papers from donors and international institutions (Hettne, 2009). The UN's sustainable development goals (SDGs) and associated targets can be viewed in the latter context with the UNWTO arguing that tourism has the potential to contribute either directly or indirectly to all the SDGs (UNWTO n.d. a) though some criticise the UNWTO's optimism in this regard (Bianchi & de Man, 2021). Similar to the preceding Millennium Development Goals, the first SDG goal notably focuses on eliminating poverty (a prerequisite to development) and while the UN notes that tremendous strides have been made with global poverty rates being halved since 2000, the global pandemic could see the extent of global poverty increasing by half a billion people (UN, 2021). However, although important and necessary steps are being taken towards achieving the SDGs, it is essential to recognise the overriding ideologies guiding any development strategy (Hettne, 1995); the SDGs, for example, remain based in the context of economic growth, as do most national development policies. Hence, the UNWTO's SDG-led agenda is contradicted by the logics of profit-making, competitiveness and growth; furthermore, their idea of 'sustained' and 'inclusive growth' does not address structural injustices which entrench inequalities and exploitative labour practices and instead 'reinforces the primacy of capital and market notions of justice and continues to perpetuate a growth driven tourism development model' (Bianchi & de Man, 2021: 353). The chapter begins, therefore, by tracing the evolution of the concept of development and examines alternatives that move beyond the reliance on GDP as a measure of it. This is followed by a critique of tourism as a driver for economic growth within the context of the political economy of tourism, whereby capitalism and globalisation, both facilitators of tourism, generate exploitation and inequity. The chapter then investigates transitional discourses and, in particular, conceptualisations centred on degrowth which place the emphasis on notions of well-being and prosperity at the individual level (which may be more equitable) rather than on tangible measures, including the accumulation of financial or material wealth (Jackson, 2016, 2021). Importantly, theorists such as Sachs (2017) and fellow writers have declared that 1992 signified the end of the 'development era' and, subsequently, called for 2017 to be recognised as the end to the so-called post-development era. More specifically, Escobar et al. (2018: xiv) argue that we need to move from development to the pluriverse 'recognizing the diversity of people's views on planetary well-being and the skills to protect it'. The principles of transitional discourses and degrowth thus represent important discussion points for re-evaluating the tourism–development nexus.

THE EVOLUTION AND MEASUREMENT OF DEVELOPMENT

The term 'development' is highly contested; it simultaneously generates images of, on the one hand, economic growth and social progress and, on the other hand, projects and policies that have led to exploitation and inequality. Writing from a critical post-development perspective, Sachs (2019) usefully identifies four main aspects of development. First, nations are viewed chrono-politically as advancing in the same direction with imagined time being linear (only forwards or backwards). Second, developed nations are seen geopolitically as leaders along the path to development showing straggling nations the direction to take and placing the diversity of all the peoples of the world on a continuum of rich and poor nations. Third, development is measured socio-politically through economic performance via GDP (a critique of which follows below) and societies emerging from colonial rule must place themselves in the custody of 'the economy'. Finally, the actors pushing for development are experts in government, corporations and multinational banks. The World Bank, for example, issues annual World Development Reports on specific topics, such as the 2021 report on harnessing data for development (World Bank, 2021).

When considering what development 'is', modern conceptions of it are often linked back, as noted in Chapter 1, to US President Harry Truman's 1949 Inaugural Address during which he discussed embarking on a bold new programme for the improvement and growth of underdeveloped areas (Schafer, Haslam & Beaudet, 2021). Subsequent initial discussions of development interpreted it more specifically as 'economic growth, structural change, autonomous industrialisation, capitalism or socialism, self-actualisation and individual, national, regional and cultural self-reliance' (Harrison, 1988: 154). Since then, definitions have broadened over time, shifting from a primarily economic focus to encompass social and environmental perspectives incorporating betterment and fulfilment through an expansion of choice (Telfer, 2015). Nevertheless, the continuing challenge in precisely defining and measuring development is reflected in its many different facets, such as examining different levels of industrialisation, considering various segments of the population, the importance of focusing on poverty and development as an aspiration for betterment (Schafer, Haslam & Beaudet, 2021).

Development theory can be examined by looking at development ideology (the ends) and development strategy (the means), whereby development strategy is a way of implementing the development process guided by an ideology (Hettne, 1995). As noted in Chapter 2, in the years following Second World War, different ideologies, policies and strategies including, amongst others, basic needs, grassroots, gender, sustainable development, human development, human rights and human security came to the forefront of development studies (see Chapter 2). Moreover, responsibility for development has fallen under the remit of a wide variety of bodies, from local to global organisations in the public, private and not-for-profit spheres (for example, local to international NGOs) utilising a range of strategies. In 1986, for example, the United

Nations adopted the Declaration on the Right to Development. The rise of sustainability in development thinking can be traced from the report of the World Commission on Environment and Development and its oft-cited and much debated definition of sustainable development – 'development that meets the needs of the present generation without compromising the ability of future generations to meet their own needs' (WCED, 1987: 43) – through Agenda 21 and successive Earth Summits to the Millennium Development Goals (MDGs) and the UN SDGs.

As development broadened in scope, efforts were made to see how tourism could contribute to these new conceptualisations (see Telfer, 2015). The push for mass tourism development in the 1960s as a form of economic growth was soon questioned as awareness over the negative impacts of tourism grew and consequently an emphasis on sustainable tourism development came to the forefront. Nevertheless, tourism continued to grow on a global scale and critics of the ensuing so-called overtourism have called for the need to degrow tourism. In addition, more specific approaches, such as pro-poor tourism, community-based tourism and responsible tourism, and questions of how tourism might contribute to the UN SDGs have been seen as ways to redirect the benefits of tourism to local communities within the guise of sustainability. Hence, Telfer and Sharpley (2016: 11–12) proposed a definition of development incorporating these broader notions, viewing it as 'a complex, multidimensional concept that may be defined as the continuous and positive change in the economic, social, political and cultural dimensions of the human condition, guided by the principles of freedom of choice and limited by the capacity of the environment to sustain such change'.

While international development is inherently normative in trying to address poverty and promote well-being both within and between countries as seen through cosmopolitanism, Schafer, Haslam and Beaudet (2021) nevertheless observe there are approaches resistant to redistributive global justice. Thus, some communitarians hold to the belief that preference needs to be given to fellow citizens whereas, in contrast, some libertarians oppose the obligatory redistribution of wealth both within and between countries. Either way, much of the criticism of development centres on the West imposing its preferred way of life on developing countries, often at the latter's expense; indeed, because of their development, the North now owes an ecological debt to the South especially in the context of climate change as well as a debt of restitution (Latouche, 2009). Sachs (2019), therefore, usefully summarises by arguing that development has gone from an intransitive subject (for example, a flower that seeks maturity) to being used transitively in terms of an active reordering of society to be completed within decades or even years.

Measuring Development and (In)equality

A principal measure of underdevelopment is poverty and there are a variety of indicators for measuring poverty and inequality at the national level. The World Bank classifies economies into four categories based on Gross National Income (GNI) which is adjusted every July 1. For the 2023 fiscal year, low-income economies have a GNI per capital of US$1,085 or less (as recorded in 2021); lower middle-income economies have a GNI per capita between US$1,086 and US$4,225; upper middle-income economies have a GNI per capita between US$4,226 and US$13,205 while high-income economies have a GNI per capita of US$13,205 or more (World Bank, 2022). The World Bank defines extreme poverty as those living on less than US$1.90 a day (the international poverty line) which is a figure utilised in the UN SDGs. The World Bank has a target of reducing the proportion of the global population living in extreme poverty to less than 3 percent by 2030 while the UN SDG Target 1.1 for 2030 is for all countries, regions and groups inside countries to have zero poverty.

Interestingly, Hickel (2017) argues there is growing consensus that the existing international poverty line is too low. He suggests that a threshold of US$5.00 a day is a more honest view of poverty and that the figure may be even higher in developed economies. Writing in the context of when the international poverty line was at US$1.25 a day, Hickel (2017) notes that if the minimum were moved to US$5.00 a day, the global poverty head count would be four times that being indicated by both the World Bank and the Millennium Campaign and that it would represent 60 percent of the world's population. Since 2017, the World Bank has been tracking poverty at US$3.20 a day for lower middle-income countries and US$5.50 for upper middle-income countries; nevertheless, it is the US$1.90 per day figure that still attracts the most attention and that determines how major international targets are being tracked. In 2022, it was suggested that the combination of the global Covid-19 pandemic, rising inflation, supply chain challenges and the war in Ukraine would result in an increase of between 75 and 95 million people living in extreme poverty (Gerszon et al., 2022). Other common country-based classifications linked to levels of development include the G7 and G20, least developed countries, landlocked and small island countries, heavily indebted poor countries, newly industrialising countries, emerging markets and human development level (Todaro & Smith, 2020).

In addition to poverty, another critical dimension for measuring development is the extent of inequality. Inequality is typically measured by the personal or size distribution of income or the functional/distributive factor share of the distribution of income (Todaro & Smith, 2020). One popular indicator of inequality, the Kuznets ratio, measures the degree of income inequality between high- and low-income groups in a country. Another common measure, the Lorenz Curve, plots the cumulative percentages of the population against income with the line of equality running diagonally across the graph. The greater the Lorenz Curve deviates from the line of equality (to the right), the greater the degree of income inequality. A third measure, the Gini Coefficient, measures inequality from the Lorenz Curve on a scale of 0 (perfect equality) to 1 (perfect inequality) by calculating the ratio of the area between the line of equality and the Lorenz Curve and the total area of the half-square where the Curve is present (Todaro & Smith, 2020). Countries with highly unequal income distribution have Gini Coefficients ranging from 0.50 to 0.70 while countries with relatively equal income distribution typically range from 0.20 to 0.35 (Todaro & Smith, 2020). Globally, inequality has been increasing with the rise of the global super-rich and the Kuznets Curve – the inverted U-shape curve which hypothesises that as societies become more sophisticated and productive, inequality transitions from low-inequality to high-inequality and back to low-inequality – has little applicability with surging income inequality becoming a worldwide phenomenon (Freeland, 2012). Income inequality can underpin other forms of inequality demonstrated through the 'web of poverty' (see Chambers, 2006) (for example, less income may lead to poorer health, fewer opportunities, etc.) leaving individuals potentially facing poverty traps and chronic poverty.

Evolution and Critique of GDP

During the Great Depression in the 1930s, the US government asked economist Simon Kuznets to develop an accounting system to measure the monetary value of all goods and services. This he referred to at the time as the Gross National Product (GNP), later becoming the basis of the Gross Domestic Product (GDP). Kuznets, however, pointed out that GDP as a measure of development or progress is flawed as it monetises economic activity but does not care if it is useful or destructive (Hickel, 2020). Nevertheless, since the Second World War, development has continued to be measured primarily by GDP and its expansion remains a dominant feature of the growth of society. Kapoor and Debroy (2019) present a critical overview of GDP. Today's GDP, they argue, was developed after the Second World War based on the work of John Maynard Keynes and, similar to Kuznets' formulation, it is an aggregate measure of the total values of all goods and services produced in an economy. Policy makers and economists have presented GDP (and GDP/capita) as an all-encompassing measure of development that amalgamates economic prosperity and societal well-being. Policies seen to promote economic growth are then viewed as being beneficial for society. Yet GDP only measures the size of the economy of a nation and not welfare; it does not consider the externalities or the negative effects of economic growth including, amongst other things, income inequality which can cause increased polarisation and discontent, health problems associated with growth (for example, increased sugar consumption), environmental degradation, deforestation, pollution and climate change (Kapoor & Debroy, 2019).

In other words, almost anything can be justified so long as it contributes to GDP (Hickel, 2020). In contrast, Jackson (2021) draws on the speeches of Robert F. Kennedy, the 1968 Presidential candidate in the United States, who argued GDP measures too many of the 'bad' things that detract from our life (for example, cigarette advertising, jails, destruction of forests and urban sprawl, nuclear warheads, etc.) as benefits, while missing out on aspects of society such as inequality, unpaid labour, the labour of those caring for children and the elderly at home, the quality of education, the health of children and so on. Kennedy went on to state 'It measures everything, in short, except that which makes life worthwhile'.

Globally, we have become addicted to growth as measured through GDP. Consequently, society's fate is based on endless accumulation and any slow-down is met with a crisis or panic; 'jobs, retirement pensions, and increased public spending (education, law and order, justice, culture, transport, etc.) all presuppose a constant rise in Gross Domestic Product' (Latouche, 2009: 16). Western nations typically embrace a geometric progression of economic growth that utilises a per capita GDP growth rate of 3.5 percent per year (the average rate of growth of France from 1949–59). This means that GDP will grow by a multiple of 31 over 100 years and of 961 in 200 years (Latouche, 2009). In an era of ecological decline and climate change, expectations of continued expansion of GDP are, therefore, utterly counter-intuitive. Furthermore, empirical evidence on decoupling GDP growth from resource use and carbon emissions does not support green growth theory (Hickel and Kallis, 2020, see also Jackson, 2021). In other words, the argument that, through efficiencies and technological innovation, GDP can continue to grow whilst overall resource use can be reduced (so-called absolute decoupling) does not stand up to scrutiny.

Inevitably, tourism's contribution to GDP is often cited as a key indicator of the importance of tourism to the host country. However, this needs to be put in context of the wider externalities that the industry causes (see also Chapter 5). With the shift towards services, tourism is becoming more resource-intensive via those working in the industry spending their wages on consumer products, whilst the industry itself requires substantial material infrastructure and resources such as planes, ships and airports (Hickel, 2020). Hence, the curious situation emerges in which overtourism is portrayed as having a negative impact in destinations yet represents a net benefit to GDP; similarly, tourism is a contributor to climate change yet investments in seawalls to protect tourist resorts from sea-level rise due to climate change contribute positively to GDP.

Relying on continued high rates of economic growth is also noted as problematic by Jackson (2021) who argues that overall growth rates of 5 percent in the USA of 1968 are long gone. Prior to the pandemic in 2020, average growth rates across OECD nations were barely 2 percent. If labour productivity becomes stationary or goes into decline (as it did during the pandemic), the only way to squeeze growth in GDP out of an economy is by increasing the overall hours spent working either by having more people work or having them work longer, neither of which is consistent with the promise of capitalism; if labour productivity declines, we have already entered a post-growth world (Jackson, 2021). Overall, then, and as Desai and Potter (2002) argue, economic growth is necessary but not sufficient for development as it needs to be broadened to incorporate human rights and other notions of welfare. Moreover, as will be discussed later in this chapter, the proponents of degrowth argue that economic growth itself needs to be reduced and brought back in line with environmental limits.

Beyond GDP as a Measure of Welfare

In his analysis of 15 years of data in West African countries, Ekpo (2016) identifies the paradox of growth without development; while average growth rates of approximately 5 percent were achieved, there was evidence of only marginal gains in some development indicators. Hence, income-based indicators only go so far in measuring development. Consequently, other measures of development have been put forward that broaden the focus beyond economic growth and GDP, whilst Kapoor and Debroy (2019) argue that there needs to be a better measure of welfare that incorporates externalities for a truer measure of development so policies can then be better generated to address externalities.

The UNDP's Human Development Index (HDI) was introduced in 1990. It measures socio-economic development based on measures in health, education and adjusted real income per capita and ranks each country on a scale of 0 (lowest human development) to 1 (highest human development). The HDI is based in part on Sen's (1985: 13) capability approach defined as 'the freedom that a person has in terms of the choice of functionings, given his personal features (conversion of characteristics into functionings) and his command over commodities'. Todaro and Smith (2020) argue that Sen's perspective illustrates the importance development economists subsequently placed on health and education (as seen in the HDI) and later, on social inclusion and empowerment; consequently, countries with high levels of income but poor education and health standards therefore represent nations with 'growth without development'. Sen (1999, 2011) also called for the expansions of freedom for development and the importance of justice. In response, the UNDP produces the Inequality-Adjusted Human Development Index (IHDI) and the Gender Inequality Index (GII) and, in 2010, refined the HDI and implemented the New Human Development Index (NHDI). Furthermore, the UNDP also publishes the global Multidimensional Poverty Index (MPI) (replacing the Human Poverty Index 1997–2009) that measures three dimensions of poverty: health (nutrition, child mortality); education (years of schooling and school attendance); and standard of living (cooking fuel, sanitation, drinking water, electricity, housing, and assets). In 2021, the MPI examined 5.9 billion living in 109 countries and found that more than one in five, or 1.3 billion people, live in multidimensional poverty (UNDP & OPHI, 2021).

Other measurements of welfare include Bhutan's Gross National Happiness Index (which incorporates socio-economic development and good governance), India's Ease of Living Index (which incorporates quality of life, economic ability and sustainability) (Kapoor & Debroy, 2019), and the Index of Sustainable Economic Welfare and the Genuine Progress Indicator, both of which attempt to correct GDP for ecological and social costs (Hickel, 2020). Other international organisational efforts include the OECD's High Level Expert Group on the 'Measurement of Economic Performance and Social Progress' and the European Commission's 'Beyond GDP program'. A range of other countries have indicated they will move away from GDP, including New Zealand, Scotland, Costa Rica, Ecuador and Bolivia. Notably, in 2019, New Zealand formally dropped GDP as its main indicator of economic success and instead is now aiming at maximising well-being by allocating resources based on their impact on five government priorities including: 'mental health, child well-being, inequalities of Indigenous people, building a nation adapted to the digital age and fashioning a low emission economy' (Pilling, 2019). Despite these initiatives to develop new measures for well-being, GDP still reigns supreme and if a country's GDP declines, governments face enormous pressures to re-establish growth. Later in the chapter, transitional discourses and degrowth will be examined in detail as options for moving away from the dominant growth model and GDP.

Development as Social Progress

In addition to definitions and measurements, development can be examined in terms of the evolution of social progress. Nederveen Pieterse (2000: 182) contends that development thinking is immersed in both social engineering and ambitions to shape societies and economies, rendering it both a managerialist and interventionist discipline; 'It involves telling other people what to do – in the name of modernisation, nation building, progress, mobilisation, sustainable development, human rights, poverty alleviation and even empowerment and participation (participatory management)'. With different ideological underpinnings in development thought (for example, conservative, liberal, radical and so on: see Goldsworthy, 1988), increased calls have been made for a better understanding of the role of power and politics within development (World Bank, 2017).

In addition, Hettne (2009) argues that schools of development thinking need to be contextualised historically as opposed to being understood as a cumulative evolution of ideas that, in turn, leads to a universal development theory. To note significant moments of change which, he maintains, can only be understood in retrospect, Hettne (2010) draws on the ideas of Polanyi's 'Great Transformations'. These transformations in economic history reflect a phase of expansion and deepening of the market system that is then accompanied by a second phase of political intervention where 'defenders of society' seek greater political intervention to control and regulate the markets. A compromise between these two different political camps can create a period of stable equilibrium. The first Great Transformation arose after the Depression in the 1930s which led to increased state intervention (Keynesian economics), whilst the second shift began in the 1970s in a time of stagflation. This resulted in a move towards freeing markets from government intervention that lasted for three decades and is noted for a market-friendly political framework that served capital accumulation and economic growth (c.f., Milton Friedman) over considerations of environmental protection and social justice. The third discursive change began with the 2008 financial crisis and numerous paradigmatic changes, from renewed calls for intervention in the markets to the Nobel prize-winning political economist Elinor Ostrom's work on sustainable resource management, the commons and civil society. In examining the evolution of these changes, Hettne (2010) called for an emerging paradigm of global development.

What these 'Great Transformations' illustrate is that the evolution of societal progress has never been in a straight line. Fukuyama (1992), who controversially declared 'The End of History' by referencing the ascendancy of Western liberal democracy spread by globalisation, has raised concerns over threats to democracy and pondered future uncertainty and crisis (Tharoor, 2017), not least with liberalism being challenged by populists on the right and a renewed progressive left (Fukuyama, 2022). In a similar vein, Harari (2018: 11) argues that Fukuyama's 'End of History' (the ascendancy of a 'liberal package of democracy, human rights, free markets and government welfare services') has been postponed as people are becoming increasingly disillusioned with liberalism which has no obvious answers to ecological collapse and technical disruption. In his final Presidential address, President Obama

(2017) also noted that, regarding democracy, 'For every two steps forward, it often feels like we take one step back'.

More recently, Steger and James (2020) have argued that, because of the Covid-19 pandemic, we are experiencing the most profound wave of what they refer to as the 'Great Unsettling', or the apparent degeneration of the current globalised system. The 'Great Unsettling' is shorthand for the intensifying dynamics of 'instability, disintegrations, insecurity, dislocation, relativism, inequality, and degradation that are threatening familiar lifeworlds' (Steger & James, 2020: 188). This, they suggest, is manifested in economic dislocation, precarious work, automation, technological transformation, inequality, migration, cultural shifts and climate change (Steger & James, 2019; Steger, 2019). Others echo the 'Great Unsettling' argument; Ghemawat (2017) states that 'business leaders are scrambling to adjust to a world few imagined possible just a year ago. The myth of a borderless world has come crashing down', whilst Kimmerer (2013: 327) complains that '[we] are deluged by information regarding our destruction of the world and hear almost nothing about how to nurture it'. Our obsession with growth has resulted in anxious, hyperactive consumers (Jackson, 2021) as part of what Bauman (2005) refers to as a 'liquid life', a precarious life lived under constant uncertainty which has led to many social challenges. In a world so connected, loneliness is sweeping the world; atomisation is rupturing social bonds and collapsing shared ambitions and civic life is defined by chronic loneliness linked to a multitude of mental and physical health problems (Monbiot, 2017).

And so, the path of social progress continues to evolve. Some predict the demise of globalisation in favour of localism while others see globalisation continuing, but in a revised form. Still others advocate that societal progress now means taking a step back from continued economic growth (degrowth), especially in the face of climate change; all the evidence suggests that growth is outpacing the Earth's ability to sustain it. Different ideologies, perspectives, systems and strategies have been offered on how to achieve progress or development. Social theories are contestable and include intricacies such as: understanding that social processes are not singular or one-dimensional/ one directional; embracing contradiction and dialectical dynamics; accepting change and continuities are not binary but intermingle; understanding new terms like 'fluidity' and 'liquidity' are not useful categories for appreciating social complexity; realising economics, even within the context of capitalist production, is not the overriding factor in all social action; and recognising 'epochs' are only names assigned to dominant characteristics and gestalt of a specific period (Steger & James, 2020). This suggests that, in the context of the 'Great Unsettling', there needs to be a redefinition of development as the objective of tourism. If tourism is to contribute towards social progress or development, however defined, it needs to be understood within the evolving field of development studies and its related theories, ideologies and strategies (Telfer, 2009). The following section will address globalisation and the political economy of tourism.

GLOBALISATION AND THE POLITICAL ECONOMY OF TOURISM: A PATH TO EXPLOITATION AND INEQUALITY?

Tourism is facilitated by the process of globalisation promoted by economic neoliberalism as open borders allow for the flows of investment and tourists. Multinational tourism operators tend to seek out destinations with low labour costs and fewer environmental restrictions, often repatriating profits outside the destination. Much of the exploitation and inequality in tourism can, therefore, be attributed to the ambitions of capitalism facilitated through globalisation which has been critiqued within the political economy of tourism. While there is substantial research on how tourism functions in terms of capitalist political economy, there has been no systematic analysis of what post-capitalism tourism may look like (Fletcher et al., 2021a). Nevertheless, Koch and Buch-Hansen (2020) argue that contemporary political economy and its emphasis on the social, political, ideational and institutional context where capitalism is embedded, as well as its focus on power relations, struggles and interests, can offer important insights for degrowth, especially in the areas of the environment and the ecological downsides of economic growth. Focusing on managerial ecology, for example, Hall (2019) stresses the need to rethink human–environment relationships as there is a mistaken belief that more effort and greater efficiencies will solve sustainable tourism's problems. Therefore, drawing together globalisation and the political economy of tourism, the following sections set the stage for examining degrowth and reconsidering development as the objective of tourism.

Globalisation

Social progress, development and underdevelopment have been profoundly influenced by globalisation. Globalisation is the process through which the economies of the world have become more integrated and increasingly open to international trade, direct foreign investment and financial flows. This in turn has led to a global economy in which global economic policy is increasingly set through agencies such as the World Trade Organization, the International Monetary Fund or the World Bank (for example, Structural Adjustment lending) (Todaro & Smith, 2020). Nation states have been encouraged to adopt the neoliberal economic policies of the Washington Consensus in order to liberalise trade, leading to time–space convergence (a shrinking world) guided by the 'invisible hand', Adam Smith's metaphor for the free market (Todaro & Smith, 2020).

In his book *The World is Flat*, Friedman (2005) argues there have been three great eras of globalisation. The first began in 1492 with Columbus setting sail and the opening of trade between the Old and New World. This lasted until 1800, and the dynamic force in this Globalisation 1.0 was countries globalising. The second era (Globalisation 2.0) covered the period from 1800–2000 (interrupted by the Great Depression and two World Wars) with the key agent of change being multinational companies globalising. Finally, Globalisation 3.0 began in 2000 with the world shrinking from small to tiny accompanied by a flattening of the playing field. Here, the dynamic force has been the newfound power of the individual collaborating and competing globally, facilitated by the flat-world platform or personal computing linked to the wider world. Sadiku, Okhiria and Musa (2020) have elaborated on Friedman's work, arguing that Globalisation 4.0 has just begun, one feature of which will be the impact on the service sector as service-sector employees will be more exposed to both the opportunities and challenges of globalisation. Examples of indices for measuring globalisation include the 'KOF Globalisation Index' which incorporates economic, social and political dimensions while the 'Maastricht Globalisation Index' incorporates similar categories in addition to technological and ecological domains.

There has long been back and forth sentiment, known as the globalisation 'yo-yo effect', whereby the virtues of globalisation are contrasted with more pessimistic views emphasising its negative attributes and calling for a revival of localism and protectionism (Ghemawat, 2018). de la Dehesa's (2007) title *Winners and Losers in Globalization* illustrates these tensions, whilst Todaro and Smith (2020) also outline the benefits, opportunities, costs and risks of globalisation. Broadly speaking, some argue that globalisation presents new business opportunities and efficiencies gained from trade and growth in innovation and knowledge as well as via knowledge and technology transfers to developing countries. An interconnected world may also be less likely to engage in conflict or war; certainly, a globalised world is an environment in which tourism thrives.

Globalisation is also inherently linked with capitalism and the drive for economic growth. The global economic order since the end of the Second World War, of which globalisation is a part, has contributed to the fastest rate of global economic growth and created a new global middle class (Stiglitz, 2018). Jackson (2021: 3), however, notes that 'Every culture, every society, clings to a myth by which it lives. Ours is the myth of growth. For as long as the economy continues to expand, we feel assured that life is getting better'. On the one hand, there is no question that economic development has resulted in tremendous advancements, lifting millions out of poverty and offering comfort, luxury and complexity for those who can afford it (Jackson, 2021). Economic growth has also led to social progress via 'nutrition, medicine, shelter, mobility, flight, connectivity, entertainment, to name just a few of the many rewards (Jackson, 2021: 4). Yet, on the other hand, all this progress and continued economic growth has come at a tremendous cost to the natural world as species are disappearing, forests are being decimated, habitats are being lost and agricultural land is under threat through economic expansion. As discussed in more detail in Chapter 4 of this book, anthropocentric-induced climate change has led to a myriad of crises including sea-level rise, ocean acidification, drought, forest fires and storm intensification (Jackson, 2021).

Concerns over globalisation have focused on growing inequalities both across and within countries and the dominance of rich countries expanding, leaving some regions and people behind as noted by Todaro and Smith (2020). Poorer countries are at greater risk of becoming locked into dependency if dualism becomes entrenched or if the poorest are bypassed by globalisation, aggravating the challenges of breaking out of poverty traps. The operations of multinational corporations (MNCs) and unbalanced international trade negotiations / rulings (for example, under the General Agreements on Tariffs and Trade (GATT), World Bank and the IMF) often reduce the power of the state with the poorest developing countries facing trade protectionism from developed countries, especially in the areas of agriculture. Countries, and in particular developing countries, also face a threat to cultural identity with the emergence of a 'global culture' in which English becomes the dominant language and where globally, people start consuming similar goods and services (Todaro & Smith, 2020). Tension and hostility have evolved alongside globalisation as people and nations strive to enhance selfish interests and to become winners in an economic battle, placing everyone else in the position of losers; consequently, there has been an alarming rise in nationalism, xenophobia, fear and mistrust (Yunus, 2017). From a structural perspective, Standing (2014) argues that globalisation has aggravated the capitalist exploitation of the working class, in so doing trashing their social fabric. Therefore, there needs to be a reassessment as to whether growth, and tourism's contribution to growth, can continue along the same path given these significant concerns over the consequences of globalisation.

Foreign direct investment, which is a key component in globalisation (and tourism), also does not always generate purported benefits as contended by Todaro and Smith (2020). Although MNCs provide capital, they can lower domestic savings and investment rates, stifle competition and inhibit the expansion of domestic firms. While MNCs provide investment, thereby improving the foreign exchange earnings of the receiving country, this can be offset by the importation of products rather than using local supplies and the repatriation of profits. Similarly, while MNCs contribute to public revenue through corporate taxes, this is often offset by liberal tax concessions, investment allowances, transfer pricing, public subsidies and tariff protection offered by the host government. Finally, the management, entrepreneurial skills and technology delivered by MNCs may inhibit the development of these skills locally and stifle Indigenous entrepreneurship. A specific example of the limitations of globalisation, and major shock to it, was the global 2008 financial collapse which the Nobel Peace Prize winner and founder of the Grameen microcredit bank Muhammad Yunus (2017) argues was linked to excessive greed in the marketplace, the failure of regulatory institutions and the effective transformation of the investment market into a gambling casino. Although there were subsequent attempts to reform the liberal policies of globalisation, the 2008 crisis served to intensify income gaps, to contribute to environmental degradation, to foment nationalistic responses (for example, Brexit) and to generate political competition between superpowers (Beaudet, 2021).

The global pandemic, the recent global supply chain problems and the resulting inflation all present further threats to globalisation. In the context of the current 'Great Unsettling' and calls from some for a 'de-globalisation', Steger and James (2020) argue that this era represents an opportunity to evaluate globalisation. They highlight the principal task to be profound social reform with the aim of 'managing globalisation better' via the enhancement of institutional capabilities. The route to this, they suggest, lies in strengthening global solidarity and building a stronger global governance architecture; equally, however, they note this is unrealistic given the current national populism era as well as the emerging crisis conditions. Their proposed framework for moving forward incorporates the following four principal formulations of globalisation: (i) embodied globalisation (physical mobility of humans – migrants, refugees, workers, tourists, etc.); (ii) object-related globalisation (mobility of physical objects like consumer goods, tangible exchange tokens such as coins/notes but also industrial refuse, greenhouse gas emissions, pollution, and viruses); (iii) institutionally related globalisation (mobility conducted through agents of states, institutions, TNCs, INGOs, etc.); and (iv) disembodied globalisation (intangible things and processes including exchange of ideas, software, cryptocurrencies, etc.). Steger and James (2020) go on to argue that globalisation is far from finished and the current crisis may in fact lead to the regeneration of a new globalisation. In a similar way, Stiglitz (2018) proposes three options for the future of globalisation (noting the first two will not work): (i) doubling down on the Washington Consensus; (ii) new protectionism; and (iii) fair globalisation with shared prosperity. As will be highlighted later, some degrowth supporters claim that restructuring global markets is a way to a post-growth society.

Globalisation has changed the world outlined in President Harry Truman's 1949 Inauguration Speech, from three worlds with two competing development projects to the contemporary situation in which we now have one development project that is 'losing both its sustainability and its traditional guardians' (Anderson, 2020: 112), a further reflection of the 'Great Unsettling'. Countries at the upper end of modernisation trajectories are encountering serious social problems while growth in China and other emerging markets is generating new upper-middle classes living 'modern role lives'. As Anderson (2020) notes, these global 'role model lives' are increasingly lived behind barbed wire and security cameras with security companies protecting those who can afford it as the new social geopolitics of poverty takes hold. It is, according to Anderson (2020), the economic and material provisioning of these 'role model lives' that needs to be changed to save the planet. Moreover, the globalisation of information also raises concerns in terms of privacy and human rights. This is very much echoed in tourism in terms of, for example, access to personal records by accommodation establishments and security screenings at airports (Hashimoto, Härkönen & Nkyi, 2021). Hence, overall, globalisation's promises of inclusive growth and better living conditions for everyone has become elusive whilst, ironically, the rise of the global civil society through protests, networks and movements has actually challenged the very foundations of globalisation (Beaudet, 2021).

The Political Economy of Tourism as a Lens for Redefining Development as the Objective of Tourism

Studies in political economy investigate the socio-economic forces and power relations involved in the production of commodities for markets and the resulting divisions, inequalities and conflicts that arise (Bianchi, 2018). The application of this critical lens to growth, globalisation, capitalism and tourism offers a pathway to redefine development as the objective of tourism.

The early foundations of political economy include the work of Adam Smith, David Ricardo and Karl Marx. Smith and Ricardo focused on the nature of capitalism with Smith famously arguing that free individuals motivated by self-interest without state interference and guided by the invisible hand of the market would generate a peaceful and productive society (Heidrich, 2021). Ricardo is best known for his theory of comparative advantage, whereby countries should specialise in the production of goods they are best at (that is, at the lowest opportunity cost) resulting in benefits in international trade for all. In this sense, sunny beach destinations then have a comparative advantage in tourism. In contrast, Marx adopted a much more critical perspective, claiming that the rules of the market benefit employers or landowners and leave workers at a disadvantage. International trade and investment flows result in similar exploitative relations between countries. There are four main approaches to political economy that are popular in social sciences (Mosedale,

2011): Marxian political economy; examinations of regulatory frameworks or the structure of capitalism; comparative and international political economists' analysis of regulatory structures and trade relationships between states; and political economy based on post-structuralism or post-Marxism focusing on alternatives to capitalism.

Early critical research on the political economy of tourism focused primarily on the analysis of the contributions of tourism to economic development scrutinised from various strands of development theory, such as modernisation or dependency, while more recent approaches in the political economy of tourism reflect critical scholarship, including post-structuralist perspectives on cultural political economy and Marxian-influenced studies drawing on contemporary radical political economy (Bianchi, 2018). These various perspectives within the political economy of tourism offer potentially valuable insights into the need to redefine development as the objective of tourism.

Tourism has, as discussed in Chapter 2, long been used as a driver of economic growth. Importantly, this economic growth has been equated with development measured by visitor numbers, income, jobs, foreign exchange and investment, all geared to increased consumption. However, studies on the political economy of tourism highlight that growth does not always necessarily lead to development; indeed, in the context of tourism, growth can lead to exploitation, inequality and ecological destruction. Early works in the political economy of tourism focused on state-centric approaches epitomised by the neo-colonial dependency model but, more recently, these have been eclipsed by the need to critically evaluate the reconfigured power relations that have arisen due to capitalistic restructuring and economic globalisation dominated by transnational tourism corporations (Bianchi, 2015). This continued drive for growth though tourism as a globalised capitalistic endeavour reflects Jackson's (2021) comments that the affluence we aspire to through sustained economic growth more generally has been purchased at an unpayable price and that the myth of economic growth which we have relied on is now undoing us. Interestingly, David Attenborough (2020), the British naturalist and broadcaster, identified tourism in a list of parameters that is used to measure growth. This list also includes GDP, energy use, water use, dam construction, telecommunications and the increase in farmland as indicators that have all shown a marked rapid increase in the period of the so-called Great Acceleration after the Second World War. Commensurately, however, measurements of carbon in the atmosphere, ocean acidification and the loss of fish populations and tropical forests all demonstrate the same sharp rise which, according to Attenborough (2020), cannot be allowed to continue.

In a critique of the reign of speed in a globalised society, Cronin (2012: 90) draws on Virilio's (2009) political economy of speed and comments: '[the] cult of mobility, the economic premium of speed, and the diminution of responsibility which comes with rapidity of displacement (transnational corporations leaving locals to clean up the ecological mess they leave behind) does indeed make being in the sky as opposed to being stuck on the ground a more attractive proposition for global elites'. 'Being in the sky' relates to a further index of globalisation, namely, the volume of air traffic, with airports focused on mobility, transition and acceleration. While airports are physically grounded, they are about being up in the air and events such as security delays and company collapses are such bleak scenarios that they often feature in national news (Cronin, 2012). Indeed, in the desire to return to travel in the wake of the global pandemic (so-called revenge travel), international news continues to highlight airline passengers struggling with significant flight cancellations, long delays and lost luggage as airports struggle to meet rising demand.

Despite the significance of tourism to many national economies and global trade as a whole, research in tourism development has largely been disconnected from or marginalised in political economy (Bianchi, 2018; Mosedale, 2011; Yrigoy, 2019). More specifically, Britton (1991) – a pioneer of tourism political economy – argued that the capitalist nature of tourism as an avenue in capitalist accumulation had not been fully grasped by scholars, even though as Bianchi (2018) notes, there is considerable corporate concentration most notably in international tour operations, hotel chains and airlines. This concentration affords an examination of the political economy of tourism across a multitude of firms that vary in size, ownership and scope (Bianchi, 2018). For instance, the political economy lens illustrates how overtourism occurs as a result of the pressure from multinational tourism organisations pursuing pro-growth approaches to tourism development (Higgins-Desbiolles et al., 2019). The tourism value chain identifies the complex horizontal and vertical linkages of tourism organisations and is a window into power structures and resulting multipliers in both the formal and informal economy (Telfer & Sharpley, 2016). A more detailed examination of the capitalist nature of the supply of tourism is provided in Chapter 5. For the purposes of this chapter, however, a few examples are presented to demonstrate briefly the value of the political economy of tourism lens in redefining development as the objective of tourism. In her book on disaster capitalism, Klein (2007) observes that following the 2004 Indian Ocean tsunami, Sri Lankan coastal towns that had been destroyed were initially restricted as buffer zones but later developed for tourism, though with limited local involvement. She also documents the intensification of neoliberal policies at work in tourism-dependent Puerto Rico after Hurricane Maria in 2017 left the island vulnerable to outside developers taking advantage of reduced tax rates (Klein, 2018). Another issue is that the globalisation of the tourism industry has allowed it to search for low-cost labour in both developing and developed countries. In Dubai, much of the futuristic metropolis tourism infrastructure was built by migrant workers whose working conditions have been criticised (Jacobs, 2018), whilst in Niagara-on-the-Lake, Canada, tourism is built around the narrative of a historical idyll, gastronomy and farm-to-table but is dependent on a globalised labour force of migrant farm workers (Lozanski & Baumgartner, 2022). The latter study highlights the invisibility of migrant labour and the precarity of transnational workers in global capitalism. Similarly, the tourism industry in Spain took advantage of changes in government labour regulations in 2012 to outsource hotel cleaning services, resulting in reduced wages for hotel cleaning staff and increased precariousness of employment (Badcock, 2017).

Tourism is often portrayed as a 'smokeless' industry yet involves considerable resource use not only in terms of the consumption of natural resources but also in terms of the spread of new forms of tourism, such as through the sharing economy (a notable example being Airbnb). During the Covid-19 pandemic, for example, water usage in the Balearic Islands fell by 24.4 percent, which therefore can be considered as the percentage of water directly used by tourism (Garcia et al., 2022). The development of online sharing platforms is another example of the global reach of tourism and resource use expansion. While the rise of the sharing economy, including Airbnb, offers local people the opportunity to rent out spare rooms in order to generate additional income, it leads to further commodification as empty rooms have value (and cost less than hotels) and may in the end lead to more travel and more resource use (Kallis, 2018). Property rental ownership and the concentration in this sector is also causing speculation and gentrification, thereby pricing locals out of the housing market. Under the auspices of degrowth, tourism planning instruments were implemented to deal with overtourism in Spain. However, they were met with crippling contradictions as they were not able to deal with the capitalist accumulation model that underlies tourism growth they set to address (Blázquez-Salom et al., 2019).

These brief examples illustrate how the political economy of tourism can provide a range of critiques on the capitalist nature of tourism, its inherent unbalanced power relationships and the resulting inequalities and resource use that occur with the industry. These critiques further amplify the need to question the role that tourism plays in the development process. Even sustainable tourism is based on the premise of continued economic growth, illustrating the need to redefine development as the objective of tourism especially in the context of the crises facing the planet. The following section, therefore, introduces transitional discourses as a means to bring about a transformation of society and, particularly, a shift away from the dominant growth model. Transitional discourses, including degrowth, have embraced new meanings and strategies of development that focus on equity and well-being. It is, therefore, important to explore what tourism would look like in a post-growth world in which it could contribute equitably to well-being and in which throughput is reduced to be in balance with the planet. Degrowth, as one transitional discourse, represents a re-enchantment of the world based on the values of altruism, conviviality and respect to nature (Latouche, 2009).

FROM CRISES TO TRANSITIONAL DISCOURSES AND THE PLURIVERSE

Social progress tied to the growth imperative has generated a range of crises that reveal the necessity for new perspectives and strategies. 'The relentless pursuit of eternal growth has delivered ecological destruction, financial fragility and social instability (Jackson, 2021: 13). The environmental crises and their implications for tourism are the focus of Chapter 4 while this section introduces transitional discourses. Transitional discourses advance profound transformations (cultural, economic and political) by demonstrating the damaging effects of the dominant social model and its focus on the individual, consumption, the market, capitalism and separation from nature in order to direct attention towards the pressing need to transform our culture and economy (Escobar, 2015). The emergence of transitional discourses, which has accelerated in recent decades in both academia and activist life, reflects not only the multiple crises facing the planet but also the 'inability of established policy and knowledge institutions to imagine ways out of such crises' (Escobar, 2015: 452). Transitional discourses represent a radical departure from the pressures of neoliberal globalisation (both in the Global North and the Global South); a commonality in many such perspectives is the need to step out of existing institutional and epistemic boundaries to envision new worlds and new practices that can result in significant transformations (Escobar, 2015).

Early notable work includes Illich's (1973) proposal for a transition from an industrial society to a convivial society, in which he set out not to describe a utopian fictional community of the future but, rather, to establish guidelines for action to endow each community with choice in terms of its unique social arrangements. Since then, a range of the different transitional discourses have emerged in both the North and South (Escobar, 2018; 2015). Examples in the North include degrowth, transition initiatives (for example, Transition Town Initiative, UK; Great Transition Initiative; the Great Turning (Macy & Johnstone, 2012)), the Anthropocene debates, forecasting trends, inter-religious dialogues as well as some of the UN processes. In the South, transitional discourses comprise post-development and alternatives to development; Buen Vivir and the rights of nature; crisis of the civilisational model; communalisation; and a transition to post-extractivism. The recent collection *Pluriverse: A Post-Development Dictionary* edited by Kothari, Salleh, Escobar, Demaria and Acosta (2019a: xix) presents 85 entries on transformative initiatives that represent a range of worldviews and practices, both new and old and local and global 'emerging from indigenous, peasant and pastoral communities, urban neighbourhoods, environmental, feminist and spiritual movements'.

In her book *Braiding Sweetgrass*, Kimmerer (2013: 111) focuses particularly on Indigenous wisdom, scientific knowledge and what plants can teach us. She discusses multiple Indigenous concepts including the Honourable Harvest and the Haudenosaunee 'Thanksgiving Address' or, in the Onondaga language, the 'Words That Come Before All Else', which sets gratitude before all else. This notion is the direct opposite to a market economy. 'In a consumer society, contentment is a radical proposition. Recognising abundance rather than scarcity undermines an economy that thrives by creating unmet desires. Gratitude cultivates an ethic of fulness, but the economy needs emptiness'. She goes on to state that cultures of gratitude must be cultures of reciprocity and laments the loss of the Honourable Harvest that cannot be found in the marketplace of the shopping mall.

In *Out of the Wreckage: A New Politics for an Age of Crisis*, Monbiot (2017) calls for a transformation of politics with a 'politics of belonging', while Anderson (2020) argues that there is a need to reconstruct the global political economy. Focusing on climate, Klein (2019, 2014) argues that we have not done the things required to lower emissions as such actions would fundamentally conflict with deregulating capitalism. An alternative proposal, the Green New Deal, focuses on meeting basic material needs, offering solutions to gender and racial inequities and rapidly transitioning to renewable energy (Klein, 2019). Solón (2022) calls for an approach of complementarity in systematic alternatives which are multidimensional alternatives that begin to challenge 'capitalism, productivism, extractivism, patriarchy, anthropocentrism, plutocracy, xenophobia, colonialism and other structural factors of the systemic crises' that we face. However, in order to build such systematic alternatives, Solón (2022) contends that we need to start with different theoretical postulates, experiences and visions of approaches such as 'the commons, degrowth, Vivir Bien, ecosocialism, the rights of Mother Earth, ecofeminism, food sovereignty, just transitions, deglobalisation and many others'. None of these alone can address the complexities of systemic crisis but, rather, these approaches need to engage in a process of complementarity (Solón, 2022). He goes on to argue that systemic alternatives cannot be reduced to a list of good practices; rather, good practices need to deepen and transform themselves, and this evolution may be fraught with crises, contradictions and conflict, without which the 'good practice' may be captured by the system it aspired to change. An example of this can be found in the concept of the green economy which originally promoted a different relationship between the economy and nature but has now become a new approach to the commodification of nature and paying for environmental services. Solón (2022) highlights REDD+, a framework created by the UN Framework Convention on Climate Change to reduce emissions from deforestation and forest degradation while enhancing forest carbon stocks and sustainable forestry management as a case in point.

Within the wide range of transitional discourses, Escobar (2018; 2015) advocates that conversations should be generated between proponents of degrowth in the North and of post-development in the South to enrich both movements and, in so doing, divisions between the two will tend to dissipate as pluriversal perspectives emerge. Simon (2007) also argues for convergence in alternative, critical and post-development thinking, suggesting that it is important to move beyond critique alone if poverty and profound inequality are to be confronted. The various discursive storylines of transitional discourses can converge on key issues, such as resistance to neoliberalism, which then may highlight synergies and points of convergence (Feola & Jaworska, 2019). Escobar (2018; 2015) postulates the features of the age to come in the North denote post-growth, post-materialist, post-economic, post-capitalist and post-human, while in the South features of the age to come denote post-development, non-liberal, post/non-capitalist, biocentric and post-extractivist. In setting out the degrowth hypothesis in particular, Kallis (2018) argues that the transformation of society will either occur through a broader political project embracing the need to reduce throughput and improve living conditions or through catastrophe where only a few will be able to maintain their lifestyles which will come at the expense of the many. Nevertheless, within these varying proposals for change, it is important to consider the politics of the real and the politics of the possible or, to put it another way, between pragmatism and utopianism (Escobar, 2018). Yet significantly, all transitional discourses point to the end of development as it is currently framed and raise important questions for all.

INTRODUCTION TO DEGROWTH

Degrowth is found amongst the transitional discourses and, as the term implies, it is first a critique of the ecological consequences of economic growth (Kallis, 2018). At a broad level, degrowth represents a political vision of radical societal transformation built on ecological, economic, philosophical and cultural critiques of growth, development, capitalism and the market (Escobar, 2018). Degrowth incorporates a range of perspectives on the pathway to a post-growth world. Related terms include 'conviviality, decolonisation, political ecology, socio-ecological economics, happy sobriety, voluntary simplicity, ecofeminism, municipalism, green new deal, transition, permaculture, prosperity without growth and autonomy', bringing the movements associated with these expressions into a veritable convergence with degrowth (Liegey & Nelson, 2020: 12). The dominant paradigm of society is continued progress and so post-growth is a necessary thought-world, a way of thinking about the world when the obsession with growth has passed; an unchartered territory where 'plenty isn't measured in dollars and fulfilment isn't driven by the relentless accumulation of material wealth' (Jackson, 2021: xv). Kimmerer (2013: 31) puts it another way by reminding us of the importance of the commons and the difference between the market economy and the gift economy. 'The market economy has spread like wildfire, with uneven results for human well-being and devastation for the natural world ... If all the world is a commodity, how poor we grow. When the world is a gift in motion, how wealthy we become.'

Kallis (2018: 113) argues that, unlike growth, 'degrowth is nowhere to be observed – but neither are "green growth" or "sustainable development" and that does not prevent a proliferation of research on these topics.' It is these explorations of new frontiers of social progress that allow us to explore '*Life After Capitalism*' (Jackson, 2021) or, more specifically, '*The Day the World Stops Shopping*' (MacKinnon, 2021) and, in the context of this book, what tourism could look like in a degrowth world. So, degrowth is currently a 'thought process' with a variety of perspectives, a plural, interdisciplinary conversation with multiple strands of knowledge, experiences, perspectives and cultures (Kallis, 2018).

From an economic perspective, there are two main outlooks on degrowth which partly reflect a geographic or cultural split (Kallis, 2018). The first perspective aligns with the work of Latouche (2009) (his eight 'Rs' of degrowth are presented below), Illich (1973) and some authors from the South, all of whom criticise how economists frame reality. From this perspective, there is a need to exit existing economics and mobilise different forms of knowledge and models of reality to engage with what economists engage in as 'economic'. The central objective is decentring the economy both as a unit of analysis and as a focus of political action. The authors from the South in particular critique colonialism and Western ideas of progress as a way of living imposed on everyone else. The second perspective on the economics of degrowth is one of heterodox – ecological and political – as evident in the works of Northern economists such as Daly (1996) and Jackson (2008); it develops a critique within the field of economics. Working within economic models, theories and data, these authors investigate how economic stability could be maintained without growth. In other words, they aspire to a new economics, but still an economics.

Ultimately then, degrowth is not rigid dogma but, rather, a challenge to the logic of growth for growth's sake and a source of diversity (Latouche, 2009). Perhaps unsurprisingly, degrowth in tourism is an emerging area of research, exploring what tourism would look like in a post-capitalist world (Bianchi, 2018; Fletcher et al., 2020); however, its incorporation into tourism practices is limited (Lundmark, Zhang & Hall, 2020). Tourism and degrowth will be the focus of Chapter 7. The following section will therefore explore the history, key concepts, different perspectives and criticisms of the thought-world of degrowth as a foundation for that chapter and its arguments on rethinking tourism and development.

History of Degrowth

Kallis (2018) usefully traces the roots of degrowth, noting key authors and movements during its emergence as part of transitional discourse. The concept of degrowth gained traction in France in the early years of the new millennium before spreading elsewhere, though its roots lie in early environmentalism, the bioeconomy of Georgescu-Roegen, the voluntary simplicity movement and the cultural critique of development and modernity (Kallis, 2018). Key environmental works, including *Silent Spring* (Carson, 1962) and *Limits to Growth* (Meadows et al., 1972) revealed the negative impacts of human activity on the natural environment and that exponential growth would eventually exhaust resources and pollute the planet (Kallis, 2018). Galbraith (1958) wrote about the 'affluent society' and the role of advertising in creating false needs for private goods, which increased levels of consumption and GDP at the cost of resources needed for public goods. Similarly, Hirsch (1976) focused on the 'social limits to growth' and 'positional goods' such as an expensive car or, in the case of tourism, a trip to an exotic location as a reflection of your position in society; with everyone pursuing these goods, the ultimate outcome is inflation and frustration. The rise of ecological economics, which focuses on the conflict between growth and the environment, is noted in the work of Georgescu-Roegen (1971) who employed a thermodynamic rethinking of economics whereby the economic process transforms low-entropy (high order) valuable resources into high-entropy (low order) waste and pollution. The result of this irreversible process is scarcity and, hence, consumption of these valuable resources needs to be reduced. In a similar vein, Daly (1991) argued that, over the long-term, only a steady state of economic activity can be sustainable; he went on to publish *Beyond Growth: The Economics of Sustainable Development* in 1996.

The 'degrowth' term originated in France during a 1972 debate between André Gorz, Herbert Marcuse and Siccco Mansholth (President of the European Commission at the time) subsequently published by *Nouvelle Observator*. Having read *Limits to Growth*, Gorz raised the question of whether capitalism was compatible with the '*decroissance*' (degrowth) in material production needed to restore the Earth's balance (Kallis, 2018). Gorz (1977) was part of the political ecology movement that was criticising industrialism and the pursuit of growth in the West, as well as criticising both capitalism and socialism (as a continuation of capitalism) and arguing for well-being through degrowth. Gorz (1991) would later highlight the difference between the economic imperative of productivity and the ecological imperative of resource conservation. On the one hand, maximising economic productivity focuses on selling the greatest quantity of goods with maximum efficiency at a high profit, which requires maximisation of consumption. While viewed as growth, from an ecological perspective this is waste. The ecological view, on the other hand, focuses on satisfying material needs with a small quantity of goods with high use value and durability with the minimum of capital, work and natural resources. However, if savings are to be gained from the ecological perspective, including increased product durability, prevention of illness and accidents and lower energy and resource consumption, these would result in a reduction in GNP and at the macro-economic level, a source of loss.

In 1979, Professors Jacques Grinevald and Ivo Rens published a French translation of a collection of Georgescu-Roegen's essays in a volume titled '*Tomorrow Degrowth*' [*Demain la Decroissance*] with *Decroissance* taking on a new meaning in the French lexicon as well as becoming a slogan for radical ecologists (Kallis, 2018). During the late 1990s and early 2000s, activists in Lyon (Darragon, Divry, Clémentin & Cheynet) published the weekly *Décroissance*, promoted a car-free city and implemented direct action against advertising (Kallis, 2018). By 2001, degrowth had been launched by French environmental activists as a provocative slogan to re-politicise environmentalism (Demaria & Latouche, 2019). Hence, as Kallis (2018: 4) notes, since its inception in France, degrowth has evolved as a combination of research and action undertaken by a collection of 'researchers, professors, activists and downshifters who lived as they professed'.

Another important contribution to the degrowth narrative has been made by those writing in the post-development camp. In the often-cited *Development Dictionary*, Sachs (1996: 1) equated development to a lighthouse guiding sailors to the coast and, therefore, it was *the* idea that oriented emerging nations through post-war history; 'Today the lighthouse shows cracks and is starting to crumble. The idea of development stands like a ruin in the intellectual landscape. Delusions and disappointment, failures and crimes have been the steady companions of development and they tell a common story: it did not work.' One of the contributors to this volume was Serge Latouche from the Université Paris-Sud who has become one of the most well-known authors in the field of degrowth. His 1996 *The Westernizing of the World* illustrated how development programmes had Westernised south-east Asia and Africa. As noted in Chapter 2, those writing in the post-development camp question the very notion of development and they also criticise how Western ideas of development destroy Indigenous ways of life (Kallis, 2018). In *Farewell to Growth*, Latouche (2009: 9) notes the goal of degrowth is to 'build a society in which we can live better lives whilst working less and consuming less.' He goes on to state that, at a theoretical level, we should be referring to 'a-growth' in the same manner as 'a-theism' rather than degrowth; this involves abandoning a faith/religion in the economy, progress and development and rejecting the cult of growth for growth's sake. Latouche's work, which is explored in greater detail later, includes an 'ecological, economic, and sociological critique of the limits to growth, post-colonial critique of development and the Polanyian thesis against the expansions of the market', as well as a critique of sustainable development (Kallis, 2018: 6). He suggests that to create a degrowth society we need a re-enchantment of the world, but we have not yet agreed exactly what this means (Latouche, 2009).

In 2008, the first international conference on degrowth took place in Paris organised by 'Research & Degrowth' and the conferences have been held every two years since. Mastini (2017) dates the emergence of the economic 'paradigm' of degrowth as 2008 based on the holding of this conference, which also saw the birth of an international community of research activists (Kallis, 2018). At the second international conference, the Barcelona Degrowth Declaration was published. A key publication was Jackson's (2008) *Prosperity Without Growth*, which argued that it was impossible to avoid climate change and at the same time grow the economy. In his more recent *Post Growth: Life After Capitalism,* Jackson (2021) argues the economy of tomorrow will be built centred on renewable and regenerative technologies, fair wages, transparent governance, protection and restoration of social and environmental assets (as opposed to their destruction), enterprise for the service of community, and living in harmony with nature. The literature on degrowth continues to expand, incorporating a range of perspectives. The rich meanings in degrowth are linked to the plurality of its philosophical currents which Demaria et al. (2013) outline as: ecology, critiques of development and praise for anti-utilitarianism, meaning of life and well-being, bioeconomics, democracy and justice. The wide range of influences on degrowth can inspire an assortment of action strategies from local to global levels which include oppositional activism, building alternatives (creating new institutions) and reformism which involves preserving and acting within some existing institutions (Demaria et al., 2013).

Key Concepts of Degrowth

The term 'degrowth' has been found to be misleading as the prefix 'de' is associated with terms like 'decline' and 'diminish', leading some to incorrectly claim degrowth means austerity, puritanism and poverty (Liegey & Nelson, 2020). However, degrowth should not be interpreted literally (Demaria & Latouche, 2019); rather, degrowth is about the decolonisation of the imaginary and implementation of other worlds to create not just 'another growth' or 'another development' but rather another kind of society based on frugal abundance (Demaria & Latouche, 2019). More specifically, Hickel (2020: 206) defines degrowth as 'reducing the material and energy throughput of the economy to bring it back into balance with the living world, while distributing income and resources more fairly, liberating people from needless work, and investing in the public goods that people need to thrive. It is the first step toward a more ecological civilisation.' Degrowth, then, challenges the hegemony of economic growth through democratically-led redistributed downscaling in both production and consumption in industrialised nations to achieve environmental sustainability, social justice and well-being (Demaria & Latouche, 2019). More broadly, Cronin (2012: 103) argues that a 'politics of re-enchantment is not simply a matter of seeing the world anew, it is also about conceiving of the very ability to live differently'.

Importantly, degrowth has been distinguished from sustainable development which Demaria and Latouche (2019) argue is an oxymoron, the aim of which has been to save 'the religion' of economic growth while denying ecological breakdown. Additionally, Kerschner (2010) argues that degrowth is not a goal but, rather, a transition to a sustainable steady-state economy. A central question that arises, however, is whether the move to a low carbon, post-growth economy can be done within the existing system of global market capitalism or if institutional changes are required to create a qualitatively different system (Büchs & Koch, 2017). In answering this question, Büchs and Koch (2017) identify three perspectives: system reform (capitalist ownership and traditional markets retained but reformed); anti-capitalist (capitalism must be rebuilt); and alternative-open (focus on core values and functions needed) (see also Anderson, 2020: 164).

Latouche (2009) suggests moving to an autonomous degrowth society which is serene, convivial and sustainable through the articulation of eight interdependent changes (the eight 'Rs') which have the ability to reinforce each other. The eight 'Rs' comprise: re-evaluate, reconceptualise, restructure, redistribute, relocalise, reduce, re-use and recycle. *Re-evaluate* involves re-examining the values of society, including moving away from the belief that we need to dominate nature. Egotism should be replaced by altruism and cooperation should replace unbridled competition. The importance of leisure should be stressed over an obsession with work; social life should be emphasised over consumerism and local should take precedence over global. *Reconceptualise* includes redefining the concepts of wealth and poverty and deconstructing scarcity/abundance. The current economic model transforms natural abundance into scarcity as a self-fulfilling prophecy, putting a price on things such as water and then selling it. Degrowth calls for a recognition of the challenges of natural resource depletion. *Redistribution* focuses on how wealth is distributed not only between the North and South but also within societies; its purpose is to reduce the power and wealth of the consumer class and big predators and thereby reduce incentives for conspicuous consumption. It also incorporates recognition of the ecological debt owed by the North to the South and includes concepts such as the ecological footprint as a way to determine a country's 'drawing rights'. *Relocalise* means producing on a local basis to meet local needs. In addition to economics, it also encourages politics, culture and the meaning of life to rediscover local roots. *Reduce* incorporates a range of features including reducing the impact of consumption and waste. It also involves reducing health risks and working hours. Here, Latouche (2009: 38) specifically targets mass tourism, stating that the 'golden age of kilometric consumerism is over'. While the desire for travel and the taste for adventure are, of course, part of human nature (see Chapter 6) and must not be allowed to dry up, the tourist industry has transformed curiosity and inquisitiveness into consumerists' consumption that destroys the environment, social fabric and culture of the destination or 'target country'. Latouche (2009: 39) refers to 'travelitis' to describe our obsession with travelling further, faster more often and for less; to him, it is largely an artificial need created by 'supermodern' life exacerbated through the media, travel agents and tour operators and it needs to be reduced. Whether ecotourism, often presented as ethical, fair and responsible and an alternative to mass tourism, is an oxymoron colluding with sustainable development is posed as a legitimate question, and one that is addressed in Chapter 6. Latouche (2009: 39) also asks the question of whether ecotourism is just 'designed to prolong the survival of a commodified, condemned and condemnable activity'. He disputes the argument that mass tourism is helping the South, calling it fallacious as very little of the money spent on a package holiday remains in the host/destination country. With impending oil shortages and climate change, travel in the future will be very different: 'not so far, less often, slower and ever more expensive' (Latouche, 2009: 39). He asserts (p. 40) that advances in technology will allow us to travel virtually without leaving home while 'adventurous souls can always windsurf to the Seychelles … if the islands have not been swallowed up by the sea.'

Reduce also involves shortening the working week and promoting job-sharing to ensure that all who want employment can find a job. People need to reduce their addiction to their 'jobs', which will also allow them to have more leisure time to focus on arts, crafts, play and mediation and to enjoy being alive. The final two 'R's, *re-use* and *recycle* are discussed together. Society needs to reduce conspicuous waste, recycle waste that cannot be re-used and combat planned obsolescence. In summing up the eight 'R's (which should be viewed as revolutionary as opposed to reactionary), Latouche (2009) notes that while they point to a utopia which is an intellectual construct, it is also concrete in that the starting point can be elements which already exist or to which changes can be implemented. Degrowth emphasises local autonomy, a reaction against the 'invisible hand' of the market as well as the importance of reciprocity and conviviality.

The reliance on GDP as a measure of development was critiqued earlier in this chapter. Interestingly, Hickel (2021) proposes that degrowth is not about reducing GDP; rather, moving to a degrowth world may reduce GDP but that is okay as GDP should not be the indicator used to measure well-being. Nevertheless, although criticisms of degrowth are addressed below, one claim by those opposed to degrowth is that it will result in a recession (a decline in GDP). In refuting this claim, Hickel (2021) sets out six reasons why degrowth is, in effect, the opposite of a recession. These reasons are presented here as they demonstrate some of the key concepts of degrowth. First, degrowth is focused on a planned and coherent policy set out to reduce ecological impact and reduce inequality while improving well-being, whereas recessions are not planned and do not target these outcomes. Second, degrowth adopts a discrim-inating approach in reducing economic activity for things that are ecologically destructive and/or less socially necessary (for example, the production of SUVs, private transportation, arms, beef, advertising, planned obsolescence) while simultaneously expanding socially important sectors such as education, health care and care and conviviality. Third, while recessions cause mass unemployment, degrowth seeks to establish policies to prevent unemployment and improve livelihoods through a shortened working week, job guarantees with living wages and retraining programmes. Fourth, degrowth tackles inequality by developing policies to share global and national incomes more fairly through initiatives such as a living wage and progressive taxation while recessions increase inequality. Fifth, degrowth expands universal public goods and services including education, health, housing and transportation while recessions often incorporate austerity measures based on cutting public ser-vices. Finally, degrowth is focused on a rapid transition to renewable energy, reversing ecological breakdown and restoring biodiversity and soils while, during recessions, governments often abandon these projects in order to restart growth. It is essential to recognise the diversity within degrowth, as noted by Demaria and Latouche (2019) below. Degrowth brings together a heteroege-nous group of actors to focus on a range of issues (with different policies and strategies) from agroecology to climate justice. It also both complements and reinforces these wide-ranging topics as a connecting thread or a platform of networks. Degrowth is, then, more than an alternative – it is a matrix of alternatives that opens up a plurality of destinies. As a result, degrowth soci-eties will be very different in different parts/nations of the world as degrowth focuses on diversity and pluralism. Consequently, degrowth in tourism will also take different approaches in different destinations. In other words, there is no one 'turnkey' solution for degrowth but, rather, the approach should be one of creating fundamentals for a non-productivist sustainable society which can be shared through transitional programmes (Demaria & Latouche, 2019). One set of fundamentals is the eight 'Rs' model outlined above by Latouche (2009) which shares values with other approaches. For instance, Latouche's (2009) concept of relocalisation is evident in the work by Cronin (2012) in his politics of 'microspection'. Cronin (2012) argues that, rather than focusing on the shrinking world in the context of globalisation, it is better to concentrate on the 'expanding world' which examines more closely our immediate surroundings or microspection. Websites for the 'Global Tapestry of Alternatives' and the 'Post Growth Institute' also illustrate the diversity of organisations that are committed to a post-growth world.

As there is a diversity of approaches to a post-growth society, there will inevitably be disagreements on policies and strategies for its achievement. Trainer (2021), for example, raises the concern that a particular type of degrowth defined by a specific/particular/selected/preferred degrowth path or system has been put forward that not all members of the degrowth movement would support. Specifically, he is referring to the comments by Hickel (2021) who, as noted above, has suggested more specific degrowth policies on: preventing unemployment and improving employment by shortening the working week, introducing job guarantees with living wages, and developing retraining programmes to move people out of sunset sectors; sharing national and global income in a fairer manner through progressive taxation and living wages; and expanding universal public services including transportation, etc. In response, Trainer (2021) suggests there are those in the degrowth camp who conceive the concept of degrowth quite differently and, hence, would not advocate for all of these policies. Thus, these policies should not be promoted as that is what the degrowth movement stands for. In another example, Hickel (2020) identifies the following five steps in setting a pathway to a post-capitalist world: end planned obsolescence, cut advertising, shift from ownership to usership, end food waste, and scale down ecologically destructive industries. Again, Trainer (2021) argues it is better for the degrowth movement not to be identified with a particular form of society; rather, it is better to offer a general sense of society with a reduced GDP. This approach, he argues, allows for debates over which forms of society are preferred. Finally, taking degrowth in a more provocative direction, Romano (2020) is highly critical of 'mainstream' notions of degrowth which, he claims, share some of the same institutional frames as growth. He therefore advocates that degrowth should be examined within the context of resource abundance rather than resource depletion and in the notion of anti-utilitarianism.

Selected Criticisms of Degrowth

Degrowth has faced a wide-ranging critique with regards to its practicality – its main objective is to move away from a reliance on economic growth, but many argue that those who currently enjoy political power would not risk questioning growth (Kallis, 2018). Another criticism is that, as Romano (2020) suggests, moving towards degrowth requires the whole citizenship to adopt a set of degrowth values, but this is an impossible precondition. In other words, the challenge becomes that degrowth is only conceivable in a degrowth society that has a different logic than that of a society based on growth (Latouche, 2009). Critics also cite the disastrous results when economies go into decline, such as during the 2008 economic crisis and the more recent Covid-19 global pandemic in which tourism was hardest hit. Destinations, companies and individuals that were heavily reliant on tourism faced extreme hardship during the pandemic, and degrowth in tourism would involve at a minimum a reduction in the number of trips and a change in tourist behaviour for those fortunate enough to travel. In a similar vein, Anderson (2020) argues more generally that it is the global upper classes who are responsible for most of the ecological destruction, yet they cannot be expected to silently accept having their lifestyles and future plans disrupted through global economic restructuring: 'Their protests and resistance is likely to be strong and potentially damaging, since they control vast resources and often have considerable influence on politics and the media' (Anderson, 2020: 109). An advocate of degrowth, Romano (2020) also cautions against the catastrophe narrative prevalent in the degrowth literature, as this may lead to an anti-democratic drift in the pursuit of ecological compatibility.

Büchs and Koch (2019) have examined extensively the structural barriers identified by critics to the political feasibility of degrowth, particularly in terms of intergenerational conflicts regarding needs, satisfaction and well-being in rich nations. They also reflect on how the transition away from a society with locked-in growth may impact well-being. Hickel (2020), however, argues that a false equivalence has been established between growth and human progress. In addition, a debate within the degrowth community focuses on whether degrowth should be applied universally in both developed and developing countries or whether it is primarily for developed nations where resource and energy use is high, and if applied in the Global South, how it should function (MacKay, 2021; Trainer, 2021). Moreover, criticisms of degrowth are similar to those levelled at post-development inasmuch as it is claimed that proponents of degrowth have not created detailed plans on how to make the transition (for example, Schwartzman, 2012). This reflects in part the wide diversity of perspectives and strategies within the degrowth school, with some calling for changes within the existing global economic system while others call for an entirely different system with a logic not based on economic growth. In this context, Latouche (2009) interestingly raises the question of whether there should be a degrowth political party. He answers in the negative, claiming that it is doubtful that a degrowth society could be built on the outdated framework of nation states and while there is seduction to move into politics, it is more important to influence debate, persuade people to consider different arguments and to help change attitudes.

Ultimately the challenge is how to create societies in which the lack of growth is not a disaster and in so doing, how to discover a 'prosperous way down' (Kallis, 2018). In the context of tourism, Butcher (2021a) argues that reversing economic growth is unrealistic and misguided, not least because it would contribute to levels of poverty already compounded by Covid-19 while it would also mean a retreat from 'mobility, economies of scale, divisions of labour, specialisation and scientific innovation'. This point of view is, however, countered by Higgins-Desbiolles and Everingham (2022) who claim that degrowth in tourism is not about diminishment and poverty but, rather, about championing 'thriving, well-being and care where humans and other beings share this finite Earth system with driving principals of equity, responsibility and justice.' In other words, the criticisms of degrowth all ultimately run up against the fact we are living well beyond planetary means and, as a consequence, we are facing growing environmental crises, biodiversity loss and rising inequality. Hence, we all need to face some difficult questions about the future, and these realities have implications for tourism.

CONCLUSION: FROM GROWTH TO DEGROWTH AND REDEFINING DEVELOPMENT AS THE OBJECTIVE OF TOURISM

'We are trapped in an iron cage of consumerism. But the cage is of our own making. We are locked in a myth of growth' (Jackson, 2021: 14). Or as Latouche (2009: 22) alternatively argues, 'if growth automatically generated well-being, we would now be living in paradise'. Growth is a myth because we are not living in paradise; rather, we are living in a world in which growth is ironically exacerbating the very problems it seeks to solve. Yet, we are locked into the need for ever-expanding tourism as set out in most national tourism plans, for it is believed that more tourism feeds growth. Moreover, although new measures have been developed to replace GDP, as explored earlier in this chapter, development in the growth society still largely is measured by GDP and therefore, destinations are keen to witness an increase in the contributions of tourism to GDP. At the same time, as the world continues to see a shift towards the service economy, it has become the accumulation of experiences, particularly in tourism, that has become the basis of our sense of belonging and status. This, in turn, feeds the growth in tourism, while even the concept of sustainable tourism remains based on growth, relying on a resource-intensive globalised industry to supply tourists.

However, given the range of crises confronting the planet (see Chapter 4), degrowth as part of transitional discourse has evolved as an alternative to the 'myth of growth'. Degrowth represents a radical social transformation which, in turn, leads to reducing the throughput of the economy to be more in balance with planetary boundaries (Kallis, 2018). Latouche (2009) argues that degrowth means neither an impossible return to the past nor a compromise with capitalism; equally, it does not reject modernity but, rather, transcends it, seeking out a re-enchantment of the world. As discussed in this chapter, there exists a diversity of perspectives on degrowth, with some advocates mapping out detailed plans that could serve as an election platform while others promote more generalised notions of degrowth and movement away from GDP. Either way, while most would agree that we need to abandon the idea of growth, no one wants to take the first step irrespective of the type of government (Latouche, 2009).

What, then, will tourism look like in a post-growth world? This question is further explored in Chapter 7 but, in doing so, it is important first to more fully recognise the capitalistic model inherent in most tourism (see Chapter 5). As discussed in this chapter, the political economy of tourism provides a lens into the unequal power relations in the globalised industry and the inequity it creates, giving rise to the second point, that there needs to be a redefinition of development as the objective of tourism. Development and tourism's contribution to it has been locked into growth and now faces a range of social, economic and environmental crises that necessitates a radical shift called for by those in transitional discourse. Thus, tourism will need to embrace concepts of well-being, equity and reciprocity (concepts fundamental to degrowth) within a global society in which throughput has been reduced. As Hickel (2020: 289) suggests, the contemporary ecological crisis requires a radical policy response involving high-income countries scaling down excess energy and material use, a rapid transition to renewables, a shift to a post-capitalist economy focused on ecological stability over perpetual growth and a new relationship with the living world. Degrowth begins by taking less but ends up opening new possibilities as it moves society from scarcity to abundance, dominion to reciprocity, extraction to regeneration and loneliness and separation to a world of connection 'fizzing with life' (Hickel, 2020). Exploring how tourism responds to this multi-layered and complex agenda is the ultimate aim of this book.

4. Tourism and the global environmental crisis

INTRODUCTION

That the world is facing an existential environmental crisis is indisputable. And the cause of that crisis is equally indisputable; it is the excessive demands placed by humanity on the Earth's natural resources, demands that, as noted in the introduction to this book, mean that 'we are using up the planet at a rate 1.7 times faster than it can regenerate' (MacKinnon, 2021: 6). In other words, humanity is living out of balance with the global ecosystem on which it depends – we are living not with the planet, but off it.

Of course, this has not always been the case. As Hickel (2020: 39) observes, 'We humans have been on this planet for nearly 300,000 years…[and]… for approximately 97 percent of that time our ancestors lived in relative harmony with the Earth's ecosystems'. In fact, it is only over the last century or so that the relationship between humanity and the natural world has fallen increasingly out of kilter, for two principal reasons. The first is the exponential growth in the global population, particularly since the beginning of the twentieth century. To put things into perspective, in 10,000 BCE an estimated 4 million people lived on the planet, a total that increased to 190 million by the year 0 (Roser, Ritchie & Ortiz-Espina, 2019). By 1800, the world's population had increased to 990 million, the rate of growth limited by low average life expectancy (less than 30 years) and events such as the Black Death which, in the fourteenth century, killed around a third of the popuation of Europe. Hence, it was only in the early years of the nineteenth century that the one billion figure was first reached, rising to 1.65 billion by 1900. Since then, the growth in the global population has been nothing short of remarkable, most notably since 1950 (see Table 4.1). As is evident from Table 4.1, during this period a further one billion people were added to the global population roughly every 12 years (from 3 billion in 1960, 4 billion in 1975, 5 billion in 1987 and 6 billion in 1999 to 7 billion in 2011 – see Roser et al., 2019). Hence, although the world's population is expected to stabilise at around 11 billion by the beginning of the next century (and despite continuing technological advances in, for example, food

Table 4.1   *World population growth, 1950–2100*

	1950	1970	1990	2000	2005	2010	2015	2020	2030	2050	2075	2100
Total Population (billion)	2.536	3.701	5.331	6.145	6.542	6.958	7.383	7.795	8.551	9.772	10.772	11.184
	1950– 1955	1965– 1970	1985– 1990	1995– 2000	2000– 2005	2005– 2010	2010– 2015	2015– 2020	2025– 2030	2045– 2050	2070– 2075	2095– 2100
Annual rate of change (%)	1.8	2.1	1.8	1.3	1.3	1.2	1.2	1.1	0.9	0.6	0.3	0.1

Source: Adapted from UN (2017: 3).

production), simply meeting the basic needs of this huge volume of people places enormous strains on the Earth's natural resources.

Alongside the resource implications of this population growth, the second and arguably more significant factor underpinning the global environmental crisis is the increasing level of per capita consumption. More simply stated, the problem is not only the overall number of people living on the planet but also how much each individual consumes. It should be noted here that consumption cannot be separated from production; not only do suppliers seek to meet the demands of consumers but also create demand through product innovation and advertising. Therefore, producers also make an explicit contribution to the environmental crisis. Either way, and as again argued in the introduction, those living in wealthier countries and, indeed, the elite in poorer, less developed countries tend to enjoy or seek consumerist lifestyles defined by acquisition beyond the satisfaction of their basic needs; for many if not all, achieving the 'good life' – long considered a multidimensional condition (Tuan, 1986) – appears to depend specifically on the ever-increasing consumption and accumulation of stuff, both material and experiential. Such high levels of consumption amongst affluent societies and countries is, in the context of a finite global ecosytem, unsustainable; indeed, most if not all contemporary challenges related to the environment are directly attributable to excessive consumption (Mayell, 2004). Moreover, until relatively recently, it has primarily been the developed, Western nations that have been in the vanguard of this excessive consumption, as evidenced by the research of the Global Footprint Network. This identifies those nations with the most multi-planet lifestyles (the number of planets required if the world as a whole were to emulate a particular country's lifestyle). As widely claimed, the US tops the list (5.1 planet lifestyle) closely followed by Australia (4.5) (Earth Overshoot Day, 2022).

The problem is, however, exacerbated by the fact that as other countries become wealthier, they too seek to emulate these consumerist lifestyles. It is predicted that in the 13-year period between 2017 and 2023, the global consumer society will expand by about 2 billion to a total of around 5.6 billion people. The commensurate increase in demands on the Earth's resources will be disastrous. For example, in his review of the over-exploitation of the world's natural resources that he has winessed during his own lifetime, David Attenborough (2020: 154) observes that '90 percent of fish populations are either overfished or fished to capacity'. More starkly, a clock is provided on The World Counts website that counts down the time remaining until, without the imposition of global controls on fishing, the world will run out of seafood (see www.theworldcounts.com) – at the time of writing, in less than 26 years (that is, by 2048).

Much of this increase in the numbers of consumers is accounted for by China which, between 1978 and 2017, achieved an average annual growth rate in GDP of 9.5 percent. This has been reflected in the rapid expansion of the country's middle class, from 39 million people in 2000 (3.1 percent of the population) to 707 millon (50.8 percent) in 2018 (Batarags, 2021). At the same time, rapid economic growth in other emerging ecomomies, such as India, is also contributing significantly to the global spread of consumerism. Given the direct correlation between wealth and participation in tourism, it is therefore unsurprising that, at least prior to the Covid-19 pandemic, China had become the world's largest outbound market in terms of both numbers of tourists and total spending (though it should be noted that a majority of mainland Chinese outbound tourists travel to destinations in the Greater China region, namely Hong Kong, Macao and Taiwan). Interestingly, the Chinese also make around 6 billion domestic trips annually and, in 2019, domestic air travel in China alone accounted for around 13 percent of total global air travel (including both domestic and international) that year.

As impressive as these figures are, the point is that tourism is a ubiquitous factor in the global growth of consumerism. Therefore, not only should it not be considered separately from consumption more generally; it must also be acknowledged that tourism is in all likelihood adopting an increasingly significant position in worldwide consumption. This, in turn, suggests that tourism's contribution to the global environmental crisis is also increasing both relatively and absolutely and, hence, that the environmental consequences of tourism should be assessed (and solutions proposed) within the wider context of global consumption-induced resource depletion. Typically, however, this has not been the case. Certainly, attention has long been paid to the impacts of tourism on the environment, both negative and positive – whilst the emphasis has tended to be on its environmental costs, the potential for tourism to stimulate environmental protection and enhancement schemes has also been widely acknowledged (Pigram, 1980). As discussed in Chapter 1, many early texts questioned tourism's developmental role in the light of its emerging environmental and other impacts at a time when international mass tourism remained a nascent phenomenon (de Kadt, 1979; Rosenow & Pulsipher, 1979; Turner & Ash, 1975; Young, 1977) whilst, of specific relevance to the arguments in this book, one early critique of economic growth in general referred to the consequences of tourism in particular:

> Travel on this scale... inevitably disrupts the character of the affected regions, their populations and ways of living. As swarms of holiday-makers arrive... local life and industry shrivel, hospitality vanishes, and indigenous populations drift into a quasi-parasitic way of life catering with contemptuous servility to the unsophisticated multitude. (Mishan, 1969: 142)

Going on to suggest that of all the ways of supporting poorer countries, tourism 'is, surely, the most costly and the most obnoxious' (Mishan, 1969: 143), the proposed solution was to ban all air travel, a move that would undoubtedly garner support in some quarters today.

Since these initial forays into the topic, innumerable subsequent publications have explored the tourism–environment relationship, some focusing explicitly on tourism's environmental consequences (for example, Briassoulis & van der Straaten, 1992; Holden, 2016; Holden & Fennell, 2012; Mieczkowski, 1995), others considering it within broader discussions of tourism's impacts (for example, Wall & Mathieson, 2006) though the majority typically discussing it in the wider context of tourism planning, management and development. Irrespective of this diversity, however, a common feature is that tourism and its impacts are treated as a discrete activity, although this is not to say that a more holistic perspective is not sometimes adopted. For example, since Smith (1990) published what is claimed to be the first paper on the issue (Pang, McKercher & Prideaux, 2013), recent years have witnessed increasing research into tourism and climate change. Those addressing the consequences of climate change on tourism tend to be destination-focused; in contrast, the contribution of tourism, particularly air travel, to climate change is inevitably considered within a global context, although some studies attempt national-level analyses (Gössling, 2013). However, rarely if ever are the environmental impacts of tourism discussed in tandem with those resulting from excessive consumption more generally. As a consequence, not only are tourism's impacts and means of addressing them typically considered in the context of particular destinations or sectors rather than from an overarching 'tourism system' perspective – Gössling's (2002) research, and more recently that of Gössling and Peeters (2015), being a notable exception – but also the need to recognise tourism as a major contributor to the global environmental crisis (including but not restricted to climate change) and to be embraced in responses to that crisis is generally ignored.

This chapter, therefore, seeks to locate tourism within the context of the environmental consequences of ever-growing production and consumption at the global level. As such, its purpose is to demonstrate that if the only logical path to sustainability is, as is increasingly argued, to reduce our overall demands on the world's natural resources (to degrow), then tourism cannot be immune from that process. In other words, rather than tinkering with parts of the tourism system to enhance their local environmental sustainability, the focus must be on reducing tourism's overall resource use in line with degrowth policies more generally – though within the broader objective of maintaining tourism's essential developmental role where appropriate. Hence, the chapter commences with a review of the principal natural resource challenges facing the planet, followed by a brief summary of tourism's contribution to them. Amongst such challenges the most immediate is undoubtedly climate change to which tourism makes a significant contribution, particularly through fossil fuel-based travel. Hence, specific attention is paid to the relationship between tourism and climate change, but also to the implications of tourism development on other natural resources, specifically water. Given that the contemporary objective of many environmental policies is so-called 'net zero' emissions, the chapter then concludes with a critique of the technocentric concept of net zero, adding further weight to the argument for degrowth in tourism.

THE ENVIRONMENTAL CRISIS: KEY CHALLENGES

In the introduction to a recent UNDP Human Development Report, it is observed that the human race has made remarkable advances over the last century but at significant cost to the natural environment; 'Humans have achieved incredible things, but we have taken the Earth to the brink… [because of] … societies that value what they measure instead of measuring what they value' (UNDP, 2020: iii). The report goes on to argue more specifically that:

> The planet's biodiversity is plunging, with a quarter of species facing extinction, many within decades. Numerous experts believe we are living through, or on the cusp of, a mass species extinction event, the sixth in the history of the planet and the first to be caused by a single organism – us. (UNDP, 2020: 3)

This potential loss of biodiversity is not only the outcome of the exploitation of particular resources; it also reflects the delicate interdependence and balance between all species (including humanity) within the global ecosystem and the extent to which this has been disrupted by human intervention. A telling example is provided by David Attenborough in his recent TV series, *The*

Green Planet. He reveals how a tree flower in the Costa Rican rainforest – the Seven Hour Flower – provides nourishment for and is pollinated by a particular species of bat (Underwood's Long-tongued Bat). The bat's survival depends on its ability to feed off hundreds of the flowers each night, but human action (logging in the rainforest) has significantly reduced the number of flowers available to the bats. With consequential insufficient nourishment the bat population is declining so less pollination occurs, resulting in the loss of even more of the flowers. In short, the single human act of logging causes a destructive chain reaction within the local ecosystem and, as such, is an example of the so-called 'butterfly effect' (see Chandler, 2020). This suggests that a small change in one part of a system may lead to major changes elsewhere – a butterfly flapping its wings may result in a tornado elsewhere. The point is that it is difficult to predict the complexity of change within the ecosystem to particular human interventions.

As we shall suggest later in this chapter, the environmental consequences of tourism should perhaps also be viewed from this perspective – that is, a particular tourism development or activity may have environmental repercussions well beyond its immediate impacts such as those typically identified in the literature. However, to return to the Human Development Report referred to above, a central theme is that if solutions are to be found to the contemporary environmental crisis, rather than adopting a piecemeal approach it is necessary to identify and understand collectively all the environmental challenges the planet currently faces – and the connections between them – in order to find and implement the most appropriate solutions. For example, the replacement of petrol / diesel fuelled motor cars with electric vehicles (EVs) is widely considered to be an important step in reducing carbon and other emissions; hence, the UK government has banned the sale of new petrol and diesel cars from 2030. However, although there are immediate benefits associated with EVs (zero exhaust emissions while driving), questions surround the level of carbon emissions during their production, said to be almost 60 percent higher than that for internal combustion engine cars (RAC, 2021). In particular, controversy surrounds the mining of lithium for EV batteries with regards to not only the depletion of the natural stock of the mineral but, more importantly, issues of carbon emissions during extraction, the loss of fertile land for mining and excessive water use and pollution at the cost of other activities such as farming (Brooks, 2021). In short, so-called solutions may themselves have major environmental consequences which potentially outweigh overall benefits, with the EV example being particularly pertinent to tourism given that the most popular mode of tourist transport is the motor car.

The principal global environmental challenges are widely recognised and presented in different ways by individuals or organisations, with varying emphasis placed on the cause and extent of, and potential solutions to, each challenge. Some, for example, highlight single issues, such as the impacts of increasing beef production to meet growing demand (like tourism, linked to the expanding consumer society); others focus on specific environmental problems, such as deforestation. For the purposes of this chapter, a brief overview of the main challenges will suffice, followed by a discussion that considers tourism's relevance to them. It must be noted that these challenges are not mutually exclusive; deforestation, for example, contributes to global warming, is linked to the increasing use of land for agriculture and is one of the causes of biodiversity loss, whilst ocean acidification and its subsequent problems is attributable to global warming and also, according to some, plastic pollution.

Climate Change / Global Warming

Without doubt, the most pressing of all the contemporary climate emergencies is global warming. At the time of writing, the average global temperature is 1.1 degrees (1.1°C) above pre-industrial levels and the critical 1.5°C level, generally considered to be the 'tipping point' beyond which the changes in many natural systems may become irreversible, is expected to be reached at the latest by 2040. Moreover, according to a recent report from the International Panel on Climate Change (IPCC, 2022b), in order to limit warming to the 1.5°C threshold, global greenhouse gas emissions must peak by 2025 and subsequently be reduced by 43 percent by 2030. Equally if not more challenging, the IPCC report also suggests that for the average global temperature to stabilise at 1.5°C above pre-industrial levels, net zero CO_2 emissions – a politically popular but, as discussed later in this chapter, controversial target – must be achieved by the early 2050s.

There are some who, though acknowledging the rise in average global temperatures, question the extent to which anthropogenic greenhouse gas emissions are a contributory factor. For example, in a sceptical review of the tourism academy's 'buy in' to the human-induced global warming thesis, Shani and Arad (2014) not only argue that, over the millennia, there have been natural periods of significantly higher (and lower) temperatures compared to what they imply to be a comparatively limited rise in temperatures over the last half century, but they also point to studies that suggest that a causal relationship cannot be established between increased concentrations of CO_2 in the atmosphere and global warming. Specifically, they suggest that even though atmospheric CO_2 concentrations increased during the mid-twentieth century, average global temperatures actually decreased slightly. Such critical voices are, however, in a minority; it is generally accepted by the scientific community that, over the longer-term, increased levels of CO_2 (currently 420 ppm compared with 280 ppm prior to the Industrial Revolution – see NOAA,

2022) as well as of other greenhouse gases in the atmosphere will result in the continued warming of the planet.

The cause of increasing atmospheric concentrations of CO_2 is well known: excessive emissions from the use of fossil fuels beyond the assimilative capacity of the ecosystem, exacerbated in particular by deforestation that further reduces that capacity. The consequences of the resultant increase in average global temperatures are also well known, conveniently summarised by National Geographic (n.d.). These include: the melting of ice, such as the Greenland ice-sheet and glaciers around the world, leading to rising sea levels and threatening species dependent on arctic or ice environments as well as, in the longer-term, numerous coastal towns and cities; increasingly extreme weather events occurring more frequently resulting in floods, droughts, wild-fires and other events that impact on people's lifestyles and well-being and threaten food production systems; and increasing populations of some species that devastate natural habitats and crops. It is unsurprising, therefore, that since the first Conference of the Parties (COP) in Berlin in 1995 and, notably, the 1997 COP in Kyoto, Japan which established the Kyoto Protocol, there have been increasingly intensive (but, to date, largely unsuccessful) attempts to both agree on targets and to implement programmes for achieving the necessary reductions in greenhouse gas emissions at the global scale. Although one outcome of the most recent COP26 in November 2021 in Glasgow was the substantial commitment (US$130 trillion) to fund the transition to net zero (arguably evidence of support for oxymoronic 'sustainable growth'), the conference nevertheless failed to deliver actions necessary to stabilise global warming at the 1.5°C threshold.

Loss of Biodiversity

As noted above, environmental attention has in recent years focused primarily on climate change or, alternatively stated, on the planet's sink function – its capacity to absorb the excess carbon and other greenhouse gases that are a by-product of human activity. However, since Rachel Carson's seminal text *Silent Spring* was published some six decades ago (Carson, 1962), there has been increasing recognition and documentation of the excessive demands also placed on the planet's source function, or the extent to which we are using up the planet's resources faster than they can be naturally replenished. Carson demonstrated how powerful synthetic pesticides (specifically the now-banned DDT) were wreaking devastation upwards throughout the natural food chain; though improving crop yields, the use of such pesticides was directly responsible for reductions in the populations of fish, birds and other wildlife. More recent studies reveal how human activity is impacting directly and indirectly on biodiversity more generally. For example, according to the WWF's Living

Planet Report (WWF, 2020a: 7), there was 'an average 68% (range: −73% to −62%) fall in monitored populations of mammals, birds, amphibians, reptiles and fish between 1970 and 2016' whilst other research has revealed not only that more than 500 terrestrial vertebrates (land animals) are at immediate risk of extinction (Ceballos, Ehrlich & Raven, 2020) but also that a quarter of all species face extinction within decades.

This reduction in biodivesity is both directly and indirectly attributable to human activity. Over-exploitation and poaching have directly reduced the populations of many species to dangerously low levels, sometimes impacting on the survival of other species; for example, the overfishing of small pelagic fish, such as sardines and anchovies (the latter predominantly used for fish-meal) off the coast of southern Africa has resulted in a 73 percent reduction in the population of breeding African penguins for which the fish are the primary food source (Kretzman, 2021). In particular, though, it is the destruction of or change in the use of natural habitats such as forests, grassland and mangroves, most commonly for agricultural use, that is considered to have the most signifi-cant negative impact on biodiversity. Examples abound, but perhaps one of the most publicised and emotive has been the expansion of oil palm plantations in countries such as Indonesia. There, vast tracts of tropical rainforests have been replaced with oil palm trees (palm oil accounts for more than 10 percent of Indonesia's exports), threatening the survival of numerous endangered species and, most notably, halving the orangutang population owing to the destruction of their natural habitat. Another example is biodivesrity loss related to climate change; the melting of ice in the Antarctic is leading to a reduction in krill – shrimplike crustaceans that are a staple food for penguins and which feed on algae that grow on the bottom of the ice. This is in turn impacting negatively on the penguin population which depends on krill and, subsequently, on whales that feed on penguins (Reardon, 2011).

Pollution

Environmental pollution refers to the introduction of harmful substances – in the form of solids, liquids, gases and energy (such as radioactivity) – into the natural environment at a rate that is greater than at which they can be absorbed, decomposed, diluted, recycled or safely stored. Putting it another way, pollu-tion is the addition of contaminants / pollutants into the natural environment to the extent that they cause adverse change to that environment and, in some cases, to human health. Evidently, then, it is a broad category of environmental impact that embraces an enormous variety of activities, processes, behaviours, substances and consequences, many of which are considered in their own right. Currently, much attention is being paid and publicity accorded to the problem of plastic pollution, often identified high on the list of the biggest contemporary environmental problems facing the planet. For example, Earth.org (2022) states that in 1950, the world annually produced around 2 million tons of plastics, a total that increased to 419 million tons by 2015. Others suggest a slightly lower current volume of plastic production (figures vary from 300 to 400 million tons annually) but the important point is that, globally, less than 10 percent of plastic is recycled with much of the remainder being placed in landfill or polluting the natural environment, often ending up in the oceans. It is estimated that up to 10 million tons of plastic are dumped in the oceans every year (Plastic Oceans, 2022), not including microplastics which have now been identified as being present in the human food chain (UNEP, 2016). The environmental consequences of this plastic pollution are enormous and not yet fully understood, but it is very much a human behavioural problem and market failure; up to 50 percent of plastic waste is from largely unnecessary single use, such as plastic water bottles. In the case of the latter, tourism is a particular culprit; there tends to be a high rate of consumption of bottled water by tourists while on holiday, not least because bottled water companies have been able to convince tourists through their marketing that bottled water is safer (which admittedly in some cases, such as some developing countries, it is). More generally, globally the bottled water industry is worth some US$280 billion.

Pollution is evident in all natural environments and arguably represents one of the greatest threats to humanity; bluntly stated; pollution is destroying the resources the human race depends on. Air pollution is perhaps most evident in the context of greenhouse emissions and consequential global warming but air pollution more generally, caused by vehicle emissions, industrial processes, dust, wildfires, volcanoes and so on, is also manifested in poor air quality. According to the World Health Organization, 4.2 million people die prematurely each year as a result of outdoor air pollution (Roser, 2021), whilst many more suffer from poor health that is directly attributable to poor air quality. The 1982 Bhopal disaster in India was an extreme example of air pollution, when the accidental release of a highly toxic gas from a pesticide plant resulted in the eventual death of around 15,000 people in the surrounding towns. Land pollution refers to the contamination and subsequent degradation of land and has various causes, such as industrial waste, mining, the incorrect disposal of waste and, in particular, contemporary agricultural practices. Specifically, intensive farming, whilst increasing crop yields, eventually degrades the soil through the practice of monocropping but also the widespread use of chemical pesticides and fertilisers that pollute and diminish the health of topsoil. As noted shortly, some 33 percent of the world's adequate to high-quality agricultural land has been lost in this way. Finally, water pollution is the outcome of human-induced contamination of both fresh and salt-water sources, including lakes, rivers, reservoirs, groundwater and the oceans. Pollutants include domestic waste (sewage) which, if untreated, reduces the oxygen content of water, industrial and agricultural waste, solid waste (including, of course, plastics), toxic waste and oil. According to Denchak (2022), agriculture is the leading cause of water degradation whilst an estimated one million tons of oil enters marine environments each year, much of it from land-based human activity but also from regular shipping operations which account for about one third of the oil in the oceans. Water pollution in all its forms has a significant impact on water quality and consequently all species that depend upon sources of healthy water; an estimated 1.2 million people die each year because of unsafe water.

Deforestation

Forests are essential to the ecosystem in general and to human life in particular. 'They're home to more than half of the world's land based species and, globally, over 1 billion people live in and around forests... After oceans, forests are the largest storehouses of carbon' (WWF, 2020b). However, deforestation, or the permanent removal of trees from land that is then converted into other uses, is significantly reducing the proportion of the world's land mass (currently around one third) that is forested. This is not of course a new phenomenon; throughout history, wood has been exploited for fuel, construction and other uses whilst the land covered by woods and forests has long been cleared to make way for human occupation. For instance, most of the world's contemporary croplands were at one or another time forested. Nowadays, however, deforestation is, according to most observers, increasing at an alarming rate, although primarily in the tropics and subtropics which account for around two thirds of the contemporary loss of forests. It is estimated, for example, that around 60 million hectares of the world's tropical forest were lost between 2002 and 2019, an area greater than the states of California and Missouri combined (Butler, 2020). In contrast, in some other parts of the world, land is being successfully reforested – in Europe, some 90,000 square kilometres of land (roughly equivalent to the size of Portugal) was reforested between 1990 and 2015 (Wood, 2019). Nevertheless, globally the net loss of forests amounts to about 4.7 million hectares annually.

The principal cause of deforestation is the conversion of land to agriculture – for crops, such as soy and palm oil, and for livestock; as noted in the next section, the increasing amount of deforested land devoted to beef production (much of it for growing cattle feed) is particularly controversial. Deforestation also occurs because of illegal logging, the collection of wood for fuel and infrastructural developments such as road building, urban expansion and so on. It is also a direct outcome of tourism development, often in mountainous regions (Kuvan, 2010; Stevens, 2003). Whatever its causes, however, deforestation has significant consequences at both the local and global scale.

At the local level, it impacts biodiversity and diminishes the enormous variety of ecological services that forests provide within the local ecosystem and to humans, from flood prevention to the supply of natural resources, eventually threatening the well-being of those who depend on forests for their livelihood. Deforestation may also impact local weather patterns, particularly leading to significant declines in rainfall. At the global level, the most evident consequence of deforestation is its contribution to global warming. The clearing and burning of forests releases enormous amounts of CO_2 into the atmosphere whilst reducing their overall carbon capture function. Hence, reversing deforestation is an essential action to combat climate change, though only in combination with policies for reducing carbon emissions.

Agricultural Land Use and Soil Erosion

At the end of the eighteenth century, the English philosopher and economist Thomas Malthus famously predicted that global population growth would outstrip food production and, hence, over time, the human race would be unable to feed itself. Some 170 years later a similar Malthusian perspective was adopted by Paul Ehrlich (1968) who, controversially, proposed that population control was necessary to avoid disaster. Although more recent studies have suggested that the time is approaching when the demand for food will exceed supply (Turner, 2008), to date history has demonstrated Malthus' concerns to be largely unfounded. Sufficient food is currently produced to meet the needs of the global population; the problem is one of inefficient distribution and food waste – as noted in the introduction to this book, one third of all food produced is, for a variety of reasons, lost or wasted (UNEP, n.d.).

In other words, over the last two centuries remarkable advances have been made in food production in terms of overall volume and yield. However, this success has been achieved at substantial environmental cost with regards to both the extent of land appropriated for agriculture and, more importantly, how that land is used. It is estimated that 38 percent of the world's land area – or 50 percent of all habitable land – is used for agriculture compared with less than 4 percent a millennium ago (Ritchie, 2019). This massive expropriation of land has been achieved through the widespread destruction of forests (see section above), the draining of wetlands, the reorganisation of landscapes by, for example, straightening rivers, and the exploitation of other natural areas. The consequential environmental impacts have been enormous, not least in the loss of biodiversity but also manifested in knock-on effects such as more frequent incidences of flooding. Greater costs have, however, been imposed on the environment through the ways in which that land is used. First, and as already noted, the success in increasing yields of crops has been achieved through monocrop farming rather than traditional land rotation methods, a practice which results in the serious degradation of soil quality. The extensive use of chemical fertilisers and pesticides has exacerbated this problem, leading to the loss of fertile soil and, ultimately soil erosion – it is estimated that up to one third of all arable land has been lost in this way over the last 40 years.

Second, there is what many consider to be an imbalance in the use of agricultural land between growing crops and livestock farming. Although estimates vary, it is acknowledged that up to 80 percent of agricultural land globally is dedicated to livestock farming, with around 60 percent of that area used not for grazing but for growing animal feed. Beef production is particularly controversial. Attenborough (2020: 170) points out that beef 'makes up a quarter of the meat we eat, and only 2 percent of our calories, yet we dedicate 60 percent of our farmland to raising it'. Not only is this imbalance in agricultural land use nonsensical, it also supports the argument for a shift to more plant-based diets. Moreover, whilst overall food production contributes around a third of all greenhouse gases, meat production accounts for 60 percent of this with beef being far and away the most polluting activity – even excluding the methane produced by cattle, the carbon output of beef production is four times greater than that of chicken and significantly greater than that for plant-based food production. For example, according to a recent study (Poore & Nemecek, 2018), soybean production produces 7.28kg of greenhouse gases per kilogram of food; for beef, the figure is 59.7kg of greenhouse gases per kilogram of food (pork is 7.28kg and lamb 24.42kg per kilogram of food). It should also be noted that, overall, agriculture uses up to 70 percent of all fresh water globally and, again, beef production is the most demanding; one kilogram of beef requires an astounding 15,415 litres of water (or roughly 1,500 gallons of water per pound of beef), about double the amount of water required for lamb and nine times the amount per kilogram of cereals (Water Footprint Network, n.d.).

It is ironic, therefore, that although we currently produce sufficient food to meet the needs of the global population, in doing so we are rapidly diminishing the potential to continue doing so through the environmental damage caused by contemporary agriculture. Hence, a major transformation is required in both agricultural practices and, in particular, the consumer demand that drives these practices in order to reduce greenhouse gas emissions, to limit pollution and the degradation of topsoil and to reduce demands on increasingly scarce fresh water supplies.

Threatened Oceans

The world's oceans are facing a number of threats. Reference has already been made to the extent to which they are becoming polluted by plastics and other forms of garbage or marine waste, much of which originates on land and enters the oceans as a result of poor waste management, storm water discharge or natural disasters. Some waste may also comprise discarded marine equipment, such as broken fishing nets. Often, so-called garbage patches can be seen in the oceans (NOAA, 2020) when large amounts of material waste collect as a result of rotating ocean currents or gyres, although much debris also falls to the ocean floor. Either way, the garbage in the oceans, as well as other forms of pollution such as oil and chemicals, directly kills or harms a multitude of ocean species or damages the habitats they depend on.

The oceans also fulfil an important environmental sink function, absorbing about 30 percent of the CO_2 that is released into the atmosphere. However, as the concentration of CO_2 in the atmosphere increases, so too does the amount absorbed by the oceans and, as a consequence, the acidity of the oceans increases. Hence, it is estimated that since 1850, ocean acidity has increased by some 26 percent, 'a rate of change roughly 10 times faster than any time in the last 55 million years' (CoastAdapt, 2017). In other words, the excessive use of fossil fuels and other carbon-producing activities is not only contributing to global warming and rising sea levels, the latter representing a longer-term threat to many coastal communities; it is also evident in the warming and acidification of the oceans which is threatening the health of many marine eco-systems, particularly coral reefs which collectively support about 25 percent of all marine species (and are also important tourism attractions). So-called coral bleaching (which is also caused by natural ocean warming effects such as El Niño) has occurred extensively in recent years and many reefs are now at risk of dying. In fact, it is estimated that up to half of the world's coral reefs have been lost or severely damaged since 1950 and some suggest that by 2070, no healthy reefs will remain.

Food and Water Insecurity

Often included in lists of global environmental challenges is food and water insecurity or, alternatively stated, declining access to adequate amounts of appropriately nutritious food and acceptably clean water for an increasing number of people. Strictly speaking, such insecurity is not in itself an environmental challenge like global warming, pollution or deforestation. Rather, it is the outcome of, amongst other things, inefficient distribution systems, poverty and population growth, but it is enhanced by environmental factors including the impacts of global warming, such as droughts, and the pollution and degradation of agricultural land which reduces yields and impacts water quality.

Food insecurity is growing. Whilst the global incidence of hunger declined over a number of decades, from 2016 there is evidence of a reversal in this trend (FAO, 2017), particularly in areas that have suffered drought or flooding as well as conflict. Indeed, a causal link exists between food insecurity and conflict; not only is a scarcity of food often more evident in areas suffering conflict but it may also lead to or increase conflict: 'The impacts of … food scarcity can undermine basic livelihoods and exacerbate social tensions, which can lead to instability and conflict if left unaddressed or when compounded by other social or political grievances' (Kenney, 2017). The same can be said with regards to climate change-induced water insecurity. Both a lack of and surfeit of water resulting from extreme weather events may significantly impact food production, transport, living conditions in densely populated urban areas as well as ecosystems, potentially leading to competition and conflict over water supplies. Hence, UNICEF's WASH (Water, Sanitation and Hygiene) programme seeks to provide access to sufficient clean water and hygienic systems (see unicef.org/wash). Moreover, as food and water insecurity increases in those parts of the world most affected by climate change, increased demand will be placed on natural resources in other less affected countries in which many existing environmental problems will be exacerbated.

TOURISM AND GLOBAL ENVIRONMENTAL CHALLENGES

From the above, it is evident that, to put it bluntly, the human race is trashing the ecosystem of which it is a part and upon which it depends. In our desire for happy, satisfying lives we are, quite simply, extracting too many natural resources from the ecosystem and dumping too much of our waste back into it. As David Attenborough succinctly puts it, 'We live our comfortable lives in the shadow of a disaster of our own making. That disaster is being brought about by the very things that allow us to live our comfortable lives' (Attenborough, 2020: 7). In other words, the environmental crisis that the world now faces is, as continuously (and intentionally) emphasised in this book, directly related to excessive consumption that occurs primarily within wealthier countries and societies but impacts most severely on the poorer, less developed countries and regions. And of course, one of the many activities that comprise that excessive consumption is tourism.

All the environmental challenges reviewed above are to a lesser or greater extent contributed to by tourism, many of which have long been acknowledged. More than 40 years ago, for example, the OECD (1981) proposed a framework that identified four 'tourism stressor activities' that impose stresses on the destination environment (widely discussed in the literature; for example, Wall & Mathieson, 2006) which result in primary (environmental) and secondary (human) responses (see Telfer and Sharpley, 2016: 278–287 for more detail). The four stressor activities in the framework remain a useful means of categorising tourism's environmental impact: (i) permanent environmental restructuring through tourism development, leading to loss of natural habitats and a reduction in biodiversity; (ii) the generation of pollution and waste, exceeding the environment's assimilative capacity; (iii) tourist activities that have direct and indirect impacts, from physical damage to fragile environments to endangering wildlife through discarded waste; and (iv) population dynamics or, more specifically, the temporary movement of large numbers of people to destinations, increasing the local population density and placing excessive demands on often scarce local natural resources, such as water. These stressors are not of course unconnected; the generation of waste, for example, can be related to the other three stressors.

The important point, however, is that the consumption of tourism has environmental impacts beyond the destination, the causes of which are often related to or indistinguishable from other activities and forms of production and consumption. Perhaps the most obvious is global warming which, in the tourism context, is most frequently discussed in terms of flying and aircraft emissions. This is explored in more detail below but the focus on the act of flying draws attention away from the often significant emissions generated, for example, in the production of concrete and the construction of airports, hotels and other travel and tourism infrastructure (the cement industry contributes about 8 percent of global CO_2 emissions), the construction of aircraft and other modes of transport, the emissions from other modes of transport and from the accommodation sector, agricultural production and so on. Regarding the latter, it is unlikely that, as they survey with anticipation the typically wide variety of dishes on offer at the hotel buffet, tourists consider or are even aware of the CO_2 emissions (to say nothing of the water usage) involved in the production and transport of that food provided for their enjoyment. Moreover, much of that food is often wasted; as Okumus et al. (2020) point out, food waste is a major environmental and economic challenge facing hotels, not least for those operating on an all-inclusive basis, whilst buffets in particular are a notorious source of food waste as opportunities for re-use or redistribution tend not to exist (Juvan, Grün & Dolnicar, 2018). The extensive use of bottled water amongst tourists, referred to earlier in this chapter, is also of relevance here.

To take another simple example, many tourists are concerned with protecting their skin from the sun whilst on holiday. It is not surprising, therefore, that a large volume of sunscreen is bought each year; more than 1 billion units of sun protection products were sold in 2018, generating revenues of around US$13 billion. Although so-called ethical sunscreen products are increasingly available, most popular brands use palm oil in their production, often disguised by different names. Hence, although sun protection products are by no means the only ones that contain palm oil – according to the WWF, it can be found in around half of all packaged products in a typical supermarket, from food and household cleaning to skincare products – the widespread consumption of sunscreen contributes directly to deforestation and habitat loss in countries such as Indonesia. In addition, it is estimated that some 10 percent of the world's coral reefs are at risk of dying owing to the up to 14,000 tons of sunscreen that washes off swimmers and divers each year (Saner, 2021). The chemicals present in sunscreen more generally adversely impact marine life whilst the microplastics commonly used in their production also inevitably contribute to the pollution of the oceans, to say nothing of vast quantities of plastic sunscreen bottles that end up in landfills and other waste dumps.

There are innumerable other examples of the wide-ranging (and often unrecognised) consequences of tourism which clearly and inevitably imposes direct and indirect impacts through the ecosystem. This point was made some 30 years ago (but arguably since continues to be ignored by many) when, in the very first issue of the *Journal of Sustainable Tourism*, McKercher (1993: 7) highlighted some fundamental truths which, he suggested, are the 'inherent and unavoidable consequences of embarking on the path of tourism development'. Foremost amongst these truths is that tourism is a 'voracious consumer of resources' (McKercher, 1993: 8), not only through the permanent and destructive restructuring of natural environments but also through often excessive consumption on the part of tourists. Moreover, tourism has a tendency to overuse resources and, as a popular development tool, to successfully compete for scarce resources at the cost of local communities and other sectors. McKercher (1993: 8) also refers to the significant waste produced by tourism, waste that he interestingly describes as 'more typical the type of waste produced by urban communities, rather than that normally associated with traditional industrial activity'. Listing sewage, garbage and car emissions as the 'most common and problematic', however, he falls into the trap of a destination focus, overlooking the pollution and waste from tourism infrastructure construction and from food and drink production and perhaps not foreseeing tourism's contribution to global warming. Certainly, sewage pollution has long been a major problem around coastal resorts whilst tourists are responsible for large amounts of trash in destinations – in the Maldives, for example, tourists generate more than 7kg of waste per day compared with less than 3kg per day amongst the local population and until recently, 700 tons of waste were dumped daily on 'trash island' where the waste created toxic fumes. However, if greenhouse gases and all forms of tourism-related waste are taken into account, then pollution must arguably be the single greatest environmental impact of tourism.

A notable example of this is cruising. Concern has long been expressed about the contribution of the cruise industry to the global environmental crisis and, as both the number and size of cruise ships has increased (in 2022, more than 320 cruise ships with a combined capacity of over half a million passengers were operated by more than 50 cruise lines), so too have criticisms of their environmental impacts. These are explored in detail in a recent review of more than 200 publications addressing the consequences of cruising for environmental and human health (Lloret et al., 2021) but the 'headline' impacts relate primarily to air and water pollution. Generally, a single large cruise ship has a carbon footprint larger than that of 12,000 cars (Dunne, 2021) whilst, more specifically, the widespread use of heavy fuel oil generates high levels of sulphur oxide (SO_x) and nitrogen oxide (NO_x). Indeed, according to one report (Transport & Environment, 2019), in 2017 the world's largest cruise operator, Carnival Cruises, emitted almost 10 times more SO_x around Europe's coastlines than did all the roughly 270 million cars on Europe's roads. Both SO_x and NO_x are damaging to the built and natural environment, falling in acid rain, and contribute to ocean acidification. In addition to air pollution, cruise ships are a major source of water pollution; Lloret et al. (2021) suggest that the cruise sector, although representing less than 1 percent of the global shipping industry, accounts for a quarter of all the waste produced by shipping. Such waste includes solid waste (plastics and other inorganic waste), 'black' (from toilets) and grey (from washing and bathing) wastewater, poorly treated sewage, bilge water and oil which, collectively have a significant detrimental impact on the marine environment and wildlife. In addition, up to 30 percent of the food produced on cruises may be wasted; this is typically liquified and discharged as 'fish food' although this again may be harmful to marine life – food served on a cruise ship is not part of a fish's natural diet.

To summarise, then, although the environmental impacts of tourism have long been acknowledged, attention has primarily focused on the immediate impacts at the destination, from transformations in land use to the excessive use of local resources, waste generation and the pollution of the natural environment. As important as it is to take these into account when managing and developing tourism, of equal if not greater importance is the need to recognise the less immediate 'upstream' and 'downstream' impacts of tourism, whether from the production and transport of products to serve tourists' needs or as the outcome of their typically excessive consumption whilst on holiday. In so doing, it becomes evident that, as argued earlier in this chapter, tourism cannot be considered separately when addressing the global environmental crisis, particularly as the consumption of tourism is forecast to continue growing in the post-pandemic era. Consequently, the need to reduce production and consumption on the global scale (to degrow) is as pertinent to tourism as to any other socio-economic activity, not least, as the next section discusses, to meet the challenges of climate change.

TOURISM AND CLIMATE CHANGE

As suggested earlier, climate change or, more precisely, global warming is widely considered to be the most significant of all contemporary environmental challenges. In terms of its consequences, it is also the most visible. Whilst extensive scientific data provide evidence of the Earth becoming warmer and of the consequences of that warming process, from receding glaciers and polar ice caps (and commensurate rises in sea levels) to transformations in agricultural productivity, reports and images of the impacts of extreme weather events appear in the media with ever-increasing frequency. During 2022, for example, numerous occurrences of extreme weather attributable to global warming were experienced around the world. Much of Europe suffered prolonged heatwaves, record temperatures and extensive drought; devastating wildfires ravaged parts of France, Spain and Portugal and some of the continent's major rivers, including the Rhine, Danube and Po, fell to dangerously low levels, impacting negatively on agriculture, trade and transport, including river cruising. India and Pakistan both experienced unusually early and prolonged heatwaves, the latter country subsequently suffering catastrophic flooding that left a third of the country under water, destroyed or damaged millions of homes and caused death and injury on a wide scale. Similarly, North America experienced weather extremes, from heatwaves to flooding; in August, flash flooding in California's Death Valley, described as a 'once-in-1000-year event' (Canon, 2022) stranded hundreds of tourists.

There are numerous other recent examples of extreme weather events occurring around the world, many of which impact tourism in one way or another, yet recognition and analysis of these impacts is not new. Researchers have been concerned with the relationship between tourism and climate for more than 30 years and there now exist numerous publications that address the topic. It is not our intention here to review this literature; this has been undertaken with regularity (for example, Arabadzhyan et al., 2021; Becken, 2013; Kaján & Saarinen, 2013; Pang et al., 2013) whilst many books discuss tourism and climate change in detail. Rather, the purpose is simply, in the context of this chapter, to emphasise the extent to which the tourism sector contributes to global warming by way of its overall greenhouse gas emissions which are predicted to increase into the future.

Curiously, perhaps, much of the initial research into climate change and tourism adopted what Pang et al. (2013: 10) refer to as a 'victim, winner, loser' perspective. In other words, tourism occupies an interesting position inasmuch as it both contributes to and also is (unsurprisingly, given the weather-dependent nature of many tourism experiences) adversely affected by climate change. However, there was a tendency in earlier studies to focus on the latter 'tourism as victim' perspective. Assessments of the potential consequences of a changing climate for destination attractions and resources, tourism flows and so on revealed that whilst some destinations might suffer, others might take advantage of new opportunities (hence, winners and losers). Inevitably, the research evolved to propose adaptation or mitigation models and strategies – how destinations might seek to minimise climate-related disruption to their tourism sector or to adapt to new climatic conditions, although more recently the concept of resilience, or developing new capabilities to become stronger or more resilient to challenges, has entered the climate change lexicon (Wong-Parodi, Fischhoff & Strauss, 2015). Examples of adaptation include seaside resorts shifting the high season from the (increasingly hot) summer to shoulder months whilst ski resorts in particular have long been in the vanguard of adapting to a warmer climate (Steiger et al., 2019). Amongst other challenges, an increasing lack of snow, particularly at lower elevations, has resulted in the almost ubiquitous use of snow-making machines. However, although enabling ski resorts to stay in business, thereby enhancing their resilience, the production of artificial snow is environmentally damaging; not only do snow-making machines devour enormous amounts of water and energy – an estimated 49 million gallons of water were used to create artificial snow for the 2022 Beijing Winter Olympics (Boneham, 2022) – but chemicals in the artificial snow as well as its higher water content and weight compared with natural snow both impact local ecology and increase the risk of snow-melt flooding. Moreover, in an ironic twist, snow machines have recently been used to fight summer wildfires, at the Sierra-at-Tahoe ski resort in California in 2021 and at the Apex Mountain Resort in Canada's British Columbia in 2022. Hence, the production of artificial snow is at best a shorter-term adaption strategy to maintain business; it is not a longer-term sustainable solution for the ski industry.

The example of snow machines points to a criticism that can be directed towards the mitigation / adaption focus of much of the tourism and climate change literature more generally. To use an old idiom, it is, in essence, 'shifting the deckchairs on the Titanic'. Whilst destinations might achieve short-term benefits through the implementation of mitigation or adaptation strategies, they do not address the unpalatable truth that such strategies are a response to a problem which is, to some extent, of the tourism sector's own making. It is not surprising, therefore, that greater attention is now being paid to estimating tourism's overall level of greenhouse gas emissions and relative contribution to global warming. Such an endeavour is, however, fraught with difficulty, not least because of the fragmented and diverse structure of the tourism sector. In other words, although some elements of the tourism production system, such as airlines, cruise ships, accommodation facilities and so on are relatively discrete, facilitating the calculation of their carbon and other emissions, other products and services consumed by tourists, such as food, drink, clothing, sports equipment, shops, local transport and so on, are also produced for markets other than tourism. Hence, estimating the tourism carbon footprint for these elements of tourism consumption and production is more difficult. Similarly, the proportion of all car journeys dedicated to tourism can at best be broadly estimated.

Nevertheless, attempts have been made to calculate the contribution of the tourism sector as a whole to global carbon / greenhouse gas emissions. For example, one report (UNWTO/UNEP, 2008: 33) estimated that 'International and domestic tourism emissions from three main sectors … represent between 3.9% and 6.0% of global emissions in 2005, with a best estimate of 4.9%'. At face value, this might appear to be a relatively small contribution to global greenhouse gas emissions, an argument usually employed by those seeking to defend the environmental record of airlines in particular. However, as Pang et al. (2013: 14) observe, drawing on data from the UNWTO/UNEP (2008) report, if tourism was a country, it 'would be the world's fifth leading contributor of GHG, behind only China, the USA, India and Russia'. Given that 'all tourism is dependent on energy, and virtually all energy use in tourism is derived from fossil fuels' (Gössling & Peeters, 2015: 642), the scale of its contribution is unsurprising.

From a sub-sectoral perspective, all modes of transport collectively contribute 75 percent of tourism's total carbon emissions, with 40 percent of the total attributable to flying alone and car transport 32 percent (UNWTO/UNEP, 2008: 33–34). This immediately points to the argument that the need exists for a reduction in tourist trips by air, both long haul and typically low-cost short haul (the latter more easily substitutable with land-based modes of travel). At the same time however, the emissions of car-based tourism trips – fundamental to domestic and, certainly in Europe, regional tourism – must also be addressed. The accommodation accounts for a further 21 percent of emissions whilst tourist activities at the destination an estimated 4 percent.

The UNWTO/UNEP (2008) report is limited to the extent that it includes only direct tourism services and activities, such as transport and accommodation. Not included are the emissions from the production and supply of tourism-related goods and services, a point acknowledged in the report: 'Taking into account all lifecycle and indirect energy needs related to tourism, it is expected that the sum of emissions would be higher, although there are no specific data for global tourism available' (UNWTO/UNEP, 2008: 133). Indeed, it is likely that the sum of emissions would be considerably higher. A more recent study by Lenzen et al. (2018) goes some way to addressing this limitation. Basing their calculations on both direct and indirect supply chains in tourism as well as taking into account not only CO_2 emissions but also those of other greenhouse gases, they estimate that, in 2013, tourism contributed 8 percent of global greenhouse gas emissions. They also project the future growth in emissions based on wealth-growth induced travel patterns, concluding that, without technology-supported efficiencies, by 2025 tourism will produce up to 6.5 $GtCO_2e$ (6.5 billion tons) of emissions, up from 4.5 $GtCO_2e$ in 2013 – an approximate 45 percent increase.

Yet, this is still not the full story. Not included in calculations are the embedded emissions in tourism-related equipment and infrastructure – that is, the carbon and other greenhouse gases produced in the construction of hotels, airports, marinas, roads, railways and so on (as noted elsewhere in this book, cement production alone accounts for 8 percent of global carbon emissions), to say nothing of the emissions resulting from the construction of aircraft, cruise ships and (with reference back to the earlier discussion on the environmental consequences of lithium mining) cars. Inevitably, to embrace all these sources of greenhouse gas emissions related to the production and consumption of tourism is a monumental and, in all likelihood, impossible task. Nevertheless, simply pointing them out adds weight to the argument that, in its totality, tourism (by and large a discretionary, or non-essential, form of consumption) makes a relatively enormous contribution to greenhouse gas-induced global warming. Moreover, it also casts doubt on the potential to achieve so-called 'net zero' or a carbon-neutral tourism sector and emphasises the inarguable fact that the solution lies only in an overall reduction in tourism consumption – though acknowledging, of course, tourism's important role in development. The concept of net zero is considered shortly but a final environmental issue that deserves brief consideration is that of tourism's impact on water insecurity.

TOURISM AND WATER INSECURITY

Fresh water is essential to human existence. However, access to fresh water is becoming problematic for increasing numbers of people. According to Boretti and Rosa (2019), around half the world's population, between 3.6 and 4 billion people, suffer water scarcity at least one month each year. Alternatively, the United Nations indicate that 733 million live in high and critically water-stressed countries and a further 2.3 billion in water-stressed countries (UN-Water, 2021). This compares with 1995 when 'an estimated 450 million people lived under severe water stress and an additional 1.3 billion people under a high degree of water stress' (Gössling, 2006: 180), pointing to increasing global water insecurity.

Two principal factors influence the extent of water scarcity or insecurity: the demand for water which, globally, has increased eight-fold over the last century and is forecast to grow by up to 30 percent by 2050; and renewable supplies of fresh water, which are in decline. These trends are universal, though the availability of fresh water varies significantly within and between countries and, typically, access to safe, clean water tends to be more limited in less developed countries. Nevertheless, some developed countries also face challenges in meeting the demand for water, not least because of the increasing incidence of drought; as noted in the preceding section, some southern European countries have in recent years been suffering drought-induced water shortages with both Italy and Spain making use of desalination plants (Gössling, 2006). Desalination has also become important in the US whilst in California in particular, where drought conditions are a perennial issue, restrictions have had to be placed on both residential and agricultural water use. In 2021, more than 350,000 Californians received state help in being supplied with drinking water.

One particular demand on fresh water supplies is of course tourism. The relationship between tourism and water use is explored in some detail by Gössling et al. (2012), who highlight the various ways in which the sector utilises water. Inevitably, direct (showers, toilets, swimming pools, saunas, spas, etc.) and indirect (laundry, kitchens, irrigating gardens, etc.) use of water in accommodation facilities is a principal demand on local fresh water supplies. It is generally acknowledged that, whilst on holiday, tourists tend to consume more water than normal and also significantly more than local residents. Some tourist activities also require significant amounts of fresh water, notably golf and skiing; the watering of the greens on an 18-hole golf course can consume enormous amounts of water, particularly in warmer climates whilst, as discussed in the previous section, the use of snow-making machines in ski resorts is also highly water-intensive. In addition, a hidden source of water consumption in tourism is in food production – the amount of water embedded in food (invisible water) can be quite considerable, particularly in meat, and hence much water is used through the consumption of locally produced or imported food.

Interestingly, despite its evident appetite for water, the tourism sector generally places fewer demands on local water supplies than other sectors of the economy. Nevertheless, in some countries and regions and, in particular, island destinations, tourism is the main form of water consumption, not only putting pressure on already scarce resources but also competing with other industries and the needs of local communities. Indeed, water inequity, or the disparity in water consumption between tourists and local people, has been found to be problematic in low- to middle-income countries with implications for resource stewardship and water-related conflicts (Becken, 2014). According to Gössling et al. (2012: 13), such conflicts are likely to increase 'given the global growth in tourism, the trend towards higher standard accommodation and more water-intense activities, which are likely to coincide with changes in the global climate system' and consequential declining water resources. Interestingly, drought in South Africa between 2015 and 2018 resulted in the threat of Day Zero when water taps in Cape Town were to run dry, which not only impacted locals but also tourism (Dube, Nhamo & Chikodzi, 2020). Gössling et al. (2012) go on to suggest that tourism development may no longer be feasible in some parts of the world whilst, more generally, a reduction by whatever means in tourism's exploitation of fresh water resources is essential.

NET ZERO: A SHORT CRITIQUE

The most popular policy response to the global challenge of global warming is so-called 'net zero'; following COP26 in 2021, a total of 135 countries pledged to work towards achieving carbon neutrality. Of these, only 66 have actually committed to a target year in their policies and legislation (Zandt, 2021), typically by 2050 although some countries have set more ambitious earlier targets, such as Finland (2035), Austria and Iceland (2040). In contrast, others have adopted later dates, including Brazil, China and Russia (2060) and India (2070). Despite this varying level of commitment, however, it is evident that the world is placing its bets on net zero as the solution to the climate crisis.

In some respects, it is easy to see why this might be the case – as a concept, net zero is deceptively simple. Given that the principal cause of global warming is, as explained earlier in this chapter, the excessive emission of CO_2 from the burning of fossil fuels, then carbon neutrality or achieving net zero emissions through a combination of 'cutting greenhouse gas emissions to as close to zero as possible, with any remaining emissions re-absorbed from the atmosphere' (UN, n.d.) is the most obvious course of action. However, not only is the very idea of net zero highly controversial but also there is a growing consensus that its achievement on a global scale is impossible, at least by 2050 (Deutch, 2020; Dyke et al., 2021).

Broadly speaking, net zero is a politically attractive policy through which governments, industry sectors and others can demonstrate positive action to address climate change. Nevertheless, the typical 30-year or so timescale is widely criticised for kicking the problem down the road; many argue that reducing carbon emissions to at least net, if not absolute zero is an immediate necessity to arrest global warming whereas the 2050 target allows for continuing increases in emissions. At the same time, it is also argued that the necessary investment in technology is beyond the means of many countries.

More specifically, however, achieving net zero through primarily a significant reduction in carbon emissions along with an increase in the amount of carbon being taken out of the atmosphere through offsetting and yet to be developed carbon removal technology is considered by many to be an unrealistic objective. For example, although renewable energy accounted for around 80 percent of new electricity generation capacity globally in 2020 (IRENA, 2021) and its supply is increasing at around 8 percent annually, the global demand for electricity is increasing at a higher rate and is likely to continue doing so. Consequently, far from reducing the need for fossil fuel-generated electricity, renewable energy currently covers only about half of the increasing demand for electricity, meaning that emissions from electricity generated from gas and coal are also increasing. Similarly, growth in the demand for fossil fuels for other uses, such as heating, transport, manufacturing and household consumption, is projected to continue into the future; driven by population growth and increasing prosperity, overall global energy demands are forecast to increase by almost half by 2050. Hence, even with an increasing supply of electricity from renewable sources, the global demand for fossil fuels will continue to increase through to 2050 with a commensurate growth in emission.

If carbon emissions are likely to increase over the next 30 years or so, then the only way to achieve net zero is through carbon removal or offsetting. Various schemes and technologies have been proposed, from bioenergy with carbon capture and storage (BECCS) – essentially, using crops to generate power and then capturing and storing the carbon emissions (Dyke et al., 2021) – to highly expensive and energy-hungry direct air capture, whilst mass tree planting also offers a potential solution. However, to be effective, BECCS would require up to 80 percent of current cultivated land to be transferred from food production whilst a study suggesting up to one billion hectares of land could be used for reforestation, potentially reducing the atmospheric carbon pool by 25 percent (Bastin et al., 2019) was roundly criticised for overestimating the extent of carbon removal and underestimating competing uses for that land. More simply stated, there is simply not enough land available to plant sufficient trees to achieve a meaningful reduction in atmospheric carbon, to say nothing of the vast amounts of water required to support their growth. It is for these reasons that Dyke et al. (2021) conclude that 'Current net zero policies will not keep warming to within 1.5°C because they were never intended to. They were and still are driven by a need to protect business as usual, not the climate. If we want to keep people safe, then large and sustained cuts to carbon emissions need to happen now'. And these cuts can only be achieved in one way: degrowth (Trainer, 2022).

From this admittedly brief and simplistic discussion, it is evident that net zero is at best a significant challenge and, in all likelihood, a myth. The same can be said for a carbon-neutral tourism sector. As indicated above, tourism is fossil fuel dependent, with 75 percent of its carbon emissions in particular related to transport (40 percent from flying, 32 percent from car transport). The shift to electric vehicles may, over time, have some impact on carbon emissions, though the increased demand for electricity will to a great extent simply transfer emissions from driving a car to power generation. With regards to flying, many airlines are committed to operating on a net zero basis; indeed, at a general meeting of the International Air Transport Association (IATA) in 2021, a resolution was passed by members 'committing them to achieving net-zero carbon emissions from their operations by 2050' (IATA, 2021). This is, it is claimed, to be achieved by the use of sustainable aviation fuel, new aircraft technologies, operational efficiencies and offsetting. However, it is again highly unlikely that net zero is a realistic objective for the aviation sector, not least in the context of projected growth in the demand for flying (44 percent growth between 2019 and 2050). Not only have the potential technologies required (the development of sustainable fuels, aircraft design and materials and so on) been criticised as myths (Peeters et al., 2016) but also, as Becken (2019) points out in her damning assessment of the potential for decarbonisation in tourism more generally, many airlines are currently investing in fossil fuel-powered aircraft that will be operated for 20–30 years. In other words, the IATA resolution is little more than greenwashing.

Becken (2019) identifies other factors that, she argues, limit potential decarbonisation in tourism; she does not even mention net zero as a realistic objective. Amongst these factors are: the prevailing growth paradigm in tourism; the institutionalisation of interests in the sector; the nature of policy making; excessive reliance on technology rather than focusing on tourism consumption and behaviour; and, the global distribution of tourism. Collectively, these factors, many of which are discussed in this book, point to a belief in the oxymoronic concept of green or sustainable growth in tourism, that tourism can follow a path of continuing growth whilst also becoming more sustainable. This is, of course, a premise that we are challenging here and, having demonstrated in this chapter that tourism makes a considerable and relatively disproportionate contribution to the global environmental crisis, we now turn in the following chapter to one of the problems that Becken (2019) alludes to, namely, the nature of the supply of tourism.

5. Tourism supply in a growth-based economy

You only speak of green eternal economic growth because you are too scared of being unpopular. You only talk about moving forward with the same bad ideas that got us into this mess even when the only sensible thing to do is pull the emergency brake.
Greta Thunberg, COP24 (2018)

INTRODUCTION

Increasing in complexity, tourism supply incorporates an ever-expanding range of actors in the public, private and voluntary spheres promoting tourism as an instrument of development. However, enabled by the dominant neoliberal growth-based economy and facilitated by advances in information communication technology (ICT), international agencies, destination marketing organisations and the tourism supply chain are driving the growth of tourism in a direction which is at odds with environmental crises. Tourism is a highly competitive, profit-driven business that thrives under capitalism and globalisation. Profit is the motor behind capitalism and the market, and the quest for profit is pursued by expanding production and consumption while cutting costs (Latouche, 2009).

Prior to the Covid-19 pandemic, international and domestic arrivals had seen tremendous rates of growth and, consequently, some destinations were facing the perils of overtourism. With the rolling out of vaccine programmes and pent-up demand, recovery has begun and, at the time of writing, concerns with regards to overtourism are starting to re-emerge. Thus, the drive for tourism growth by tourism suppliers is not only contributing to the environmental crisis but also is prompting social change, often to the detriment of destination residents. While efforts have long been made to put sustainability at the forefront of policies, plans and operations (see Chapter 2), tourism organisations are nevertheless still reliant on the continual growth of the economy and tourism. Equally, tourism destinations promote their sustainable development plans yet seek more tourism revenue whilst, perhaps unsurprisingly given its role, the UN World Tourism Organization (UNWTO) (2021) argues that 'tourism is well positioned to foster economic growth at all levels and provide income through job creation' and to contribute to the SDG #1 on poverty. Moreover, tourism enterprises seek to embrace corporate social responsibility (CSR) and to achieve net zero, yet contradictorily also seek a return to travel that exceeds pre-Covid levels. Thus, it is important to recognise the underlying neoliberal philosophy that drives many of the actors in tourism supply despite their sustainability claims or the promise of 'green eternal economic growth'.

More generally, global GDP needs to grow annually by at least 2–3 percent for large firms to maintain rising aggregate profits (Hickel, 2020). Annual growth of 3 percent means the global economy doubles every 23 years (based on an exponential growth curve); and of course, throughout the entire history of capitalism, GDP growth has been linked to energy and resource use (Hickel, 2020). In other words, the continual expansion of growth is a formula for ecological disaster and must be challenged. The chapter, then, begins by examining the influence of growth, capitalism and globalisation on tourism and offers examples of how the industry has been kept on a path for growth. A selection of tourism suppliers and their policies, plans, strategies and operations are then highlighted, illustrating how they are strongly influenced by the growth model. Sustainability efforts in tourism supply are then identified before the chapter concludes with the idea of degrowth in tourism.

GROWTH, CAPITALISM, GLOBALISATION AND TOURISM

Tourism has a problem in that it is addicted to growth, yet this is incompatible with sustainability goals (Higgins-Desbiolles, 2018). Arguably, tourism is one of capitalism's most versatile and creative manifestations (Büscher & Fletcher, 2017); it is constantly searching for new frontiers as capitalism never rests, continuously looking beyond any boundary/barrier as a site for new value and new capital formation (Kovel, 2002 in Büscher & Fletcher, 2017). As a capital practice, tourism has a role in both sustaining and expanding global capitalism (Büscher & Fletcher, 2017). Hence, it has been argued that tourism research needs to engage further with the themes and debates related to the processes of globalisation, capitalism and structural power (Bianchi, 2009); when tourism growth is prioritised over social development and at the expense of the environment, the inequalities of economic neoliberalism, capitalism and globalisation become apparent.

Fletcher (2011: 446) suggests that there exist three interrelated factors that explain the growth of tourism, namely: 'alienated tourists seeking extraordinary experiences; industry operators endeavouring to provide these experiences in order to glean a profit; and development/conservation organisations seeking to harness the exchange between these two groups in order to promote their own goals'. He goes on to argue that these three groups need to be framed within a single process by which the capitalist world-system harnesses tourism to fuel expansion. This reflects on one of McKercher's (1993: 7) fundamental truths of tourism, that it 'is a private sector dominated industry with investment decisions being based predominantly on profit maximisation'. Profits are relied upon for the bottom line but also by shareholders who have invested in the sector. This means, of course, that tourism operators are pressured to achieve improvements in key performance indicators (KPIs), such as tourist arrivals and expenditures and hotel occupancy rates, whilst the tourism industry as a whole has a long history of using benchmarking through ratio analysis (for example, profitability ratios, operating ratios, activity ratios and employee ratios) (Uysal & Sirgy, 2019). To remain competitive, businesses such as theme parks, galleries, heritage sites and museums need to continually add new attractions incorporating the latest technological trends.

Profitability can also be considered at a destination level inasmuch as the growth of partnerships, networks and strategic alliances can lead to potential profits for many stakeholders. Gill (2000) refers to the growth-machine of tourism in destinations. This growth-machine incorporates local landowners and entrepreneurs, as well as businesspersons who create growth coalitions of local elites that then influence governments to pursue economic development. Governments, in turn, both facilitate tourism investment and promote destinations to drive economic development. Yet this pursuit of profit can come at a social cost. In an analysis of new tourism and capitalism in the Danube Delta, for instance, Ivan (2017) found although local people are making more money, they no longer talk to each other. More broadly, developing countries pursuing tourism as an economic tool become enmeshed in a global system in which they have little control as large-scale powerful multinational tourism operators squeeze out local entrepreneurs. It is, therefore, important to clarify the goals for tourism development which, Burns (1999) suggests, can be viewed from two main perspectives: on the one hand, 'Tourism First' places developing the industry at the forefront of planning while, on the other hand, 'Development First' is framed by national development needs.

A number of critical points on tourism development in advanced capitalism have been raised (Fitchett, Lindberg & Martin, 2021). Tourism transforms pre-existing resources into tourism resources through which local practices, traditions and aspects of economic, social and cultural life are transformed through cultural commodification, marketisation and privatisation. This is linked to Marx's theory of primitive accumulation whereby land, labour and natural resources are made available to capital which, historically, has been linked to a range of processes including, amongst others, the forceful expulsion of Indigenous populations, the suppression of access to the commons, the commodification of labour and the conversion of collective property rights to exclusive property rights (Fitchett, Lindberg & Martin, 2021). A more contemporary take on this has been linked to research into land grabbing, in what Harvey (2005: 2) refers to as 'accumulation by dispossession where resources are disposed of one set of uses and values and repurposed for the expansion of capital' (Fitchett et al., 2021). This accumulation by dispossession is essential to the ongoing operation and functioning of global capitalism, including tourism as a particular manifestation of global capitalism. While it has often been linked to fraud, violence and theft, this accumulation has also been applied in more apparently ethical and progressive tourism initiatives, such as ecotourism and sustainable tourism, in which governments and conservationists use environmental arguments in order to dispossess Indigenous Peoples of their land (Fitchett et al., 2021).

More generally, and as Büscher and Fletcher (2017) note, as tourism destinations become capital (defined by Marx as 'value in motion'), this process can provoke various forms of material violence while tourism can become a form of structural violence in its own right. Three types of tourism-related structural violence under capitalism can be identified: the systematic production of inequalities, of waste and of spaces of exception (for example, local people being excluded from resort enclaves) which are frequently rendered invisible through branding. More specifically, the drive for tourism growth has led to major forms of exploitation evident in sex tourism and human trafficking (Mehlman-Orozco, 2017) and in the growth of the number of unscrupulous operators in orphanage tourism (Higgins-Desbiolles, Scheyvens & Bhatia, 2022; see also Biddle, 2021). Moreover, as noted in Chapter 3, tourism has also been complicit in what is referred to as disaster capitalism, primarily though land grabs which result in disaster-affected communities becoming even more vulnerable, facing continued poverty, inequality and a lack of opportunities (Wright, Kelman & Dodds, 2021).

Capitalism requires ever-expanding spaces for new markets, so the establishment of protected areas favoured by wildlife tourists is one illustration of how public land is enclosed in order to transform wildlife into a commodity (Fitchett et al., 2021). Drawing on the work of Bourdieu (1991), Fitchett et al. (2021) also investigate symbolic accumulation which offers another conceptual tool to examine emerging forms of capital accumulation and development, including tourism. Symbolic accumulation refers to the monopolisation of symbolic resources as forms of capital, including language and discourse which have the power to structure reality. Specifically, in their study of tourism development in the Lofoten Islands, Norway, symbolic transformations were found in defining territory, the commodification of time and space, legitimacy and authorisations, and in symbolic power and resistance. They argue that accumulation by symbolic dispossession was the most enduring and powerful form of accumulation by dispossession in advanced capitalist contexts, yet the struggle for symbolic capital is a necessary precursor to international tourism market expansion (Fitchett et al., 2021). Examples of how tourism has been kept on a path of ever-expanding growth and profit are now highlighted below.

KEEPING TOURISM ON A PATH TO GROWTH: POLICIES, PLANS, STRATEGIES AND OPERATIONS

From destinations to tourism businesses, actions are continually taken to keep tourism on a path to growth and profitability (see Becker, 2013). The rapid spread of information technology has made tourism much easier to market, sell and purchase than ever before, with social media in particular driving tourism as visitors compete to post online images and reviews of famous, exotic and remote places (see also Chapter 6). Since the advent of the modern tourist age, tourists have been able to travel further, faster and more frequently. New forms of tourism continually expand into more remote, fragile and dangerous environments or to present the adversities of others; see polar bears before they are gone, travel to space, pretend to be a migrant crossing the US–Mexico border or take a slum tour (Büscher & Fletcher, 2017). As a consequence, fragile heritage sites, from Machu Picchu in Peru to Angkor Wat in Cambodia, have struggled with tourism capacity, while wildlife is increasingly being chased by, for example whale watching tour boats and safari companies. Even the slopes of Mount Everest have faced overcrowding with inexperienced climbers paying tour companies to get them to the summit (Wilkinson, 2019).

This expansion of tourism has been driven by the pursuit of profit and government policies to attract more tourists, investors and developers. Recent decades have witnessed ever-increasing numbers of hotels, resorts, casinos, mega-shopping malls, theme parks, larger cruise ships and more lower-cost air-lines, the latter expanding into secondary airports, all of which consume more resources (for example, land, construction materials, etc.), generate increasing volumes of waste and emissions and create social change. Ironically, more tourists will be able to see first-hand the climate change to which tourism is contributing as Greenland is expanding two airports and building another, tar-geting the North American and European market (Cassey, 2022). Elsewhere, the Beijing Capital Airport has a capacity of 50 million passengers per year; the world's largest cruise ship, Royal Caribbean's *Symphony of the Seas*, can carry close to 9,000 passengers and crew while the A380 aircraft has the poten-tial to transport up to 855 passengers. The Accor hotel group has over 5,100 hotels in 110 countries covering a range of hotel brands. The Las Vegas area in the US boasts over 150 casinos while Macau has 41. More recently, the rise of the so-called sharing economy has rapidly changed the form and function of the delivery of tourism products, from taxis to food delivery to accommo-dation. Most notably, perhaps, Airbnb which started in 2007, now has over 4 million hosts, although some suggest that the platform is losing its popularity as rentals are in some cases no longer cheaper than more traditional forms of accommodation (Ghilarducci, 2022). Tourism products and experiences are becoming more specialised, attracting niche markets with more seasoned tourists seeking to venture outside tourist enclaves to stay in non-traditional accommodation and to experience a destination as a local (Gravari-Barbas, 2020). However, recent evidence suggests the industry is experiencing difficulties in meeting growing demand and hiring sufficient employees as many left during the Covid-19 pandemic.

The structure and operation of the industry within capitalism is reflected in another of McKercher's (1993: 7) truths about tourism, namely, that it is 'a multi-faceted industry, and as such, it is almost impossible to control'. Tourism has evolved into a multi-faceted and pervasive phenomenon which has lost specificity in terms of dedicated places, such as resorts and tourist zones, and dedicated players (for example, established traditional commercial providers), resulting in different types of tourism actors playing a role in the tourism system (Gravari-Barbas, 2020). In this context, Grefe and Peyrat-Guillard (2020) refer to the '3rd tourist revolution' which is characterised by internationalisation, digitisation and hyper-personalisation, all of which contribute to the expansion of tourism. Internationalisation is leading to the renewal of business models that have been challenged by the strategies of new operators, such as low-cost airlines, while digitisation has opened the door to disintermediation, allowing more operators to be involved in the industry without having to go through traditional markets or operators. Finally, hyper-personalisation engages customers through multiple touch points and new technologies which has led to increased numbers of people working in data-driven positions in tourism (GlobalData Thematic Research, 2021). Moreover, the well-known characteristics of tourism supply – intangibility, inseparability, perishability, heterogeneity, seasonality, complementarity, a high ratio of fixed to variable costs, ownership diversity (Inkson & Minnaert, 2018) and vulnerability to crises – all influence operational decisions as companies seek to expand or respond to challenges. For example, to address the problem of seasonality, ski resorts have opened mountain bike trails in the summer, low-cost airlines often lease their planes to save costs and tour operators are diversifying their products to extend their market reach.

There are various models which can be used as a lens on tourism product expansion and resource use. For instance, Lieper's (2004) widely cited tourism system model comprises a tourist generating region, a transit region and a destination region. As tourists cross each region and return home, they encounter multiple suppliers driving tourism growth. For example, airports in the transit regions of Dubai, Hong Kong, London (Heathrow) and Singapore (Changi) have become major duty-free shopping destinations. Alternatively, the tourism value chain approach identifies all tourism providers (both direct and indirect) comprising travel planning, transportation, accommodation, food and restaurants and excursions (Telfer & Sharpley, 2016). The complexity and power structures within the supply chain can be seen in the TUI Group based in Germany. The Group includes over 400 hotels, 16 cruise ships, leading tour operator brands and marketing platforms in Europe, five airlines with over 150 aircraft, 1,600 travel agencies and online portals, incoming agencies in holiday destinations and is increasingly focusing on expanding digital platforms (TUI, 2022). All components of the tourism value chain consume a wide range of resources including energy, land, food and water, reflecting a third truth about tourism, that as an industrial activity, it 'consumes resources, creates waste and has specific infrastructure needs' (McKercher, 1993: 7). The consumption of resources increases as the industry expands, often at the expense of local communities. From Dubai to Las Vegas, tourism has expanded into desert regions while, more specifically, with climate change, more ski destinations are having to use substantial volumes of water for snow-making (Gössling, Hall & Scott, 2015). The 40 golf courses in the Algarve region of Portugal are irrigated with approximately 18 million cubic meters of water, mostly taken from boreholes (Gössling et al., 2015). In just one week, the above-mentioned *Symphony of the Seas* cruise ship consumes: 60,000 eggs, 9,700 pounds of chicken, 15,000 pounds of beef, 20,000 pounds of potatoes and 450 cases of champagne (Ross, 2019).

In Niagara Falls, Canada, the land along the top of the Niagara Escarpment overlooking the waterfalls has mostly been built out with a row of high-rise hotels. The City has been approving even taller hotels to overlook the first row of hotels to allow for even more waterfall view rooms. Butler's (1980) well-known 'Tourism Area Life Cycle' model illustrates the evolution of a destination as local hotel supply is supplanted by large-scale international resorts as the popularity of the destination and, consequently, visitor numbers increase. The model points to ways of revitalising destinations once stagnation and decline occurs, the implication being it is critical to get the destination back on track. Proposals include the addition of man-made attractions, such as casinos, or relying on untapped natural resources for year-round tourism. Hotels and shopping malls, for example, periodically require refurbishment or, in the case of the Las Vegas Strip, a dozen classic hotel casinos have faced the wrecking ball since the early 1990s to make way for modern hotel casinos (O'Neil, K., 2022). Facilitated by government investment incentives, destinations are in constant competition to attract developers and more tourists (Butler, 1980).

Place-based competition has led to the pursuit of developing signature attractions or signature events, including the World's Fair and the Olympics. Tourisitification, however, transforms an area, whether a region, a town or a neighbourhood, into 'a place for tourist consumption' with resultant changes in landscape, environment and cultural and social dynamics (Lorenzen, 2021, 65–66; see also Ojeda & Kieffer, 2020). Touristification also has links with gentrification, which can transform the social fabric of an urban area (Jover & Díaz-Parra, 2020). In particular, local people have been squeezed out of the home rental/ownership market as the sharing economy has facilitated the spread of tourist rental accommodations into residential areas, further contributing to overtourism. In addition, Nofre (2021) argues that the touristification of nightlife is emerging into one of the most aggressive forms of material, symbolic and heritage dispossession of local communities for central historic neighbourhoods in Europe.

Tourism supply also needs to be viewed within the context of consumer society which, Latouche (2009) argues, has three necessary ingredients: (i) advertising, which creates the desire to consume; (ii) credit, which gives us the ability to consume; and (iii), products with planned obsolescence, which means we will continually need new products (see also Chapter 5). Globally, over 500 billion euros is spent annually on advertising, the second biggest industry in the world after arms (Latouche, 2009). Destinations and tourism enterprises continue to pursue innovative marketing strategies to drive visitor numbers, brand recognition and sales. Notably, the rise of the Internet, social media and ICT has revolutionised how brands and marketers engage with customers (Buhalis & Sinarta, 2019). Small firms have been able to advertise at relatively low cost and destinations are rebranding themselves in what Kotler, Haider and Rein (2002) refer to as place wars. People can purchase holidays on credit ('travel now pay later'), further adding to consumer debt. Indeed, the Internet now provides access to companies specialising in customer 'point-of-sale loans' for travel products (Paul, 2022). Uplift, for example, focuses exclusively on travel loans with 200 travel partners including United Airlines, Kayak and Royal Caribbean Cruises. Customers can book and pay for a trip with loans of up to US$25,000 with interest rates ranging from 7 percent to 30 percent (although some products offer 0 percent); however, if the trip is cancelled, customers are still required to repay the loan (Paul, 2022). Hence, it is possible to return from a trip and to be faced with not only additional credit card debt but also a 'point-of-sales' travel loan. Finally, all tourism businesses utilise products, from computers and television screens to toasters and light-bulbs which, in a growth-based society, are not built to last (Slade, 2007). For instance, MacKinnon (2021) draws attention to the planned obsolescence of LED lightbulbs which, as Fox (2019) reports, are increasingly being used in luxury and full-service hotels to create more customised looks. LED lights were rapidly adopted and initially manufactured to be long lasting (50,000 hours). However, over time, these were followed by shorter-lived LEDs; people and businesses utilised the money saved (on energy) by using LED lights to buy yet more LED lights. And to sell more LED lights, producers also began installing them into products that also are subject to short lifespans (MacKinnon, 2021).

Latouche (2009: 17) argues that in a society addicted to growth, the new heroes of the day are the 'cost killers', or managers intent on doing what they can to outsource costs. Hotels, for example, have been outsourcing housekeeping while airlines have outsourced catering (Rucinski and Shivdas, 2021). Latouche (2009: 19) contends that outsource costs are borne by 'their employees, their subcontractors, the countries of the South, their clients, states and public services, future generations and, above all, nature which has become both a supplier of resources and a dustbin'. Overall product costs have been kept low through maintaining low wages. Indeed, low levels of pay is one of the main criticisms of tourism employment while other challenges include the increased precarity of employment, technological displacement, seasonality, lack of long-term contracts and reliance on migrant workers who face visa challenges. In the United States, for example, the leisure and hospitality sector is the lowest-paid industry tracked by the Bureau of Labor Statistics (Kaplan & Hoff, 2022), although local contexts do need to be considered with some tourism jobs being highly sought after (c.f. Cukier, 2002). Nevertheless, tourism has long been promoted as a labour-intensive industry and, therefore, one that is attractive to governments, not least because it does provide both formal and informal jobs for skilled and unskilled labour that are particularly taken up by women, younger people and low-income families (Su et al., 2022). In fact, Sun et al. (2022) argue that, by supporting these economically vulnerable groups with decent jobs and fair wages, tourism plays a significant role in reducing both absolute poverty (US$1.90 a day) and income inequality. However, as noted earlier in this volume, critics have argued that the absolute poverty rate of US$1.90 is far too low. As the tourism industry starts to recover from the pandemic and employers are obliged to offer higher wages to attract employees, the labour shortage may be more linked to the wage shortage (Kaplan & Hoff, 2022).

To paraphrase Latouche's (2009) degrowth argument in the context of tourism, while growth of the production/jobs/consumption trio is credited with almost every virtue in terms of capital accumulation, continued growth (of tourism) is also responsible for multiple harms, including exploitation, imperialism and various crises including the pressing ecological crisis. The following sections provide examples of the policies, plans, strategies and operations of some selected tourism supply sectors, the purpose being to demonstrate their commitment to growth. These examples are also reflected upon in order to contribute to the critique of the neoliberal capitalistic growth-based mode of tourism development although it must be emphasised that, within the politics of tourism, power is arrayed on the side of pro-growth, from the policies of UNWTO and most national tourism authorities, to the influence of multinational tourism corporations and the perspective of the tourism academy itself (Higgins-Desbiolles & Everingham, 2022).

International Tourism Organisations

Global and regional international tourism organisations are actively engaged in the promotion and development of tourism. Many of these organisations emphasise sustainable tourism, particularly in their post-pandemic recovery agendas, yet their policies and platforms are nevertheless firmly founded within a neoliberal growth framework. The UNWTO (2022), for example, 'promotes tourism as a driver of economic growth, inclusive development and environmental sustainability and offers leadership and support to the sector in advancing knowledge and tourism policies worldwide'. While the UNWTO has identified how tourism can contribute to the UN's SDGs, these remain based on the growth model. Notably Goal 8, focusing on decent work and economic growth, calls for sustained per capita economic growth of at least 7 percent per annum in the least developed countries. More specifically, Target 8.9 calls for the development of sustainable tourism which is measured by Indicator 8.9.1, namely, tourism direct GDP as a proportion of total GDP and in growth rates (UN, 2022). Gascón (2019) argues that the UNWTO has been promoting participation in tourism as a human right, in part to legitimise itself within the UN but also to defend the interests of the industry against calls for the degrowth of tourism. Recently, the UNWTO as well as the World Travel and Tourism Council (WTTC) have published numerous policy documents on how the industry might recover from the pandemic, with both organisations calling on governments for assistance. For example, in their document *To Recovery and Beyond*, the WTTC (WTTC & Wyman 2020: 6) calls on governments to do more to acknowledge the importance of tourism as a driver of job creation and growth and 'a mechanism to further equality, reduce poverty and enhance inclusivity in society. The sector now needs the right assistance to bring back the millions of jobs and people whose livelihoods have been impacted'.

International development banks and related agencies such as the International Monetary Fund (IMF), the World Bank, the Asian Development Bank (ADB) and United Nations Development Programme (UNDP) have long provided funds to support tourism as a vehicle for economic growth and development (Hawkins & Mann, 2007). For example, from 2016 to 2019 the World Bank allocated US$1,952.32 million dollars for 32 tourism projects, with Indonesia (15.37 percent), China (14.32 percent) and El Salvador (10.24 percent) receiving the highest level of funding (Carrillo-Hidalgo & Pulido-Fernández, 2019). Funding is provided through repayable loans (82 percent) and non-repayable credits (18 percent), with each tourism project being a link to other sectors in the economy. The World Bank also provides technical assistance and training in association with some of the tourism development projects (see also International Finance Corporation, 2021). The

UNDP helped finance the 2,000 kilometre *Via Dinarica* route connecting trails in seven countries and territories in the Balkans to utilise tourism to stimulate the economy in remote rural areas (UNDP, 2020b). The ADB provided funds to Nepal, India and Bangladesh for improvements in infrastructure and services at key tourism sites, including at natural and cultural attractions (ADB 2022a), and in May 2022, the ADB and the Government of Fiji signed a US$3 million grant for testing and the containment of Covid-19 at the Nadi International Airport financed through the Government of Japan (ADB, 2022b). Generally, while these international loans and grants may undoubtedly help with tourism expansion, they have also been criticised for drawing recipient nations further into neoliberal monetary policies driven by global banking institutions.

On a regional scale, tourism promotional organisations include the Pacific Asia Travel Association (PATA), the European Tourism Association (ETOA) and the Association for Promotion of Tourism to Africa (APTA). The European Union is focusing on rebuilding tourism and making it more resilient with its *Transition Pathway for Tourism*, the aim being to lead green and digital transformations to boost the EU's global competitiveness (EU, 2020). The Caribbean Tourism Organisation (CTO) represents its 24 member countries and private sector allied members in one of the most tourism-dependent regions in the world. Their vision is to 'position the Caribbean as the most desirable, year-round warm weather destination. Its purpose is Leading Sustainable Tourism – One Sea, One Voice, One Caribbean' (Caribbean Tourism Organisation, 2022). Its Aviation Task Force acknowledges air access is integral to the archipelago's tourism growth and calls for increased access to international and regional markets as well as increasing the economic benefits from the growth and development of tourism and improving the region's competitive position. Relying heavily on air transport, however, contributes to the region's already high vulnerability to the impacts of climate change (Pentelow & Scott, 2011).

The international tourism organisations referred to above all advocate on behalf of tourism and its important role in national economies. Keen to recover from the Covid-19 pandemic, many of these organisations recognise the recovery period as a time to re-evaluate and find a potentially better tourism (c.f. UNWTO 2020a), yet underlining their messages is the desire to rebuild tourism to pre-Covid-19 levels, a mandate firmly based in the neoliberal growth model.

National and Regional Tourism Organisations

National and regional tourism organisations also focus on strategies to grow tourism markets, to attract more tourists to the destination and to generate increased spending and repeat visitation (Higgins-Desbiolles et al., 2019).

Tourism policies establish the framework while marketing strategies help create an image of the destination. 'It's More Fun in the Philippines' to '100% Pure New Zealand' to 'Incredible Indi' illustrate place-based branding strategies at the national level that are also utilised at regional levels (Telfer, 2015). An important question, however, is whether tourist imaginaries match local desires. In 2019, the Government of Canada released its national tourism strategy with the title *Creating Middle Class Jobs: A Federal Tourism Growth Strategy*. To track the economic impact (target date of 2025), indicators monitored included: revenue (total spending by tourists on goods and services), the number of jobs created and tourism GDP growth. Seasonal and geographic targets were also set to increase spending outside Canada's three largest cities and to increase international arrivals in the winter and shoulder seasons. The Canadian government set aside CA$58.5 million for the *Canadian Experiences Fund* to invest in unique tourism products and experiences. In addition, a new Canadian tourism growth strategy is in development to respond to the pandemic, while the Indigenous Tourism Association of Canada (ITAC, 2020) has launched a CA$50 million strategic recovery plan to rebuild Indigenous tourism across the country to 2019 levels. Similarly, the Australian government (2022) recently launched THRIVE 2030, a national strategy for the long-term sustainable growth of the visitor economy. The plan states that the 'visitor economy is a significant driver of growth, prosperity and wellbeing for Australia'. The target is to return visitor expenditures to pre-Covid levels of US$166 billion by 2024 and then have this grow to US$230 billion by 2030. The themes within the plan are collaborate, modernise and diversify. While these national plans often highlight sustainability, they are still quite evidently grounded in the growth paradigm as they seek to rebuild tourism numbers and revenue.

Subnational jurisdictions have a similar economic reliance on tourism, illustrating widespread regional tourism hyper-dependency and hyper-accumulations of tourism capital (Weaver et al., 2022). At a state level, the Hawaii Tourism Authority's (2020) Strategic Plan (2022–25) has four pillars: natural resources; Hawaiian Culture; Community; and Brand Marketing. The Plan is linked to the SDGs through the Aloha Challenge program especially in the areas of energy, local food production and consumption and water. The four key performance indicators are resident satisfaction, visitor satisfaction, average daily visitor spending and total visitor spending. In 2019, visitor spending was US$17.75 billion, while taxes generated by visitor spending amounted to US$2.07 billion and the industry supported 216,000 jobs. One point of note in the plan is that 53 percent of the growth in arrivals between 2009 to 2018 was largely driven by visitors staying in vacation rentals and other non-traditional accommodations. This clearly indicates the diversification and geographic spread of accommodation units available to visitors, which enhances the affordability pressures on local people. Recovery is on the way in Hawaii; visitor numbers in June 2022 totalled 842,927 or 89 percent of the June 2019 figure (State of Hawaii, 2022).

While national, regional and local tourism organisations pursue tourism for growth, it is important to recognise that tourism may be based on a created narrative which may not necessarily match the 'real' image, needs and desires of the host population. *Detours: A Decolonial Guide to Hawai'i* provides alternative narratives, images, tours, itineraries and mappings to present a decolonial heritage of Hawai'i going beyond tourism marketing (Aikau & Gonzalez, 2019). Many encounter Hawai'i first through their imagination – a picture postcard, perhaps, of hula girls, *lūaus* or plenty of sun, sea and surf. However, in reality, Hawai'i is not a postcard with happy hosts; Native Hawaiians 'struggle with problems brought about by colonialism, military occupation, tourism, food insecurity, high costs of living, and the effects of a changing climate' (Aikau & Gonzalez, 2019: 1–2). Hawai'i as an ideal tourist destination is a result of the infrastructure built for the comfort, safety and pleasure of visitors; this infrastructure, as well as the values, ideas and decisions that support it, are built on the historical and present-day dispossession of *Kanaka 'Ōiwi* (Native Hawaiians) (Aikau & Gonzalez, 2019: 2): 'Unless we actively work to dismantle this infrastructure and refuse the tourist imaginary, we will (wittingly or unwittingly) contribute to reproducing the occupation and colonisation of these places, people, and practices' (Aikau & Gonzalez, 2019: 3). The edited guidebook is meant to unsettle and disturb Hawai'i as a place for tourists; it is not an open invitation. Rather, it examines the different ways in which communities and various groups are working to restore '*ea*' (the breath and sovereignty of the *lāhui*, '*āina*, and its people). The Hawaiian example, then, clearly illustrates that the tourism growth agenda of the state can be at odds with local desires to assert sovereignty.

Tourism Transportation – Airlines and Cruise Ships

Deregulation and liberalisation in civil aviation have had the most significant impact on tourism (Inkson & Minnaert, 2018). With barriers removed, the introduction of low-cost air carriers such as Southwest in the US and Ryanair and easyJet in Europe furthered the geographic spread of air travel. Low-cost carriers utilise ticketless travel, direct sales on airline websites, single cabin class with no frills, no transfers and operate a single model of aircraft (Eugenio-Martin & Perez-Granja, 2021). By utilising secondary airports with lower landing fees and point-to-point routes, costs are reduced. In so doing, low-cost carriers have allowed more people to fly at a lower price, thereby generating positive impacts on international and domestic arrivals. Global air fares fell by 60 percent between 1998 to 2018, meaning that more people could go on holiday more often, travelling greater distances for shorter periods of time (Gössling & Higham, 2021). Low-cost airline expansion has occurred globally with AirAsia, a Malaysian low-cost airline using the slogan 'Now everyone can fly' (Bowen, 2019), emphasising the democratisation of travel. In 2019, the website Flightradar24 (2022) tracked on average 188,901 flights per day globally, a 10 percent increase over 2018. Prior to the pandemic, there had also been tremendous growth in air travel in China with the country receiving 23 percent of global aircraft deliveries (Gössling & Higham, 2021). Larger airlines have capitalised on strategic alliances (for example, Star Alliance, One World) and customer loyalty programmes. The Star Alliance has 27 member companies offering over 19,000 daily departures to over 1,300 destinations in 195 countries (Star Alliance, 2022). However, it is important to recognise the power structures in these alliances and for airlines controlled by tour operators. If a route is no longer profitable, or the airline fails, the resulting reduction in flight numbers has a major impact on affected destinations.

The Covid-19 pandemic has been devastating to the airline industry with aircraft grounded and employees laid off. Compared to 2019, there was a reduction of 50 percent of seats offered by airlines in 2020, a reduction in 2,703 million air passengers (−60 percent) and a loss of US$372 billion in gross passenger operating revenue (ICAO, 2022). At the time of writing, domestic air travel has started to recover better than international flights although, unsurprisingly, the Chinese domestic air market has experienced continuing volatility given renewed outbreaks of Covid-19 and consequential restrictions on mobility in the country (ICAO, 2022). As demand for flights has increased with pressures to return to pre-Covid-19 travel levels, there has been a shortage of pilots. As a result, some regional carriers in the USA have been increasing wages to attract more pilots (Josephs, 2022). Another impact of the Covid-19 pandemic on airlines has been the rise in the use of private jets through ownership, charters or subscriptions which has not reduced as the airline industry begins to recover. In fact, what was deemed a necessary luxury during the Covid-19 pandemic for the wealthy is now becoming 'a pricey but sought-after alternative to a premium ticket on a commercial flight' (Lampert & Singh, 2022).

During the pandemic, state governments were forced to financially support airlines deemed too big to fail. Air France received 7 billion euros in state aid (loan guarantees) accompanied by a requirement to reduce carbon emissions (Macilree & Duval, 2020). Simultaneously, the French government became the first large economy to ban short haul flights if a bus or train alternative of 2½ hours or less is available (effective April 2022). The move could eliminate 12 percent of French domestic flights. Air France was also requested to accelerate its environmental transition as part of the financing which could affect 40 percent of their flights where a rail link is available and other carriers were asked to do the same. However, it should be noted that the ban only applies to local traffic and not to flights with international connections in order to keep Air France competitive (Ledsom, 2022). While apparently a step in the right direction, Garay (2022) observed that banning selected short haul flights will lead to minimal reductions in overall emissions. Shorter flights (less than 311 miles) comprised 31 percent of European flights in 2020, contributing just over 4 percent of the EU's total aviation emissions while long haul EU flights (over 2,485 miles where a train alternative is available) made up 6 percent of flights and 52 percent of emissions. Hence, Greenpeace (2021) claims the French ban will equate to less than a 1 percent reduction in the carbon emissions of the country's air transport sector. Greenpeace is also calling on the EU to ban short haul flights (if a train route is available under 6 hours), activate/revive underused train routes for day and night trains, increase funding to the rail system and make travelling by train cheaper and easier than flying.

Overton (2022) examined several reports analysing the growth in greenhouse gas emissions from commercial aviation. While difficult to predict, forecasts estimate that international and domestic commercial air travel will recover quickly by 2025 with a more typical growth pattern thereafter. In 2018, aviation produced 2.4 percent of total global CO_2 emissions, with passenger travel accounting for 81 percent and freight for 19 percent of global commercial aviation emissions. Airplane non-CO_2 effects, such as warming from airplane contrails, adds to aviation's impact on the climate, thereby increasing the aviation industry's overall contribution to global anthropocentric warming to 3.5 percent. However, with the projected growth in airline traffic, commercial aircraft emissions could triple by 2050. Although the UN International Civil Aviation Organisation (ICAO) has established CO_2 emission standards for new aircraft and has pledged support for an aspirational net zero by 2050 (Hoskin & McGrawth, 2022), and IATA (2022) has similarly committed to fly net zero by 2050, the overall projected growth in demand for both passenger and freight traffic becomes the central barrier to controlling emissions of commercial aviation. ICAO predicts that greenhouse gas emissions from international aviation could rise by a factor of two to four times the 2015 level by 2050 (Overton, 2022). Macilree and Duval (2020) thus pose the question of whether post-neoliberal ideologies and concerns over climate change will lead to deglobalisation, with a resultant contraction in global trade having an impact on passenger and cargo demand for international air transport.

In 2018, the cruise industry witnessed a global 10-year growth of 74.9 percent in cruise ship passengers (Novicio, 2021); it is an industry that represents the coming of age of neoliberal globalisation (Wood, 2004). Dominated by three large companies, Carnival Corporation, Royal Caribbean Cruises Ltd. and Norwegian Cruise Lines (Honey & Bray, 2019), in 2019 the cruise line industry created 1.8 million jobs and US$154.5 billion in total output worldwide (Cruise Lines International, 2021). As a result of the Covid-19 pandemic, global cruise passenger numbers plummeted from 29.7 million in 2019 to 7.1 million in 2020 before recovering slightly to 13.9 million in 2021 (Nilson, 2022). Numerous cruise ships were retired between 2019 and 2021 in order to save costs as revenues dropped, with significant impacts on intermediaries. The pandemic powerfully illustrated the fact that the international ship industry, and cruise ships in particular, are a potent vector for the global transmission of viruses, notably demonstrated in 2020 by the docking of the *Diamond Princess* in Yokohama in February and the *Ruby Princess* in Sydney in March (Gullett, 2021). Globally, ships were turned away from ports and voyages were cancelled or cut short (Gullett, 2021). Post-pandemic, recovery is underway with 32 new cruise ships setting sail in 2022, albeit with a shift towards boutique designs to attract a younger market (Gullett, 2021; Cruise Industry News, 2022a). The luxury and expedition cruise markets in particular are the fastest growing segments. The expedition market often operates smaller ships reaching destinations inaccessible to larger ships and has seen passenger numbers grow from 67,000 in 2012 to 356,556 in 2022, a 450 percent increase in 10 years (Cruise Industry News, 2022b). Concerns have, however, been raised over these smaller cruise ships moving into remote and fragile areas such as the Arctic.

Reflecting on the role of cruise ships in development, it is important to consider the nature of their operations. Renaud (2020) argues that the mass cruise tourism industry is firmly based in the neoliberal production of tourism space and promotes the economic, environmental and socio-cultural marginalisation of cruise destinations. Cruise ships carry most of their own supplies, reside in ports for short periods of time and endorse specific excursions and shopping locations, raising questions about the economic impact of cruise ships in destinations. In fact, Wilkinson (2017) argues that destination governments in the Caribbean have demonstrated little appreciation of the economic problems and of the less-than-hoped-for positive economic benefits of cruise ship tourism. Strong competition between destinations in attracting more cruise passengers has also forced governments to invest significant resources in new or expanded cruise ship docking facilities to accommodate larger ships (Wilkinson, 2017). In another development, some cruise lines are even creating their own destinations with Disney including stops at its own private island, *Disney Castaway Cay*, and it recently received approval to develop a second island in The Bahamas (McGillivary, 2021). Additionally, cruise ships are known to fly Flags of Convenience (FOC) which offer flexibility and cost savings (Terry, 2017). Under FOC, ships are registered in countries with less strict regulations on taxes, the environment and labour. The ships pay a fee based on tonnage rather than paying income taxes and the ships can be built wherever owners choose. The elimination of restrictions on crew and owner citizenship allows for the hiring of crew from anywhere in the world, especially low-wage countries. As a consequence, approximately 70 percent of the labour (especially in menial and semi-skilled work) comes from the relatively poorer countries in South Asia, south-east Asia, Central America, the Caribbean and Eastern Europe (Terry, 2017).

Critics have also noted a range of environmental problems both at sea and in port associated with the cruise industry, including 'air pollution, sewage, grey water, hazardous waste and solid waste in larger than life scales' (Honey & Bray, 2019: 32). While improvements have been made through legislation and industry change, cruise ships have been fined for illegal dumping, including Princess Cruises paying US$40 million after the discovery of one of its vessels had been illegally dumping raw bilge waste from the engines and fuel system into the ocean (Honey & Bray, 2019). Considering the Covid-19 pandemic, Renaud (2020) questions cruise tourism and argues that the future of the industry should be aligned with deglobalisation and degrowth. He contends that destinations need to utilise the industry's reliance on global mobility as leverage in order to transform the balance of power to their benefit and promote local mobility. Destinations need to transition from 'growth for development' to 'degrowth for liveability' by banning or restricting mega-cruise ships, promoting the development of niche cruise tourism with small ships and creating a fleet controlled by local actors (Renaud, 2020).

Tourism Accommodation: from International Hotel Chains to Airbnbs

The evolution and progression in tourism accommodation has been critical to keeping tourism on a path to growth. Traditional globalisation driven by multinational firms in North America, Europe and Japan is being challenged by so-called 'Dragon Multinationals', or multinationals from the 'periphery', with investments in hotels (Mathews, 2002). The 'Asian Wave' of hospitality and tourism represents a geographic shift in power from Europe and North America to Asia (Chon, 2019). In 2020 alone, there were 928 hotel projects with 215,433 rooms in development in the Asia Pacific Region (Chon, Park & Zoltan, 2020). The largest hotel groups in the world in 2021 included Marriott (over 7,500 hotels and 1,400,289 rooms), China-based Jin Jiang International (over 10,000 hotels with close to 1,100,000 rooms) and Hilton Hotels (6,619 hotels and 1,010,257 rooms) (Tourism Review, 2021; Lock, 2022). India is also experiencing a hotel development boom in domestic and international brands, with room rates having regained 2019 levels and the country is on track to being the third largest lodging market in the world within 10 years (O'Neil, S., 2022). While international hotel chains control 60 percent of the market share in Africa, there is a growing number of Indigenous African hospitality brands, such as Tsogo Sun with over 90 hotels and casinos across Africa, while

80 percent of the safari lodges in South Africa are managed by Indigenous brands (Emelike, 2020). Large hotel companies operate a range of brands in their portfolio operated through management contracts, lease contracts, franchises and consortiums (Inkson & Minnaert, 2018). Britton (1991) argues that many foreign investors prefer contractual agreements with Indigenous or other foreign parties as it gives foreign companies effective corporate control and profits without having to invest large sums of capital to construct the resort complex.

Criticisms of the power structures of multinational hotels can be found in Britton's (1991) early work on the political economy of tourism which focuses on the state-centric neo-colonial model whereby metropolitan economies control tourism development in peripheral economies with the largest commercial gains going to foreign and local elites. Hotel management, construction materials and food are often imported and profits repatriated. The advertising campaigns of metropolitan tourism companies shape tourists' expectations and are determinants of tourist facilities which are often capital- and energy-intensive luxury hotel resorts that poorer countries cannot afford to build and operate due to import costs. Most locals can only participate through wage labour or small retail and artisan enterprises. More recently, Bianchi (2015) has argued for the need to critically analyse the increasing dominance of transnational tourism corporations and the growing structural power of the market at regional and global levels; economic globalisation and market liberalisation have underwritten a more complex and differentiated geography of tourism production, distribution and exchange.

Wall-Reinius, Ioannides and Zampoukos (2019), drawing on the work of Harvey (2013), argue that the rise in the number of all-inclusive resorts (including cruise ships) reflects capitalism's obsession with profit within an era of neoliberalism. Globally, all-inclusive resorts are becoming increasingly popular in coastal areas, such as in Turkey, Egypt, Mexico, the Caribbean and the Indian Ocean, due to policies that favour foreign direct investment. This has resulted in large-scale, planned projects controlled and managed by major multinationals or local elites (Wall-Reinius et al., 2019). At all-inclusive resorts, tourists pay for everything up front before leaving home; they enter the tourist 'bubble' with access to sports facilities, recreational amenities, activities for children and a multitude of eateries embracing a modern and 'international' style and standard. As a consequence, such resorts have weak local economic linkages and high rates of monetary leakages; they also exacerbate dependency on multinationals, reinforce socio-economic and spatial neo-colonial patterns, have limited connections to place and are criticised with regards to working conditions and labour rights (Wall-Reinius et al., 2019; Tourism Concern, 2014).

In October 2021, hospitality workers marched through Waikiki, Hawaii, calling on employers to resume full operations as the pandemic eased. The Union claimed hotels had been at full occupancy for months but only 70 percent of the workforce was recalled. In an emerging trend, hotels are automatically opting guests out of daily housecleaning and the Union claimed this would cut up to 39 percent of all US hotel keeping jobs and cost housekeepers $4.8 billion in annual lost wages (HNN Staff, 2021). On the one hand, eliminating daily room cleaning reduces hotel operating costs (and therefore generates more profits) and is more sustainable. On the other hand, the loss of employment in tourism without alternatives highlights the challenges surrounding degrowth in tourism.

While large-scale multinational tourism enterprises attract most attention, tourism is mainly comprised of small businesses. In Europe, for example, over 90 percent of all hotels are small and medium-sized tourism accommodation enterprises (Bastakis, Buhalis & Butler, 2004). A crucial component in this structuring has been the evolution of the sharing economy which has transformed the accommodation sector. Guttentag (2015) utilised the lens of disruptive innovation theory to examine the rise of Airbnb, illustrating how an alternative product can, over time, transform a market and capture mainstream consumers. The online platform has spread globally, enabling individuals to rent out their residences to tourists, thereby generating income while tourists benefit through lower costs and an authentic local experience (though, as noted earlier, some suggest the Airbnb bubble has burst). The growth in Airbnb can be seen in Santorini, Greece where there are 350 hotels with 14,298 beds and 3,796 Airbnbs with 17,082 beds (Sarantakou & Terkenli, 2019). This has, however, intensified the incidence of overtourism in Santorini, generating animosity while further impinging on landscape planning and management. Other challenges of overtourism include locals being priced out of the rental market while some rentals may be illegal with respect to short-term rental regulations and tax regulations (Milano, Cheer & Novelli, 2018). Prior to the pandemic, overtourism was creating problems in numerous cities / destinations across the globe, including Barcelona, Palma de Mallorca, Dubrovnik, Kyoto, Berlin, Bali and Reykjavik, leading to an increase in protests from locals. Milano et al. (2018) suggest that overtourism may be a symptom of the present era of 'unprecedented affluence and hypermobility' which is a consequence of late capitalism. While some have argued that overtourism has become irrelevant in light of the pandemic, others, such as Séraphin and Yallop (2020), argue otherwise. They suggest that the nature of overtourism will be transformed with the rise in the use of second homes and domestic tourism likely to engulf many tourism destinations. With the recovery of tourism in many destinations on the way, overtourism may soon again be a source of profit and concern.

Information Communication Technology and Tourism Intermediaries

One of the greatest changes in how tourists engage with tourism products and how they are increasingly created, marketed and distributed has been in the development of the Internet and advances in information and communication technologies (ICT) (Buhalis & Sinarta, 2019). These advancements in ICT have allowed suppliers to drive growth and expand profitability by targeting tourists with advertising and providing the means for consumers to purchase tourism products more easily. ICTs are both revolutionising and disrupting tourism, introducing new ways to enhance tourist experiences (Xu & Buhalis, 2021). Tourists with smart mobile devices can navigate a city, make a booking (from a taxi to an entire vacation), research a historic site and post pictures and reviews online. Navío-Marco, Ruiz-Gómez and Sevilla-Sevilla (2018), updating an early review by Buhalis and Law (2008), explore the changing role of ICTs and its impact on tourism. They note that ICTs have played a critical role in increasing the competitiveness of tourist destinations and organisations as well as shaping the market. The process of digitisation has dramatically changed the structure of the industry by altering barriers to entry, revolutionising distribution channels and optimising costs, facilitating competition and price transparency along with improving production efficiency. These advances have resulted in the tourism industry becoming the largest category of services and products sold on the Internet. Areas to watch in the future include human–device interaction with the 'Internet of Things' and wearables, whereby sensorisation is generating new usages and experiences in tourism; the vast amount of data generated also represents further sources of opportunities and innovation for tourism supply (Navío-Marco et al., 2018).

Value creation has shifted from a product-centric process to a consumer-centric approach with brands having in-depth intelligence on consumers through social media and ICTs (Buhalis & Sinarta, 2019). The integration of real-time consumer intelligence, artificial intelligence, dynamic big data mining and contextualisation is transforming service co-creation and nowness service (Buhalis & Sinarta, 2019). The adoption of blockchain technology (enabling distributive, smart, encrypted and secure peer to peer transactions) has further promoted dealings directly with service providers (Irannezhad & Mahadevan, 2021). Development of virtual reality in tourism has enhanced the tourist experience, protected fragile sites and even offered the tourist the opportunity to travel without leaving home. Three other key technological innovations in tourism include smart environments, cybersecurity and gamification (Xu & Buhalis, 2021). All of these advances are driving growth in new forms of tourism supply for those who have access to the technology and are not left behind on the other side of the digital divide. While the Internet and the utilisation of data has generated significant advances for the tourism supply side, concerns have been raised over the security of data and questionable practices of management in terms of ratings and comments posted online where economic performance is concerned (Navío-Marco et al., 2018). Moreover, increasing carbon emissions generated by the power relied upon by ICT utilised by the industry and tourists and the resources needed in their manufacture has also raised environmental concerns.

Tourism distribution channels and intermediaries have also been significantly transformed due to ICT advancements, further facilitating the growth of tourism. For instance, direct transactions between consumers and suppliers via ICT has resulted in disintermediation, benefitting small suppliers while at the same time facilitating a re-intermediation with the rise in online travel agencies (Gretzel & Fesenmaier, 2009). Traditional travel agencies have faced threats from online travel agencies such as Expedia and Priceline, metasearch engines, direct bookings of airlines and hotels and mobile applications for travel bookings, while global distribution systems have faced challenges from both low-cost carriers and legacy carriers encouraging direct bookings on their websites (Aamir & Atsan, 2020). Although the Internet provides opportunities for small providers to advertise, most tourism commercialisation (mainly accommodation and airlines) relies on a limited number of online world intermediaries and so smaller firms still need to rely on a network partner for greater visibility (Navío-Marco et al., 2018). This reinforces the importance of understanding the changing power structures rapidly evolving in the distribution system. In terms of package travel, the dominant channel leaders are large-scale integrated tour operators (Bastakis et al., 2004). By integrating their charter airlines and travel retailing with outgoing travel agencies (through acquisition or cooperation) and, in the destination, acquiring or developing accommodation establishments along with incoming coach and tour operators, they enjoy significant control. To be profitable, these large consortiums need to standardise packages and operate on a high-volume, low-cost and low-profit margin and must compete on market share. There has also been considerable concentration within the tour operating sector, with larger operators strengthening their market share by acquiring leading specialist tour operators (Bianchi, 2015). This, however, leaves independent destination hoteliers at the mercy of fewer tour operators. Bastakis et al. (2004: 153) note that 'tour operators accumulated forces have produced signs of oligopoly and unfair trade practices in the origin markets and acute oligopolistic phenomena for the destination's suppliers'. Tour operators are notorious for having minimal loyalty to specific destinations or businesses within those destinations and, instead, prefer a multi-locational approach focusing on a holiday type and not a specific location (Wall-Reinius et al., 2019). The pursuit of growth by tour operators reinforces the political economy of tourism. The changes in tourism distribution facilitated by ICT have generated tremendous advantages for large-scale tour operators and other multinational tourism enterprises, enabling them to accumulate wealth as the industry pursues profit and growth.

Sustainability Policies and Practices in Tourism Supply

While growth is the mantra for tourism, it is important to acknowledge the shift towards policies and practices amongst organisations from the UNWTO, to national and regional destination branding organisations to tourism enterprises that emphasise sustainability. Generally, there is evidence of the increasing adoption of CSR policies and certification schemes measuring sustainability against a set of standards that are then marketed with ecolabels. Current trends focus on reducing emissions, achieving net zero and adopting a circular economy approach whilst concepts such as responsible, resilient and regenerative tourism have all come to the fore. The extent to which tourists are actively seeking out these labelled products (based on genuine sustainability values) when booking a holiday is debatable and will be explored in the next chapter but, while these actions are clearly a step in the right direction, the question remains as to whether they go far enough (and fast enough) given the fundamentals of the tourism industry and the multiple crises facing the planet. 'Capitalism is fundamentally dependent on growth' (Hickel, 2020: 22) and, given current projections, the global drive for the continued growth and expansion of the tourism industry will more than offset the steps taken to make tourism supply more sustainable. Sustainability is promised, but the policies are still rooted in a growth framework seeking to increase visitor numbers, revenue and contributions to GDP.

At a global level, the UNWTO is striving for sustainability, recovery and growth. In its *One Planet Vision for a Responsible Recovery of the Tourism Sector*, the UNWTO (2020b) sets out plans that are aligned with the SDGs and the Paris Agreement. The strategy focuses on a responsible recovery, building back better and restarting tourism. It calls for long-term holistic thinking that considers the challenges facing the world and the need to transform to a sustainable model of tourism based on social inclusion, the restoration and protection of the environment and embracing the circular economy. In a similar vein, the WTTC's mission is to 'maximize the inclusive and sustainable growth potential of the Travel & Tourism sector by partnering with governments, destinations, communities and other stakeholders to drive economic development, create jobs, reduce poverty and foster peace, security and understanding in our world' (WTTC, 2022). In a recent report, the WTTC (WTTC & Wyman, 2020: 24) acknowledged that 'businesses and governments are facing scrutiny not only of their environmental track record but also for their support for diversity and inclusion'. In another illustration of the shift towards sustainability policies at a global level, the World Economic Forum (2022) revised its *Travel and*

Tourism Competitiveness Index which measured the attractiveness for tourism investment in a destination into the *Travel and Tourism Development Index*. The revised index incorporates 'the set of factors and policies that enable the sustainable and resilient development of the Travel and Tourism Sector … which in turn contributes to the development of the country'.

At a national level, Thailand has released a new sustainable tourism development strategy with the acronym 'SMILE' – Sustainability, Manpower, Inclusive economy, Localisation and Ecosystems (VNA, 2022). While embracing sustainability, however, the government simultaneously wants tourism to grow to represent 30 percent of Thailand's GDP by 2030, an increase from the 20 percent of pre-Covid-19 levels. At a regional level, the northern Yukon Territory of Canada recently launched its Yukon Sustainable Tourism Framework (Yukon, 2022) which is based on the United Nations Network of Sustainable Tourism Observatories and the Yukon Tourism Development Strategy (2018–2028). One of the goals of the Yukon Tourism Development Strategy is to double revenue attributable to tourism from CA\$262.9 million in 2016 to CA\$525 million in 2028, requiring growth at a compounded rate of 5.9 percent. Of course, the challenge inherent in all of these policies again lies in the paradox of driving for growth while advocating sustainability. In contrast, some destinations have developed policies to regulate tourism growth. In 2022, for example, the Balearic Islands issued a regulation stipulating that only three cruise ships a day can dock at Palma's cruise terminal, of which only one can be a mega-ship with over 5,000 passengers (Baratti, 2022). Other measures taken to reduce overtourism include new or revised tax arrangements, fines and demarketing as some destinations try to attract fewer but higher-spending, low-impact tourists as opposed to larger groups (Milano et al., 2018). All of these are important steps, but the question remains; if overtourism policies are implemented in one destination, will tourists, businesses and cruise ships simply go somewhere else, thereby shifting the problem to another neighbourhood, destination or port?

At the industry level, businesses have been adopting CSR policies, defined as an approach in business administration where, in addition to traditional issues of profitability and shareholder concerns, greater voluntary consideration is given to ethical, social and environmental issues along with the organisation's various stakeholders in operations and value creation (Coles, Fenclova & Dinan, 2013). CSR has been endorsed by a range of tourism businesses, intermediaries, lobbying groups, trade associations and NGOs, with large tourism corporations producing elaborate CSR programmes. As an example, Carnival Corporation & PLC is the largest cruise line company in the world and its sustainability report includes sustainability goals for 2030 and sustainability aspirations for 2050. The main components of the plan include climate action, a circular economy, good health and well-being, sustainable tourism, biodiversity and conservation, and diversity, equity and inclusion each linked to the SDGs (Carnival, 2022). Similarly, TUI's sustainability strategy, *Better Holidays, Better World*, is centred on: reducing environmental impacts of holidays; creating positive change for people and communities; pioneering sustainable tourism across the world; and building the best place to work where people are passionate about what they do. Statistics are also provided on carbon efficiency improvements and growth in sustainable holidays (TUI, 2020). British Airways' *BA Better World* establishes a roadmap to achieving net zero carbon emissions by 2050, in part by investing in new aircraft (40 percent more efficient), altering the way they fly to reduce emissions and creating partnerships to support the development of 'sustainable aviation fuel, zero emissions hydrogen-powered aircraft and carbon capture technology' (British Airways, 2022). In the accommodation sector, InterContinental Hotel Group (IHG, 2022) has implemented its *Green Engage* strategy while Hilton (2019) offers *LightStay*. A more recent trend within CSR is ESG which measures the sustainability practices of Environmental, Social and Governance factors (Chen, Su & Chen, 2022). Sample measurable indicators include carbon emissions, diversity and inclusion programmes and ethical governance. The Hilton's (2022) ESG policy *Travel With Purpose* has resulted in US$1 billion in cumulative savings in energy costs since 2009. For hotels, Chen et al. (2022) argue that 'an integrated ESG strategy can increase access to capital, strengthen corporate financial performance, and boost sustainable growth', all benefitting investors, businesses and consumers while contributing to the SDGs. While these innovative and important sustainability policies adopted by corporations, organisations and destinations represent vital steps towards limiting the impacts of tourism, there is a need to further their adoption by the wider industry to combat overall expected future growth in tourism.

Tourism businesses and destinations have adopted certification schemes often promoted in marketing materials, including the International Organization for Standards (ISO) 14001 (environmental management systems), ISO BS 8001:2107 (Circular Economy), LEED (Leadership in Energy and Environmental Design), the UN Global Compact, Blue Flag, the Global Sustainable Tourism Council's Sustainability Criteria and Green Key amongst others. Sustainable accommodation can be reserved online through Bookitgreen or ecobnb which rate accommodation through various criteria such as renewable energy and using local food while, more generally, Dunk, Gillespie and MacLeod (2016) identify over 100 tourism-related environment and social certification schemes. CSR and certifications programmes are increasingly linked to the Circular Economy (CE) which focuses on economic growth and business profit while reducing/closing resource loops to be more sustainable and creating a pathway to carbon neutrality (Prideaux & Phelan, 2022). The adoption of CE principles by all three levels of the tourism value chain (firms, destinations and transport) has, however, been inhibited by the lack of agreed national and international standards and the consumptive nature of tourism (Prideaux & Phelan, 2022). While some initial steps are being taken towards CE principles at the firm level (for example, switching to renewable energy) and at the destination level (for example, Copenhagen setting carbon-neutral targets), the transport sector, and in particular aviation will continue to face major problems (Prideaux & Phelan, 2022).

Although there is increasing awareness and adoption of green policies, there is also rising concern over the common practice of greenwashing or unsubstantiated claims of environmental policies (Gupta, Dash & Mishra, 2019). Indeed, the myth of carbon neutral airline operations has already been noted in the previous chapter, while accountability and metrics of sustainability are still in their infancy (Gilchrist, 2021; Coles et al., 2013). It is often pointed out that the benefits of ecotourism resorts following environmental policies would be offset by guests taking long haul flights, with the result that they may have a larger ecological footprint than a mass tourism destination (Marzouki, Froger & Ballet, 2012). A sliding scale of green practices exists, with some hotels simply asking guests to re-use towels while others use renewable energy, recycle, grow their own food and give discounts to guests arriving by public transit (Robbins, 2008). Williams and Ponsford (2009) examined the relationship between tourism business operators and sustainability. They claim that out of self-interest to develop market advantage, an increasing number of larger tourism operators view globalisation as a way to leverage new market opportunities, develop new products as well as launch more environmentally friendly sustainable operations. By doing so, these organisations feel they are able to create product differentiation as well as enhance brand image and stronger community stakeholder support which reduces business transactions costs. There is also the belief amongst businesses that the adoption of corporate sustainability actions will lead to a better competitive position and, therefore, a stronger bottom line (Williams & Ponsford, 2009). Wheeller (1993: 127–8), however, has long argued that while academics debate the precise definition of sustainability, in the practical world of business, these niceties can be ignored because if it can be used to sell the product, use it: 'Sustainability is being used to sustain business – a predictable, understandable ruse, but perhaps not quite what the purists had in mind.' Similarly, Bianchi (2009) refers to Rojek's (2007) concept of 'neat capitalism' in which highly successful capitalist enterprises position themselves at the forefront of socially responsible market solutions to the social, economic, environmental and cultural problems we face. 'They do all this, and they still make vast amounts of money by extracting surplus value from labourers and charging the margin to consumers' (Rojek, 2010: 46).

Carbon mitigation strategies in tourism have been directed at changing visitor behaviour (demand) and technology adoption by firms (supply) (Sun, Lin & Higham, 2020). On the supply side, tourism businesses are encouraged by either incentive or punitive schemes to realise emission efficiencies per service unit. Examples include the acceleration of fleet renewals, hotel refurbishment with sustainability upgrades and the creation and deployment of low carbon sustainable energy. Nevertheless, empirical observations illustrate a lack of meaningful progress on both the demand and supply side (Sun et al., 2020). Appeals to consumer consciousness have been found to be ineffective in significantly altering consumer decision-making (see Chapter 6); certainly, pre-Covid-19, the trends of greater travel frequency, increasing long haul travel, more reliance on aviation and reduced stay per trip resulted in global tourism carbon emission driven by increasing volumes through number of visits and intensity through emissions per traveller (Sun et al., 2020). Although new technology can contribute to a reduction in carbon emissions, the speed at which these are being implemented is lagging behind the rate of tourism growth and so marginal gains in emissions are more than offset by the growth in tourism consumption. This problem is particularly evident in air transport, the main source of emissions, as technological solutions in this sector have largely been exhausted which has led to limited efficiency gains over the past decade and into the near future (Sun et al., 2020). Efforts to reduce emissions have also been hindered by infrastructure lock-in (for example, airports, road, and rail), superstructure lock-in (for example, aviation and cruise lines) and technical lock-in (for example, technologies). Although many older planes and cruise ships were decommissioned during the pandemic, expectations of a return to travel will likely offset these gains. It should also be acknowledged that emissions are not only a factor of distance from source markets (i.e., long haul vs. short haul international; domestic) but are also influenced by length of stay, mode of domestic transportation, visitor activities, purpose of visit and levels of consumption (Sun et al. 2020).

CONCLUSION: TOURISM IN A GROWTH-BASED ECONOMY

At its core, tourism supply is largely driven by profitability and growth facilitated by capitalism, globalisation and economic neoliberalism. The tourism industry continues to develop mass and customised innovative experiences to more remote regions of the world, a trend which is at odds with the environmental crisis and is driving social change, often to the detriment of local people. The growth and complexity of the industry has been enabled by revolutions in ICT and has been built into policies, plans, strategies and operations across the tourism value chain. Yet, while growthism stands as one of the most hegemonic ideologies in modern history, no one stops to question it (Hickel, 2020). Prior to the Covid-19 pandemic, the tourism industry saw historic rates of growth that undoubtedly benefitted destinations, businesses, communities and individuals who were deeply reliant on the industry. At the same time, however, tensions of overtourism were becoming more apparent. During the pandemic, those directly and indirectly linked to the industry faced severe hardships, although many projections predict a return to volumes of travel similar to those in 2019 in the next three to five years. Pre-pandemic, Barcelona had the highest rate of pollution of all the ports in Europe with mega-cruise ships emitting sulphur dioxide and nitrogen oxide; yet even by May of 2020, the city saw cruise traffic returning to pre-pandemic levels. The Spanish government is now looking at restricting the numbers of cruise ships (Baratti, 2022) but these large ships can simply choose another more welcoming destination, transferring the problem elsewhere. Unbalanced power structures within tourism supply have favoured large-scale multinationals; as Higgins-Desbiolles and Everingham (2022) argue, the global trading system is rigged with exploitation baked-in from historical imperialism; developing countries dependent on tourism may see this unfair system exacerbate poverty as well as undermine traditional livelihoods and subsistence modes of living.

There has been a major shift in the tourism industry towards the adoption of sustainability policies and practices with some viewing the pandemic as an opportunity to reset tourism (looking for a new normal) and to be transformative; to be responsible, resilient, and regenerative. Gilchrist (2021), however, argues that 'hopes for a green recovery may have been overblown' and sustainability initiatives may be more about business viability or the sustainability of business itself. Those in favour of the green economy argue that it offers both profitability and environmental protection, yet decoupling has proven elusive. In the opening quote of this chapter, Thunberg (2018) refers to politicians speaking of 'eternal green economic growth' when they should be pulling the 'emergency brake'. While Jackson (2021) observes that green growth has been referred to as 'better growth', he argues it is more of a convenient, compelling narrative driven by anxiety about what might happen if growth fails. In other words, green growth is still growth. Undoubtedly, sustainability initiatives in tourism have the potential to play important roles in reducing the impacts of tourism (and potentially increase profits); however, as argued throughout this book, the tourism industry still needs to be considered within the wider neoliberal growth-based economy within which it operates. With destinations and businesses driving the growth of tourism, emissions will rise again (Sun et al., 2020). Moreover, as Hickel (2020) argues, even if we were able to generate 100 percent clean energy, unless we change how the economy works, we will continue to do the same thing that we do with fossil fuels – that is, using the power for continued extraction and production. Clean energy can help reduce emissions but it does not reverse deforestation, soil depletion, overfishing and mass extinction; 'a growth-obsessed economy powered by clean energy will still tip us into ecological disaster' (Hickel, 2020: 22).

Butler (2018) states the obvious paradox; for tourism to be sustainable, it must involve little to no travel and, therefore, would not be tourism. Following this reasoning, he suggests that if only truly sustainable tourism were offered, the outcome would be an economic and social disaster for many parts of the world, cutting off travel to many markets including sensitive environments. While on the one hand this would be positive for the environment, it would not, on the other, help to meet the needs of present and future generations in these destinations (Butler, 2018). MacKinnon (2021) undertook a thought experiment in *The Day the World Stops Shopping* – in essence, the effects of just a 25 percent reduction in consumption. We have seen the reality of the 'Day the World Stops Travelling' during the pandemic; for many, the results were catastrophic. Even those destinations previously suffering from overtourism have been seeking a return to pre-pandemic tourism growth while globally, millions continue to rely on the tourism industry for their livelihoods. Yet, can the tourism industry continue to expand as it did prior to the pandemic? While tourism supply needs to be preserved where it plays an essential role in development, by adopting stricter sustainability measures and degrowth on a global basis, can both the tourism industry and tourists 'pull the emergency brake'? If MacKinnon (2021) asks shoppers to shop less, can we ask (or regulate) tourists to travel less? Will the industry accept a reduction in the supply of tourism products to facilitate degrowth in tourism? Can a more convivial tourism better contribute to well-being and equity? Chapter 7 will go on to explore degrowth in tourism in greater detail as a basis for rethinking tourism and development. However, while other strategies such as regulation, demarketing and virtual travel have a role to play, what is also required is a reimagination of the larger economic system based on continuous growth within which tourism is embedded, a system that sociologist Max Weber (in Romano, 2020) argues is one of the main distinctive features of modern Western capitalism. According to Latouche (2009: 90), 'degrowth can only mean the contraction of accumulation, capitalism, exploitation and predation'. The following chapter explores the consumption of tourism where excesses in the accumulation of tourism experiences have helped fuel the growth of tourism and the exploitation of resources and considers the extent to which such excessive accumulation might be reversed.

6.   The (over)consumption of tourism

INTRODUCTION

Some years ago, a vicar in the north-east of England was talking with one of his parishioners, a 70-year-old farmer who lived and worked on the coast near to Lindisfarne, an island that at low tide is connected to the mainland by a causeway. The discussion turned to Lindisfarne's popularity as a tourist and pilgrimage destination; also known as Holy Island, its main attraction is the ruins of a priory which was founded in the seventh century by St. Aidan and which became a centre of early Christianity in Anglo-Saxon England. The vicar was surprised when the farmer said that he had never been to Lindisfarne. 'What?' he asked; 'You've lived here all your life but you've never been over to Lindisfarne?' 'No', was the short response. 'Why ever not?', asked the vicar. 'Never needed to', replied the farmer.

This is not an apocryphal tale. It was related by the vicar himself during a church service attended by one of the authors of this book who, at that time, lived in the English county of Northumberland close to where Lindisfarne is located. The point of the story, used to illustrate a sermon on the spiritual limitations of an acquisitive, materialistic lifestyle, was that the farmer did not feel he was missing out because he had never visited Lindisfarne. In fact, quite the opposite; he was content knowing that he did not need to visit the island, that doing so would not make him happier or more fulfilled. In other words, the farmer recognised that, in broad terms, he had what he needed and that seeking what for him were unnecessary experiences would add nothing to his life.

As such, the farmer in this story was displaying one example of what might be described as a sense of 'enoughness'; in terms of his well-being, he considered he had enough to live a content life. This is not, however, a commonly held attitude. As observed in the first chapter of this book, modern contemporary societies, especially those in the wealthier developed nations but also those in many emerging economies, are defined by a pervasive consumer culture. Members of those societies seek identity, meaning and fulfilment through their consumption practices or, as Trueman (2020) argues, drawing on the work of the Canadian philosopher Charles Taylor and others, the 'modern self' more generally engages in expressive individualism to validate their identity, usually in relation to other members of society. This expressive individualism is manifested in a variety of social and cultural practices (see Taylor, 2009) but primarily, and as discussed earlier in this book, through consumption; consuming stuff, both material and experiential, is considered to be what Trueman (2020) describes as therapeutic – a path to psychological well-being or happiness. However, that sense of well-being is also inevitably measured against the well-being of others, with the result people seek to have more in both relative (to others) and absolute terms. This, in turn, drives the continuing growth in consumerism at both the individual and global level that lies at the root of the contemporary environmental crisis.

The environmental consequences of excessive consumption, reviewed in Chapter 4, are described by Kimmerer (2013: 303–309) as 'Windigo footprints'. In her book *Braiding Sweetgrass*, referred to in the previous chapter, Kimmerer (2013) draws on her knowledge and understanding of Indigenous North American cultures to introduce a mythical monster: the Windigo. Originating in the folklore of the early North American Indigenous population and associated with the harsh winters, famine and starvation they suffered, the mythical Windigo was a human creature that became a cannibal; as Kimmerer (2013: 304) explains, 'Windigo stories reinforced the taboo against cannibalism, when the madness of hunger and isolation rustled at the edge of winter lodges'. Anyone succumbing to such an urge would themselves become a Windigo, destined to 'suffer the eternal pain of need, its essence a hunger that will never be sated. The more a Windigo eats the more ravenous it becomes. It shrieks with its craving…consumed by consumption, it lays waste to humankind' (Kimmerer, 2013: 305).

The myth of the Windigo, then, was a warning or perhaps an early prophecy of the dangers of unbridled consumption. It is also a metaphor for contemporary consumer culture for, as Kimmerer (2013: 308) goes on to suggest, 'We seem to be living in an era of Windigo economics of fabricated demand and compulsive overconsumption', the environmental consequences (or footprints) of which are all too evident. Hence, addressing the environmental crisis is dependent on defeating the Windigo in all of us or, in other words, reducing levels of consumption on a global scale as one means of adopting more sustainable and reciprocal (with the natural environment) lifestyles. This is not of course a new idea. The Genevan philosopher Jean-Jacques Rousseau, writing in the eighteenth century, hinted as much in his argument that social ills arise through competition and the quest for social status through property and position; a better society could be achieved by individuals living more simple lives in a hypothetical rural nature and, in so doing, being true to themselves. In more recent times, promoting and achieving more sustainable levels of consumption have become central to the sustainable development discourse ((IUCN/UNEP/WWF [1991] 2009; Middlemiss, 2018) whilst innumerable popular books provide advice on how to live more in a more sustainable fashion (for example, Olivia, 2020).

To a great extent, to suggest that we need to reduce how much we consume (or in the context of this book, to degrow) in order to live sustainably is to state the obvious; from data detailing the declining stock of natural, non-renewable resources to the more headline-grabbing annual announcement of Earth Overshoot Day (see www.overshootday.org), it is patently clear that humanity is over-exploiting the Earth's finite natural resource base. Sooner or later, without a significant reduction in what we extract from the Earth combined with an increased supply of renewable resources, as well as reducing the amount of waste we deposit back into the ecosystem, that natural resource base will no longer exist. The problem, however, is that although this immutable fact is generally acknowledged, there is relatively limited evidence of a transformation towards more sustainable, less consumptive lifestyles. This is not to say there are not some who are adopting behaviours (beyond the basics such as recycling waste) that are more sustainable, from following plant-based diets or engaging in circular consumption to giving up flying or 'divorcing' their cars (Alvord, 2000). Moreover, some countries are striving to achieve net zero and other environmental policies through alternative production processes. In Finland, for example, wood from sustainable sources is increasingly replacing concrete and steel in building construction (Savage, 2022). Yet, despite all the publicity surrounding climate change and the environmental crisis, succeeding in getting people to change their consumption habits (to consume less) remains, as Porritt (2007) acknowledged some years ago, one of the greatest challenges to sustainability. Furthermore, in the degrowth literature Latouche (2009: 90) argues it even goes beyond reducing consumption with the point being 'not just to slow accumulation down but to challenge the concept of accumulation itself so as to reverse the destructive process'.

Amongst all forms of consumption, tourism is perhaps one of the most visible and significant manifestations of this challenge. Despite increasing awareness of the negative consequences of tourism, particularly those related to flying, as well as the alleged growth in the number of so-called responsible tourists (Goodwin, 2016; Weedon, 2013) – to say nothing of the predominant policy focus at the local, national and international levels on sustainable tourism – participation in tourism (both international and domestic) on the global scale has long demonstrated consistent and remarkable growth, at least up to the onset of the Covid-19 pandemic and the resultant widespread restrictions on mobility. Indeed, in the years prior to the pandemic, the annual rate of growth in worldwide international tourism receipts outstripped that of the global economy more generally. Moreover, despite geopolitical tensions and, in some areas, continuing travel restrictions, international tourism experienced a significant rebound in 2022 (catching the airline sector unprepared, if reports of cancelled flights and chaotic scenes at many international airports were anything to go by); though not attaining pre-pandemic levels, many regions welcomed large numbers of international tourists. Notably, beach tourism destinations in Europe experienced the biggest recovery of all regions, also demonstrating that, contrary to the hopes of some that post-pandemic tourism would in some way or another be different, more meaningful or 'better' (Stankov, Filimonau & Vujičić, 2020), there has been little change in the way in which people consume tourism experiences. In short, the consumption of tourism has long defied political, economic, health and other constraints and, of particular relevance in the context of this book, all attempts to transform its scale and character and to reduce its environmental and other impacts. In a world where degrowing overall levels of consumption in general has become imperative, people appear to have an insatiable appetite for tourism; the consumption of tourism continues on an unsustainable growth trajectory.

It is also important to mention here the continuing growth in tourism or, more specifically, the ever-increasing consumption of tourism experiences as measured by levels of participation in tourism (arrivals, trips, visitor nights and so on) also feeds other forms of consumption – notably shopping. Tourists often spend not insignificant sums of money on the various things they need for their holidays or travels, such as clothing or luggage, which although not usually measured as a form of tourism expenditure, collectively add considerably to tourism-related consumption. In addition, so-called 'shopping tourism' is becoming an increasing popular form of tourism recognised by the UNWTO for its potential economic contribution. Destination choice may be determined by perceived opportunities for shopping; in some instances, shopping may be the primary motivation for tourism (Timothy, 2005). For example, prior to the Covid-19 pandemic, Japan was an important destination for Chinese cruise ships known for 'bakugai' or 'explosive shopping'. Buses transported cruise tourists to nearby shopping malls in ports such as Fukuoka where they would purchase significant quantities of household consumer products, in so doing causing disruption for local residents (Kalosh, 2016). The weight of luggage on cruise ships is not restricted in comparison to air travel and a 2012 survey of 40 Chinese cruise ships calling at Fukuoka revealed that Chinese cruise tourists spent a total of US\$43 million on shopping at an average of US\$1,391 per person. In short, the consumption of tourism drives consumption more generally.

Exploring why tourism continues to grow in defiance of economic, political and, in particular, environmental challenges is the focus of this chapter. More specifically, we set out to ask why the sustainability message appears to be having little or no effect on the consumption of tourism. For instance, although surveys consistently suggest that not only are tourists aware of the social and environmental consequences of tourism but also that many are in principle prepared to pay more for sustainable experiences, in practice few if any change their behaviour. In other words, a significant value–action gap exists in tourism; despite claims that they would do so, most people appear unwilling to adapt or reduce their participation in tourism. Only through seeking answers to this question might we begin to identify ways of necessarily reducing (degrowing) the demand for tourism within a broader shift towards 'post-growth' (Jackson, 2021) consumption, albeit whilst striving to maintain tourism's developmental role as appropriate. First, however, it is important to offer evidence of the challenge of degrowing the consumption of tourism by reviewing briefly not only the incessant growth in the demand for tourist experiences but also some of the characteristics of that demand.

TOURISM CONSUMPTION: A STORY OF GROWTH

When extolling the benefits of tourism as a vehicle of development (which is, of course, the broader context of this book), academics, organisations such as the UN World Tourism Organization or the World Travel and Tourism Council (see Chapter 5), development agencies and so on all typically emphasise the fact that tourism is a growth sector. The reason for doing so is self-evident; over the last seven decades and prior to the onset of the Covid-19 pandemic in 2020, there had been only three occasions when the annual increase in overall arrivals (and commensurate tourism receipts) was negative (see Chapter 2 and Table 2.1). So, despite these occurrences and other occasional volatility at the local or regional level reflecting political crises, health scares and other factors, tourism has proven to be a safe economic sector on which to base development policies.

There is no need to discuss this growth in detail here (again, see Chapter 2); suffice to say that both the absolute scale of international tourism (close to 1.5 billion international arrivals in 2019) together with domestic tourism – estimated to be six times greater than international tourism, with 9 billion domestic (overnight) trips in 2018 (Carvao, 2021) – as well as their annual growth rates have been nothing short of remarkable. However, a vital point must be made with regards to the inherent inequality in both participation in international tourism in particular and also in international tourism flows and benefits. First, and as pointed out elsewhere in the book, the headline data refer to arrivals, not individuals. Many tourists make multiple annual trips; in major tourism regions, such as Europe and North America, continuing growth in arrivals is largely accounted for not by more people travelling but by existing tourists travelling more frequently. Hence, the actual number of people travelling internationally – a highly privileged minority in global terms – is perhaps around half the arrivals total – or around 10 percent of the global population (see also Peeters & Landré, 2012). It is worth re-emphasising

Table 6.1   *Regional shares of international tourism arrivals / receipts 2019 (%)*

	Americas	Africa	Asia & Pacific	Europe	Middle East
International Arrivals	15	5	25	51	4
International Receipts	23	3	30	39	5

Source: Adapted from UNWTO (2021: 7).

here too that much of this activity is discretionary leisure consumption; most people do not have to travel; they simply want to and, in so doing, make a highly disproportionate contribution to the global environmental crisis. Here, it is worth mentioning the Travelers Century Club, a 'social club for serious travellers' founded in Los Angeles in 1954 with membership limited to those who have travelled to 100 or more countries or territories. With currently over 1,500 members, one of the membership benefits mentioned on their website is 'worldwide recognition or "bragging rights"' (TCC, 2022).

Second, the benefits of tourism in development terms are, on the global scale, unequally distributed. Becken (2019: 427) notes, for example, that 'over half of [international] tourism arrives at only 10 recipient countries. The top ten outbound and inbound countries are almost the same'. In other words, around half of all international tourism is shared by just ten countries. The same point can be illustrated more broadly by a summary of regional shares of international tourism arrivals and receipts (Table 6.1)

As can be seen from Table 6.1, Europe maintains its position as the leading tourism destination region, attracting more than 50 percent of all international visitors, followed by Asia and Pacific (25 percent) and the Americas (15 percent). What these figures do not reveal, however, is the long-recognised polarised and regionalised nature of international tourism (Shaw & Williams, 1994). That is, not only does much international tourism occur within three main regions, but also tourism flows typically from one point to another within these regions, such as from northern to southern Europe and from North America to the Caribbean. Particularly in the European case, this is evidence of tourism occurring primarily between modern, developed wealthier counties and, whilst the balance is shifting, generally those countries that arguably need tourism the most for their developmental contribution benefit the least. As Becken (2019) suggests, this rather ineffective global redistribution of wealth points to potential policy directions in degrowing tourism, an issue we return to in the next chapter.

Following on from this, an interesting point is that, particularly within the United States and Canada, there are substantial flows of tourists over distances that, in the European context, would inevitably be international but in North America are domestic and, hence, another (unacknowledged) manifestation of tourism within wealthy regions. For now, however, it is important to consider the characteristics of this increasing demand, particularly in the context of the alleged widespread adoption of environmentally responsible attitudes and behaviours on the part of tourists. In other words, since the notion of the 'new' tourist was first proposed some 30 years ago (Poon, 1993), it has been claimed that increasing numbers of tourists are rejecting the 'traditional' mass package holiday in favour of more individualistic, meaningful and 'co-created' (Campos et al., 2018) tourist experiences. In support of this, surveys consistently suggest that a majority of tourists are in favour of more responsible, sustainable holidays, allegedly often seeking out or being willing to pay more for such experiences. For example, one report suggests that 87 percent of all global travellers want to travel sustainably, with 39 percent claiming that they often or always manage to do so – though 48 percent never or rarely do so (Booking.com, 2018).

Other studies have revealed more nuanced responses, pointing to the fact that although many tourists express a willingness to pay more for sustainable tourism experiences, this is moderated by a number of factors such as the actual increase in costs, perceptions of how sustainable the destination actually is or suspicions of greenwashing (Durán-Román, Cárdenas-García & Pulido-Fernández, 2021; Jurado-Rivas & Sánchez-Rivero, 2019). It should also be noted here that much of the continuing increase in the demand for tourism in recent decades has been driven by the expansion of low-cost airlines. Not only have these had a major influence on short haul tourism flows – in 2020, low-cost airlines collectively accounted for 35 percent of all air travel (Statista, 2022b) – but their success is also evidence of the continuing significance of cost in travel decision-making (see Chapter 5). In other words, paying more for a sustainable tourism experience is unlikely to occur widely in practice.

More generally, cynics might argue that most people would claim to want to act sustainably even if they do not intend to, whilst research into green consumerism often reveals a significant discrepancy between intended and actual behaviour (Moraes, Carrigan & Szmigin, 2012) – the value–action gap. Nevertheless, in the specific case of tourism, many point to the increasing demand for ecotourism in particular as evidence of more responsible tourism consumption. It is suggested, for instance, that participation in ecotourism is growing at up to 30 percent annually and now accounts for one in five of all tourists (CABI, 2022) whilst another report indicated that the ecotourism market would be worth US$185 billion in 2022 (Business Research Company, 2022).

Such figures must be treated with extreme caution. The prefix 'eco' is attached to an enormous variety of tourism experiences – though typically to those occurring within a natural environment – yet more often than not such products or experiences do not reflect the principles of ecotourism from a development perspective (Fennell, 2007). Moreover, research has long demonstrated that those who participate in ecotourism are not typically motivated by environmental values; as Sharpley (2006) observes, any environmental concerns that (eco)tourists may possess tend to be subordinated to a variety of other, usually egocentric, values, motivations and desired benefits more typically associated with 'conventional' tourist experiences. Indeed, a recent study identified eight motivational dimensions amongst ecotourists, from escape and building personal relationships to simply having fun, all of which relate to personal benefits and commonly associated with tourism more generally and none revealing environmental values or drivers (Carrascosa-López et al., 2021). Hence, it is erroneous to interpret the growth in demand for ecotourism or for experiences more broadly labelled as 'responsible tourism' (for example, see responsibletravel.com) as evidence of greater environmental awareness and commensurate behaviour on the part of tourists. As Wheeller (1993: 128) pithily observed some time ago, 'for eco-tourist, read ego-tourist'; for him, the growth in ecotourism and other forms of allegedly sustainable tourism are evidence not of 'good' tourists but simply of good marketing and product development aimed at 'sustaining the ego' of tourists.

This conclusion is supported by other research into environmental awareness and sustainable consumption amongst tourists. For example, one study revealed that not only is there a lack of understanding amongst the travelling public of the environmental consequences of tourism but also, more significantly, that most people are unwilling to change their tourism behaviour, believing instead that it is the responsibility of governments to address the problem (Miller et al., 2010). In another study, Juvan and Dolnicar (2014b) identified a significant attitude–behaviour gap amongst tourists. Specifically, they found even those who actively engage in environmental protection in their day-to-day lives and recognise the negative impacts of tourism behave (albeit unintentionally) in ways damaging to the environment whilst on holiday. They justify their behaviour, however, on a variety of grounds, from denial of consequences (the claim that there are no negative impacts) to denial of responsibility or control. Such justification, also referred to as 'selective moral disengagement' (Bandura, 2007), has also been identified in the context of more general consumer behaviour: 'Once [people] get wedded to rewarding lifestyles that exact a toll on the environment, they devise schemes that enable them to stick with their behavioural practices without feeling bad about their adverse effects' (Bandura, 2007: 31). Interestingly, however, tourists in particular do feel a sense of guilt (Juvan & Dolnicar, 2014b); more recent research amongst bloggers subscribing to green travel sites revealed that feelings of guilt, shame or remorse were often expressed with regards to the impacts of their behaviour as tourists. Nevertheless, justification was also expressed in terms of cost and convenience (Mkono & Hughes, 2020), reminiscent of Dresner's (2002) more general observation that people are supportive of sustainability as long as it does not cost them anything.

It is not possible here to discuss in detail the now extensive research with regards to tourists' acknowledgement and understanding of and responses to the sustainable tourism message. The point is, however, quite straightforward. Despite all the 'noise' over the last three decades surrounding sustainable tourism and the need to be 'good' tourists (Popescu, 2008; Wood & House, 1991), the demand for tourism continues to increase, driven by growth in both established and emerging (notably Asian) markets and, most recently, by so-called post-pandemic 'revenge tourism' (Abdullah, 2021). Moreover, there is little evidence of the widespread adoption of pro-environmental behaviour on the part of tourists, even amongst those with strong environmental credentials. Undoubtedly there are those who do give primacy to their environmental values as tourists – refusing to fly, engaging in cycling holidays and so on – but their numbers are relatively limited. For the most part, tourism consumption continues to grow along its unsustainable path with tourists either unaware of or ignoring the negative environmental consequences of their behaviour or justifying it to themselves or others in various ways.

So, the question now to be addressed is: why is this the case? Why do people continue to participate in tourism, particularly international tourism, more frequently and in ever-increasing numbers in defiance of the sustainability imperative?

WHY CONSUME TOURISM?

Tourism is undoubtedly one of the most studied forms of contemporary human activity. Since gaining recognition as a legitimate field of academic study, it has been explored in depth from a variety of disciplinary and practical perspectives, though largely under two broad headings: the business of tourism and tourism as a social phenomenon. The latter, concerned with what might be referred to as the 'tourist experience', has long attracted academic attention. Indeed, according to Dann and Parrinello (2007), early studies in the sociology of tourism date back to the 1930s, laying the foundations for the now extensive and diverse research into the person that is 'the tourist' (Ryan, 2010; Sharpley, 2022a). Consequently, it is safe to say that, in academic terms, we have an in-depth if not complete understanding of what it is to be a tourist, of *how* people experience tourism.

Continuing to be more elusive, however, is an understanding of *why* tourism is such a popular form of contemporary consumption. Inevitably, a major theme within the tourist experience literature is tourist motivation, or identifying the needs that people seek to satisfy through participating in tourism. As discussed shortly, such needs are often classified rather broadly as either 'escape' or 'ego-enhancement' motives (Dann, 1977) and recognition of these goes some way to explaining why people become tourists. However, they do not necessarily get to the essence of tourism consumption, of the significance of tourism within contemporary consumer culture.

On the one hand, much of the tourist motivation literature adopts a sociological perspective, viewing participation in tourism as an individual's response to forces and pressures in their social environment. On the other hand, motivation is also a psychological phenomenon (Mannell & Iso-Ahola, 1987) reflecting the need for intrinsic, psychological rewards, or 'ego-enhancement'. In reality, the distinction between these two perspectives is rather fuzzy. Needs emanating from the external, social environment are inevitably internalised, leading Iso-Ahola (1982: 257) to argue that 'motivation is a purely psychological concept, not a sociological one'. Either way, however, and irrespective of this debate, the tourist motivation literature is unable to explain fully the increasingly dominant position that tourism holds in contemporary consumption practices. Are we obsessed with or addicted to tourism (Henning, 2012)? Is tourism an effective form of expressive individualism? Is 'travel behaviour… rooted in the desire to move as a purpose in itself' (Niblett & Beuret, 2021)? Why do we persist with tourism when many would agree with Ryan's (2002) assertion that it is mindless, irrational behaviour? Why do we justify being tourists when we know it is environmentally harmful? Do we actually think about or understand ourselves why we participate in tourism? The answer to the last question is probably 'no'; it has long been acknowledged, for example, that tourists themselves cannot express their real motivations (Krippendorf, 1987), which perhaps explains the continuing dearth of empirical studies on tourist motivation. The other questions are more challenging to answer but, by going on to consider them from a number of different perspectives including tourist motivation and the framing context of consumer culture, this chapter now points to the reasons why expecting people to radically adapt their consumption of tourism by choice is, in all likelihood, wishful thinking.

The Origins of Tourism

Any discussion of the history of tourism (for example, Christou, 2022; Zuelow, 2015) inevitably traces its evolution through different periods and forms, from travel in Greek and Roman times, the pilgrimages of the Middle Ages and the early Grand Tour of the seventeenth Century (Towner, 1985), through Thomas Cook's tours in the nineteenth century to the emergence of modern mass tourism from the 1960s onwards. Yet, arguably, the origins of the contemporary phenomenon of tourism lie not in these specific manifestations of travel but within people themselves. According to Pasternak (2021: 13), 'As a species, humans are the world's great travellers'; we live in highly mobile societies and, if all travel, whether over short or longer distances and for discretionary or other purposes is taken into account, it is evident that travel is a ubiquitous behaviour. Hence, Pasternak (2021: 13) goes on to suggest that this behaviour 'must have some sort of biological basis…travel is in some way hard-wired into us'. It is, in a sense, in our DNA.

To substantiate this claim, Pasternak (2021) draws attention to the travels of our ancestors, from the initial migration of *Homo Erectus* out of Africa some 1.8 million years ago to the arguably more significant travels of *Homo Sapiens* from about 60,000 years ago, leading to the diffusion of humanity around the world. In other words, early humans evolved as travellers, facilitated by the characteristics that distinguished them from other species, notably both the physical capability and mental capacity to travel and explore. The motivation for these early travels is unknown although Pasternak (2021) surmises that curiosity was a dominant factor. Through the invention of the wheel and the domestication of animals, travelling became easier and quicker and, as the nomadic life that defined humanity until about 10,000 years ago was gradually replaced with sedentism, trade in particular became a dominant purpose. Nevertheless, the need or desire to travel remained and continues to be psychologically driven or, putting it another way, a function of our brains. Travel, according to Pasternak (2021), not only satisfies our inherent curiosity or thirst for knowledge; it may also increase our capacity to be creative. Along similar lines, Hiss (2021: 35) suggests that 'travel, even when no longer a constant state, continues to serve as a unique mental stimulus with its own unsurpassed and still much-prized ability to lead our minds in new directions'. In this context, Hiss (2021) introduces the notion of Deep Travel, which he describes as a way of using our minds through travel to be aware of and alert to both opportunities and dangers. Such awareness, or Deep Travel, was vital to the survival and progress of our ancestors but is also 'key…to understanding why, despite millennia of sedentist habits, a desire to travel persists in our minds' (Hiss, 2021: 35). For it is through Deep Travel that we achieve mental stimulation and nourishment.

Importantly, then, both Pasternak and Hiss imply that the perceived benefits of travel – learning, experiencing, broadening the mind and so on – are intrinsically understood and have 'a neurological basis' (Pasternak, 2021: 25); through the evolutionary process, humans are biologically tuned to travel for the benefits it brings. Hence, seeking adventure, spirituality, education or, perhaps, the authentic self through tourism are all ways in which the biologically inherent traveller in all of us is manifested. Equally, the idea of wander-lust or the impulse to travel, rarely explored in the tourism research (Shields, 2011), may similarly be attributable to a deep-rooted, instinctive human need. Of interest here is the fact that 'wanderlust' is a popular contemporary term sharing the same meaning as the historical psychiatric diagnosis of dromoma-nia, or the uncontrollable urge to wander. As a perceived medical condition, dromomania might simply reflect the neurological roots of the desire to travel. And if this condition exists to a lesser or greater extent in all of us, then the objective of degrowing tourism becomes all the more challenging.

However, it must be acknowledged that much contemporary tourism behav-iour does not necessarily display the curiosity or a thirst for knowledge that is fundamental to this biological need to travel. Nor does it reflect the concept of Deep Travel; indeed, Hiss (2021) himself admits that the benefits of Deep Travel are short-lived or go unrecognised. In other words, much contemporary tourism is passive and primarily recreational. Although now dated, Cohen's (1972) much-cited concept of the organised mass tourist travelling in an 'environmental bubble' can still be applied today, albeit to a relatively small segment of the global tourist market; in contrast, his subsequent categories of recreational or diversionary tourists (Cohen, 1979) – those seeking only recreational or diversionary (temporarily forgetting about home) experiences, with little or no interest in learning or experiencing new things – remain much more relevant, although there are undoubtedly many tourists who combine recreation with some discovery whilst on holiday. Hence, if the desire to engage in tourism cannot be explained by a deep-seated psychological desire to broaden the mind, then the factors that inspire or drive much contemporary tourism must emanate from our social world. This, in turn, suggests that we need explore the sociological roots of tourist motivation.

Tourist Motivation: a Brief Overview

Contemporary tourism is both facilitated and motivated by modern society. In other words, modern society has on the one hand democratised tourism (Urry, 1990). It has enabled ever-increasing numbers of people to become tourists through the well-known triad of factors: first, technological advances in transport, allowing people to travel faster, further and more cheaply; second, increases in wealth and disposable income, providing the financial means to participate in tourism; and third, widely enjoyed socially sanctioned leisure time in the form of paid holidays. To this list can be added advances in communication technology, particularly the smartphone, which have made it significantly easier and quicker to access tourist services as well as reduce the perceived risk of being a tourist (Benckendorff, Sheldon & Fesenmaier, 2014), whilst the role of a highly innovative tourism industry must not be overlooked

(Chapter 5). Indeed, since the early days of Thomas Cook's tours in the late nineteenth century, the tourism sector has proved to be highly effective in not only creating and packaging an increasingly wide variety of affordable tourist experiences but also encouraging us to buy their products and services by convincing us that we 'need' a holiday. This latter point is of fundamental importance in the context of this chapter. To survive and make a profit, tourism businesses must, like all capitalist endeavours, convince people that consuming their products will make them happier or more satisfied, hence the substantial resources dedicated to marketing and advertising. In so doing, they are directly instrumental in motivating people to become tourists – which is why limiting advertising is seen as vital to degrowth more generally (Hickel, 2020).

On the other hand, modern society has created the perceived need for tourism. More specifically, the nature or condition of life in modern, contemporary society is such that, for one reason or another, people are motivated to remove themselves temporarily from it, to have a holiday. Whether to simply rest for a couple of weeks on a beach, to participate in physical or cultural activities which the hectic pace of life at home does not allow for, or to search for meaning, fulfilment and authenticity in other places and cultures (MacCannell, 1989), people are motivated to escape briefly from their day-to-day life at home. Inspired by the exhortations of the tourism industry, we have come to 'learn to desire vacations...for escape purposes and... to think of such vacations as essential for [our] psychological well-being' (Mannell & Iso-Ahola, 1987: 324). Putting it another way, tourism has acquired a functional role in modern society; 'tourism is social therapy, a safety valve keeping the everyday world in good working order' (Krippendorf, 1986: 525) – and it is in recognition of this that some countries implement so-called social tourism policies (Minnaert, Maitland & Miller, 2009).

There are varying perspectives on the manner in which the nature of contemporary life is translated into tourist motivation, more commonly described as motivational 'push' factors (Dann, 1981; Sharpley, 2018). For example, some consider the driving force behind tourism, particularly international tourism, to be the sense of alienation or 'anomie' – 'a situation of perceived normlessness and meaninglessness in the origin [tourist generating] country' (Dann, 1981: 191) – that characterises modern societies. As MacCannell (1989: 3) has famously suggested, the alienating, inauthentic condition of modern societies motivates tourists to become, in a sense, contemporary pilgrims seeking reality and authenticity in 'other historical periods and other cultures, in purer, simpler lifestyles'. Others point to more specific factors that create a felt need that, we believe, can be satisfied through participating in tourism or, more precisely, a need that is translated into the demand for tourism as a specific form of goal-oriented behaviour. Typically, it is the need to escape that underpins much tourist motivation – to escape from the pressures of work, from the routine of everyday life, from the 'rules' of society or even simply from the weather. Inevitably, however, such escape cannot be separated from the search or need for physical or mental well-being, for 'ego-enhancement' (Dann, 1977). Hence, as noted above, not only is the distinction between social and psychological motivating factors rather fuzzy, but much of the research into tourist motivation focuses on the various ways in which people consume tourism to satisfy their combined escape / ego-enhancement needs.

There is, of course, an extensive literature on tourist motivation, a discussion of which is well beyond the scope of this chapter – for a recent critical review, see Huang (2022). However, for our purposes here (and acknowledging the risk of very much over-simplifying some complex issues), drawing attention to some key themes will suffice. Primarily, it is evident that people consume tourism in the expectation of some form of reward or compensation, perhaps for what is missing in their day-to-day lives or for what makes them feel in one way or another unhappy. Indeed, given the substantial amounts often spent on buying tourism experiences, it is logical to assume that some return on that investment is anticipated, that tourism may enhance people's happiness (Nawijn & Strijbosch, 2022). For example, for those whose lives are determined by the restrictions and responsibilities of obligated time, such as work, family commitments and so on, tourism might fulfil the need for a sense of freedom. Indeed, the notion of freedom is implicit in much tourism marketing and advertising (Caruana & Crane, 2011) and might be seen simply as the ability to choose how to spend time free of commitments. Alternatively, tourism might offer temporary freedom from social norms and the opportunity to 'let one's hair down' in a liminal space where the rules of home life no longer apply (Lett, 1983; Sharpley, 2022b). Equally, tourism is often motivated by inter-personal needs, such as sharing time with friends, family and loved ones; as such, tourism compensates for a lack of social interaction during normal, day-to-day life. It has also been suggested that tourism can satisfy the need to live like a king for a day (Gottlieb, 1982), to temporarily enjoy a lifestyle that is not normally affordable – in many respects, tourism epitomises both conspicuous and excessive consumption.

It may be, of course, that the need for ego-enhancement, for a heightened sense of well-being, whether physical, psychological or, most likely, a combination of the two, outweighs the need to escape. Putting it another way, many people undoubtedly enjoy satisfying 'normal' lives but are in the position (possessing sufficient time and financial resources) to augment that satisfaction though tourism. Falling into this category are the older generations; the so-called 'silver market', comprising those over 50 years of age who are 'empty nesters' and particularly those who have retired, is widely recognised as a valuable and growing market segment in tourism. Such silver tourists, who may have progressed to a higher level on the 'travel career ladder' (Pearce,

2022), may well be motivated by the opportunity, if not need, to seek pleasurable, meaningful experiences simply because they are able to do so. Equally, it is the older generations who are probably better placed to finally 'tick off' items on their bucket lists – the bucket list arguably being a powerful contemporary driver of tourism (Zascerinska, Sharpley & Wright, 2022) – whilst promoting silver tourism is seen as a means of both injecting economic resilience into the tourism sector and encouraging 'active ageing' and well-being amongst the older generations (Taloş et al., 2021). Whatever the case, tourism for many people may not be motivated by a need to escape; rather, it is simply a popular and pleasurable form of experiential consumption.

This points to another important issue relating to tourist motivation. Although continuing to be a topic fundamental to tourism studies, much of the research is now very dated. Many of the key concepts, from push–pull or escape-seeking models (Huang, 2022) to tourist typologies can be traced back more than four decades (Dann, 1981), yet continue to underpin the relevant literature. Over this period, however, not only has tourism expanded remarkably in scale and scope but also the significance of tourism as a form of consumption has also changed. Some years ago, the sociologist John Urry explored the dynamic historical relationship between tourism and culture, suggesting that whilst initially tourism represented a distinctive cultural practice, over time it evolved to reflect cultural change, specifically through the emergence of mass tourism as a reflection of the culture of mass production and consumption. Eventually, according to Urry (1994: 234), tourism simply became cultural: 'Tourism is no longer a differentiated set of social practices with its distinct rules, times and spaces' but, rather, has merged into day-to-day life and practices to the extent that most people are, in one way or another, tourists most of the time. Whether this is indeed the case remains debateable but what is certain is that tourism has become a democratised, accepted and expected social institution. It is part of the fabric of modern, contemporary societies; it is simply something that we do, possibly unquestioningly and probably unaware of what motivates us. Indeed, perhaps in the era of the 'post-tourist' (Feifer, 1985; McCabe, 2015), we intuitively acknowledge that tourism is one, albeit significant, element of the game of consumption and, hence, attempting to understand the motivation for tourism becomes less important than considering its role in contemporary consumer culture.

This is not to suggest that tourists are no longer motivated by the fundamental need for escape and ego-enhancement. Quite evidently, many people experience the need to get away ('I need a holiday') and to enhance their sense of well-being – to re-create. And inevitably, most turn to tourism to satisfy this need. Yet, tourism is a discretionary form of consumption; there are other ways to spend leisure time and other forms of recreation. Hence, it is necessary to look beyond motivation and to consider tourism in the wider context of consumer culture to understand why tourism has become a dominant form of consumption and one that continues to defy the environmental message.

Tourism and Consumer Culture

The concept of a consumer culture can be variously defined. Arnould (2011), for example, refers to it in a rather convoluted manner as a 'social arrangement in which the relations between the [lived cultural experience of everyday life] and social resources, between meaningful [valued] ways of life and the symbolic and material resources on which they depend, is mediated through markets'. Alternatively stated, it is a culture within which consumption, or buying goods and services, 'is a cultural activity... imbued with meaning and driven not just by practical or economic factors' (AQR, n.d). In essence, then, in a consumer culture, people buy stuff not only for the practical, utilitarian benefits they provide but also for the socio-cultural meanings they convey, typically as a means of establishing and conveying social identity and status.

That contemporary societies, at least in wealthier developed nations, display the characteristics of a consumer culture is beyond dispute – although it must be noted that some would disagree (Lodziak, 2002). Such characteristics include, amongst other things: an ever-growing and widely available variety of goods and services both on the high street and online; ever-greater opportunities for consumers to spend, such as extended opening hours for stores, access to 24/7 online shopping with efficient home delivery, including for take-away food; increasing access to credit facilities; pervasive advertising, both direct (in print, TV / radio, online) and indirect or subliminal (for example, social media, influencers); the popularity of leisure shopping, either on the high street or browsing the Internet; and, the existence of effective legislation to protect consumers. Collectively, these point to the fact that, as Lury (2011) observes, it is impossible not to have to make choices about consumer goods and services.

This is certainly the case in tourism. Some 40 years ago, the range of organised tourism experiences (as opposed to independent travel) was relatively limited; they were typically marketed via brochures, sold through high street travel agents and produced by intermediaries (tour operators), the larger of which enjoyed significant influence over tourism consumption through their vertical and horizontal ownership of the tourism supply chain. Similarly, access to international air travel was relatively restricted (by both cost and supply) within a highly regulated market. Consequently, potential tourists arguably had quite limited choice and control with regards to their consumption of tourism. Since then, of course, a number of well-known factors have served to transform the supply of and access to tourism experiences to the extent that empowered tourist-consumers now face a seemingly infinite and bewildering array of choices limited only by their financial and temporal resources. The liberalisation of the tourism sector has resulted in much greater choice and cheaper prices, most notably manifested in the evolution of low-cost airlines. In addition to significantly influencing the nature, volume and direction of international tourist flows (for example, popularising international 'stag' and 'hen' weekends in Europe), many low-cost airlines have in effect become online tour operators – when buying a plane ticket, tourists must now often navigate choices of whether or not to also book airport parking or a hotel, hire a car or purchase travel insurance before finally being able to pay for their ticket. More significantly, however, developments in information communication technology, from the Internet to the smartphone, have directly connected potential tourists with the suppliers of tourism products and experiences (including, of course, low-cost airlines), facilitating so-called dynamic packaging (Cardoso & Lange, 2007); tourists can easily construct and purchase their own combination of travel, accommodation and other experiences. As a consequence, the future of charter flight operations, once fundamental to traditional package tourism, is uncertain (O'Connell & Bouquet, 2015). At the same time, a whole host of online businesses similarly provide access to and booking facilties for tourism services (for example, booking.com; trivago.com) whislt others, such as travelzoo.com, provide regular lists of discounted travel and tourism offers. In short, consumers can, if they wish, be bombarded with information about tempting tourism experiences and, should they succumb to such temptation, quickly and easily purchase those experiences with a few clicks on the computer, touches on a smartphone or through a voice-controlled virtual assistant.

That they do so is evident from the consistent growth in the demand for tourism worldwide. As noted earlier in this chapter, in the years prior to the Covid-19 pandemic, the annual rate of growth in international tourism receipts outstripped that of the global economy more generally, suggesting that tourism was accounting for a relatively increasing share of global consumer spending. Moreover, all the indications are that, post-pandemic (albeit subject to global political-economic uncertainties), that trend will continue. But, can this be explained from a consumer culture perspective? In other words, does tourism, as a specific form of consumption, possess a particular significance that undepins its continuing and growing popularity?

The answer to this question perhaps lies in an exploration of the factors that led to the emergence of a consumer culture. For many, its foundations lie in the broader cultural tranformation of contemporary societies from a condition of modernity to postmodernity. The concept of postmodernity first emerged in the 1980s (Lyotard, 1984) and has since remained highly controversial – it continues to be questioned whether it is simply a period in history, a phase in economic development, a cultural phase or even just an academic craze (Eagleton, 1992; Harvey, 1990). Irrespective of these issues, however, there is broad consensus that the character of contemporary societies has changed inasmuch as the structure, organisation and rationality that defined modernity no longer exists. Rather, the 'dominance of an overarching belief in "scientific" rationality and a unitary theory of progress' (Jary & Jary, 1991: 487) has been replaced with an emphasis on choice, a plurality of ideas and viewpoints, image and the ephemeral and the 'eclectic borrowing and mixing of images from other cultures' (Voase, 1995: 67). Putting this another way, following on from the eighteenth century Enlightenment, reason, objective knowledge, scientific progress and rational institutions (and the commensurate rejection of myth, superstition and ideology) came to be seen as the bedrock of social betterment. Consequently, modern societies were defined by social and institutional distinctions, between work and leisure, between gender and race, between occupations and wealth, between the past and the present. In short, modernity was represented by '"structural differentiation", the separate development of a number of institutional and normative spheres, of the economy, the family, the state, science, morality and an aesthetic realm' (Urry, 1990: 84). This, in turn, endowed members of modern societies with a sense of certainty, of who they were, of their identity.

The advent of postmodernity heralded the 'de-differentiation' (Lash, 1990) of society. What occurred was the breaking down of the distinctions in the social and cultural spheres and the emergence of a corresponding plurality of viewpoints and ideas, along with: the merging of high and popular cultures; the disappearance of traditional social structures based on, for example, class or gender; the blending of the past and present; and, the fusion of reality and image resulting in lifestyles increasingly influenced by spectacle and lacking in cultural depth. The consequence of such de-differentiation has been to endow members of postmodern societies with a lack of certainty of who they are, with a lack of identity.

Others seek to explain the social and cultural transformations of society from alternative perspectives. For example, the American sociologist Philip Reiff argues that individuals learn who they are by learning to conform to the purposes of the community to which they belong (see Trueman, 2020). Throughout history, according to Reiff (2006), four ages of man are identifiable. In ancient times, political man was defined by his engagement in public affairs; religious man in the Middle Ages identified with the religious practices in which he engaged, to be replaced by economic man whose sense of self was related to his work or economic activity (a period that can be aligned with the era of modernity discussed above). Finally, psychological man has taken centre stage, one who no longer finds identity through community engagement or their economic / work role in particular but through 'an inward quest for personal psychological happiness' (Trueman, 2020: 45).

Nevertheless, both the postmodernity thesis and Reiff's (2006) analysis arrive at the same conclusion, that contemporary society no longer provides people with markers of identity. In other words, people are no longer able to turn to established social and cultural institutions to understand who they are. Rather, they are obliged to find other ways of determining their identity, a need that is primarily fulfilled by consumption; as Featherstone (1991: 85) observes, contemporary capitalist economies (in which tourism plays a significant role) 'must not be understood as the consumption of use-values, a material utility, but primarily as the consumptions of signs'. That is, consumption practices have become signs or signifiers of identity and status, to the extent that, quite simply, we are what we buy.

However, this still does not explain why tourism in particular has become a dominant form of consumption; it does not explain why people might forgo other forms of consumption in favour of tourist experiences or, during challenging economic times, continue to consume tourism, albeit less frequently or less expensively, rather than giving it up all together. Certainly, throughout its history tourism has been a marker of social status. In the eighteenth and nineteenth centuries, for example, participation in the Grand Tour or, more precisely, simply being able to travel internationally for essentially leisure or cultural purposes was a sign of social distinction, whilst early twentieth century international tourism to places such as the French Riviera separated the wealthy and leisure classes from the masses. Moreover, although it has become increasingly democratised, the consumption of tourism is itself subject to social roles and status. Those who rue the 'lost art of travel' (Boorstin, 1964) continue to distinguish between 'the traveller' and 'the tourist' (the word 'tourist' being seen as possessing derogatory connotations) whilst mass tourism, once described as the 'degenerate offspring' of early travel (Crick, 1989: 307) is widely looked down upon in contrast to 'good', alternative forms of tourism. Additionally, tourists now seek status through the type of tourism they consume, the destinations they travel to, how frequently they travel and so on; tourists, as Culler (1981: 130) observes, 'can always find someone more touristy than themselves to sneer at'. In short, not only is tourism in general widely consumed to achieve social status and identity; different forms of tourism are similarly consumed for the same purpose, perhaps to the extent that tourism has arguably come to epitomise consumer culture or, to repeat Urry's (1994) assertion, tourism has simply become cultural.

CONCLUSION

So, where does this leave us? From the discussion in this chapter, is there any evidence that people will willingly not only adapt but reduce their consumption of tourism in order to address the global environmental crisis in general and global warming in particular? The answer to this question appears to be 'no'. From a demand perspective, the consumption of tourism has long demonstrated remarkable and consistent growth. The onset of the Covid-19 pandemic in 2020 halted that growth but it would be safe to assume that, in time and notwithstanding the dynamic political and economic environment, that growth will resume. Moreover, there is little to suggest that there exists any substance to claims that, despite this constant growth in tourism, eco-conscious or environmentally aware travel behaviour is in the ascendency. In other words, although numerous surveys point to an apparent propensity on the part of tourists to seek out more sustainable forms of tourism, research consistently reveals a value–action gap, that for the most part, environmental values are reflected neither in the motives nor the actual behaviours of eco-conscious tourists. In short, the actual demand for tourism, particularly for international tourism for which data exist (though it might be safely assumed that in most countries domestic tourism is also on the increase) tends to contradict the environmental message.

Similarly, from the interrelated perspectives of tourist motivation and consumer culture, it is evident that the significance of tourism lies in its ability to satisfy the need for both escape and ego-enhancement, the latter inevitably being related to the (post)modern search for identity through consumption. By definition, tourism involves 'getting away' but it has also always been a powerful indicator of social status. That role of tourism in creating status and identity has, however, been enhanced by cultural transformations that have resulted in the emergence of expressive individualism or the act of determining identity though consumption, a principal manifestation of which is tourism. Indeed, as a result of the tourist experience becoming increasingly a performance framed by the taking and sharing of images (notably the 'selfie') on social media, it is likely that in contrast with other forms of consumption, tourism is further cementing its role in identity creation. This, in turn, suggests that wide-scale voluntary reductions in the consumption of tourism are unlikely to occur, that tourists will not buy in to a degrowth agenda. The implications of this are considered in the following concluding chapter which seeks to draw together the various strands of this book within the context of degrowth to propose a rethinking of tourism and development.

7. Rethinking tourism and development: towards equitable degrowth

INTRODUCTION

The overall purpose of this book is, as its title suggests, to rethink the relationship between tourism and development. In other words, over the last 70 years or so, tourism (both domestic and international) has assumed an increasingly important role as an agent of what is broadly termed 'development'. More specifically, as the scale and scope of tourism has expanded, so too has its economic significance; as a powerful engine of economic growth, it has become an integral element of the development policies of many regions and countries around the world. This role of tourism has, however, been viewed in overly simplistic linear terms, not least by those organisations and agencies tasked with supporting and promoting tourism for developmental purposes. Typically, the aim has been to increase the scale of tourism at the destination level, in so doing increasing its contribution to the local or national economy (jobs, income, foreign exchange, government revenues and so on), the assumption clearly being that such economic growth translates one way or another into development.

At the same time, however, it has of course long been recognised that tourism incurs a variety of economic, social and environmental costs – hence what we refer to elsewhere as the tourism–development dilemma (Telfer & Sharpley, 2016) – and that development, however understood, is not an inevitable outcome of tourism. Consequently, much attention has been paid to alternative forms of tourism falling under the conceptual umbrella of sustainable tourism – tourism that, in principle, optimises the benefits to destination communities whilst minimising the negative outcomes. Yet, sustainable tourism remains firmly adhered to the growth imperative, as indeed does its parental paradigm of sustainable development (Adelman, 2017).

Therefore, as we have argued throughout this book, there now exists a pressing need to reconsider the tourism–development nexus, for two main reasons. First, consumption on a global scale has reached an environmentally unsustainable level; the contemporary environmental crisis, embracing not only global warming / climate change but also the irreversible destruction of the world's natural resources, demands that overall levels of consumption must be reduced. Tourism, as an increasingly significant element of global consumption (enjoyed by a privileged minority), cannot be immune from this process (see Chapter 6). There is nothing special about tourism. Yes, it has evolved into a major sector within the global economy and yes, there is no doubt that the economies of some destinations have become highly dependent on it, but the 'what about all the jobs?' argument cannot justify tourism globally being permitted to continue on its current growth trajectory, irrespective of over-optimistic policies for carbon neutrality. Tourism is a discretionary, resource-hungry socio-economic activity that makes a relatively high contribution to the environmental crisis and, consequently, is a prime candidate for degrowth within a reduction in global consumption more generally.

Second, the concept of 'development' as the objective of tourism demands reconsideration inasmuch as what continues to be seen as a fundamental prerequisite for (and, indeed, measure of) development – namely, economic growth (measured by GDP) – has become increasingly discredited. Many have argued in the past that there are limits to economic growth (Daly, 1991; Meadows et al., 1972; Mishan, 1969) whilst more recent critiques highlight the ways in which it serves not to solve but, rather, exacerbate social challenges (see Jackson, 2016), notably inequality within and between nations. According to the UNDP (2019), inequality remains the most significant developmental challenge on the global scale; the achievement of well-being for all people requires, by definition, equality (economic, social, legal and so on) but economic growth and the neoliberal capitalistic system that drives it promotes the opposite – greater inequality. Indeed, Hickel (2017) convincingly argues that global development policies have simply served to maintain, if not increase, what he refers to as the 'divide' between wealthier and disadvantaged people, societies and nations. And tourism is a manifestation of and contributor to this continuing divide in terms of both access to tourist experiences and its developmental outcomes.

For an increasing number of commentators, the solution to both the environmental crisis and the lack of progress towards meaningful and equitable development lies in the concept of degrowth. As discussed in Chapter 3, degrowth is not only (as commonly misinterpreted) about reducing how much we produce and consume to 'save the planet'. Certainly, this is a fundamental objective – to achieve a more sustainable level of consumption – but proponents of degrowth also suggest that a reduction in consumption is but one element of a post-growth society, an alternative approach that rejects acquisition and social competition in favour of more collaborative, reciprocal and meaningful lifestyles in which how we both work and enjoy our leisure is reassessed. In this sense, and as proposed earlier in this book, degrowth offers an interesting and potentially viable framework for rethinking tourism and development (see Table 2.3). The preceding chapters, in addition to introducing degrowth as what is, in effect, a new and arguably radical development paradigm, have highlighted the key issues surrounding the tourism–development nexus as a basis for justifying why the concept of degrowth might provide a new direction for tourism development. The purpose of this chapter is to consider how the principles of degrowth might be applied to tourism. Before doing so, however, it is important to summarise the key arguments made so far in the book.

Essentially, tourism is but one (though increasingly significant) element of global consumption. Driven by both increasing levels of wealth around the world and a capitalistic system that depends upon and promotes economic growth as a pathway to 'development', levels of consumption in general and of tourism in particular continue to follow a growth trajectory. Consequently, enormous pressure is being placed on the global ecosystem in terms of both natural resource exploitation and climate change, to the extent that current levels of consumption are environmentally unsustainable. To repeat the words of David Attenborough (2020: 7), we are living 'our comfortable lives in the shadow of a disaster of our own making. That disaster is being brought about by the very things that allow us to live our comfortable lives' (see Chapter 4). Moreover, tourism can be seen as making a relatively high contribution to this impending disaster, particularly when all elements of the tourism value chain are taken into account (see Chapter 5). Indeed, as emphasised repeatedly in this book, tourism must not be considered separately from but as part of global consumption more generally in terms of both its environmental consequences and potential solutions.

One such proposed solution is, of course, sustainable development. For more than three decades, the concept of sustainable development has informed development policy from the local to the global levels (most recently manifested in the SDGs) whilst also providing a framework for tourism in particular. However, since its conception, sustainable development has remained controversial; not only is it inherently oxymoronic but it continues to promote high levels of economic growth as a basis for development. Similarly, sustainable tourism development has proved to be unworkable, not least because of the continuing dominance of the growth imperative in tourism planning and production. In a similar vein, the concept of net zero has emerged as the dominant response to the challenge of climate change; from national policies to sectoral strategies, the objective of restricting global warming to 1.5 degrees Celsius above pre-industrial levels rests on achieving carbon neutrality through a combination of offsetting, carbon capture and other 'yet to be developed' technologies (though not through reducing the levels of production and consumption that result in greenhouse gas emissions in the first place). Yet not only is there increasing consensus that net zero is an unrealistic objective but also that it is, in effect, a means of promoting so-called green growth. In other words, carbon neutrality would in all likelihood encourage growth in economic activities, with commensurate negative consequences on the ecosystem. This is certainly the case with tourism. In the event that carbon-neutral travel, particularly by air, was possible, the outcome would probably be the even greater consumption of tourism with all the environmental consequences that would entail.

The only solution to the global environmental crisis, therefore, is to reduce the demands on the ecosystem through slowing down or reducing consumption on a global scale. Tourism cannot be immune from this, not least because, as observed earlier, it is a non-essential activity enjoyed by a privileged minority who, at the individual level, make a relatively enormous contribution to natural resource depletion and global warming. However, the contemporary significance of tourism as a form of consumption is that voluntary transformations (that is, a reduction) in the demand for tourism are unlikely to occur. Hence, degrowth as an alternative social project offering a pathway to sustainable lifestyles becomes a potential framework for rethinking tourism and development. The chapter now turns to reviewing briefly some of the key concepts of development and degrowth covered in Chapters 2 and 3, thus setting the foundation for a closer examination of tourism and degrowth.

A REVIEW OF DEVELOPMENT AND DEGROWTH CONSIDERATIONS FOR TOURISM

In proposing degrowth as a potential framework for reconsidering the relationship between tourism and development, it is important to recognise the seductive nature of the development rhetoric or developmentalism which has been internalised across virtually all countries (Kothari et al., 2019b). The problems of development (and therefore tourism) centres on it being perceived as linear, unidirectional and based on both financial and material growth driven by capitalist markets and commodification (Kothari et al., 2019b). In other words, development in today's global economic system requires growth and if 'growth stops, companies go bust, governments struggle to fund social services, people lose their jobs, poverty rises and states become politically vulnerable' (Hickel, 2020: 100). This continuing and extensive growth centres on mobilising more and more work through the commodification of goods and services that previously were not produced for profit (in tourism, for example, rooms converted into Airbnb units) (Kallis, 2018). Moreover, such developmentalism prioritises the modern Western myth that is built on assumptions with regards to the linearity of time, anthropocentrism and the separation of nature and society (Querejazu, 2016). Yet the recent 'Great Unsettling' (Steger & James, 2020) has upended both this myth and modernity's globalised system and so our familiar lifeworld, which tourism relies upon, seems unrecognisable. Hence, it has become even more pressing that new approaches, or approaches that have been marginalised in the past (for example, Indigenous ways) are brought into focus (Querejazu, 2016).

Degrowth is, however, complex as it incorporates a minimum of three main denotations: (1) degrowth as reduction in environmental pressures; (2) degrowth as emancipation from ideologies such as neoliberalism, consumerism and extractivism; and (3) degrowth as a utopian destination where society is grounded in care, sufficiency and autonomy (Parrique, 2019, cited in Fitzpatrick, Parrique, & Cosme, 2022). As such, degrowth is rooted in transitional discourse with contributions from both the Global North and the Global South that focus on shifting away from the growth model to reducing throughput and embracing equity, reciprocity, conviviality and well-being while living within ecological limits (see Chapter 3). Transitional discourses in turn cultivate the pluriverse which incorporates a variety of visions and ontologies that seek solutions to crises where previous attempts have failed, solutions not only from within the current globalising development model but that also include non-modern and self-defined alternatives (Kothari et al., 2019b; Querejazu, 2016). Overall, degrowth is concerned with well-being, a complex concept involving both individual and community perspectives that have historically been viewed through a Western lens; in contrast, Indigenous well-being embraces holistic and multidimensional concepts that connect people to land and to each other through kinship systems (Scheyvens, Movono & Auckram, 2023).

Given this diversity, degrowth is not a turnkey model (Latouche, 2009); rather, its agenda is open with local autonomy offering a great variety of paths within its broader principles (Liegey & Nelson, 2020). Proposals for degrowth range from simply advocating the rejection of GDP as a measure of development to more extreme radical degrowth imaginaries that not all of those who advocate degrowth (including the authors of this book) would endorse. Indeed, degrowth incorporates a significant element of utopian thinking and, as Kallis (2018) warns, it can consequently be criticised not for being unrealistic but for being monolithic and closed.

Nevertheless, four points deserve emphasis here. First, the purpose of the degrowth movement is to make a point, to be a catalyst for social change. Therefore, it must find a balance between acting within the system and acting outside and against the system (Liegey & Nelson, 2020: 90). Alternatively stated, while degrowth may adopt both reformist and revolutionary tactics, its main aim is to 'influence, engage with and incorporate sufficient numbers of people to radically transform society'; this, Liegey and Nelson (2020: 94) argue, cannot be achieved either by taking power or abandoning power to the reigning economic and political elites. Second, degrowth is not negative growth, for that is a recession or depression (Kallis, 2018). Nor is degrowth austerity; in fact, it is the opposite; austerity calls for scarcity to create more growth while degrowth 'calls for abundance *in order to render growth unnecessary*' (Hickel, 2020: 236 – emphasis in original). Third, degrowth does not propose a return to a primitive past but, rather, is future oriented. It seeks ways to escape inequality, hyper-consumption, weak democracy and environmental crises caused by growth-driven capitalism (Liegey & Nelson, 2020). And finally, whatever degrowth perspective is embraced, planning for it becomes critical because without planning we may find degrowth being forced upon us by looming crises.

It is evident, then, that degrowth scholarship confronts two formidable and related tasks (Kallis, 2018: 9). The first is to critically understand and undo the concept of growth which is the material, historical, ecological, discursive and institutional phenomenon that lies at the centre of Western imaginary and its colonial discourse. The second and consequential task is to propose alternatives to growth not only in terms of economics but also for political, social and personal change. In developing these alternatives, degrowth scholarship requires inputs from all disciplines and approaches from all parts of the world (Kallis, 2018). This inevitably means that concerns have been raised over the potential lack of internal coherence given the number of perspectives involved; however, in response, Vandeventer and Lloveras (2020: 374) offer the notion of the 'degrowth multiple', a step beyond the pluriverse drawing strength from across multiple disciplinary boundaries which leads to action. They go on to state that the degrowth multiple reflects a shift from epistemology towards ontology, 'from passively standing in front of plural degrowth perspectives awaiting acknowledgement to actively engaging ourselves within an increasingly complex assemblage of multiple degrowth enactments always in the making'.

It must also be acknowledged that, given its relatively recent emergence as a development paradigm, degrowth primarily remains a thought-world; a way of thinking about what might happen when our obsession with growth is over and we move to a post-growth world, thereby raising important questions for social theory and development (Jackson, 2021; MacKinnon, 2021). Equally, it is important to recognise there is a lot of wishful thinking in the degrowth literature (Kallis, 2018) yet, even though degrowth is in its very early stages, a range of proposals and solutions have been put forward by a growing number of authors (for examples of detailed degrowth platforms see Latouche, 2009; Kallis, 2018; Liegey and Nelson, 2020; Hickel, 2020; and Fitzpatrick et al., 2022). However, the problem with many of these proposals is that the preconditions for implementation are not in place and whilst some scenarios recommend a gentle transition towards degrowth, others such as Latouche

(2009) argue that, given present circumstances, a radical change of direction is required.

We support the philosophical approach adopted by Hickel (2020) that scholarship on degrowth need not be about doom but, rather, about hope and how we can change an economy structured around domination and extraction to one that is based on reciprocity with the living world. A similar approach is adopted by Ord (2020) in his book *The Precipice* which explores the existential threats facing humanity. Ord shares Hickel's (2020) positive perspective on the future potential of humanity and argues that safeguarding the future of humanity is the defining challenge of our time, suggesting that the greatest chance for humanity to achieve its potential is through three phases. The first phase is reaching existential security where existential risk is low and remains low; we need to extract ourselves from immediate danger and defend humanity from dangers over the long-term. Once this first phase is achieved and we have passed the precipice, we can enter the second phase, 'the long reflection' where we take the time to reflect on what would be the best vision for humanity, something that we rarely think about. The final phase is achieving humanity's full potential, which comes after reflecting on which future is best and how it might be achieved without fatal mishaps. Ord (2020) maintains, however, this can wait as the immediate task is to get ourselves to safety, to achieve existential security.

Tourism is highly integrated with complex linkages across the supply value chain (see Chapter 5) and has an important role to play in this search for existential security. However, as we have stressed throughout this book, it cannot be viewed in isolation. Degrowth in one industry or one country is not enough if this proposed framework is to offer an alternative to the crises the planet currently faces. Yet, how can tourism play its part? How can a framework of degrowth be applied to tourism to get us past *The Precipice* to a post-growth world so that we can achieve our potential in the long-term? To what extent are tourism enterprises and tourists willing to accept a shift towards degrowth and what are the barriers to this? Certainly, the 'business as usual' approach in tourism based on continual growth is no longer an option and, as argued elsewhere in this book, nor is it enough just to rely on sustainable tourism as a way forward. As Hall (2019: 1056) notes, the 'holy grail of manageability espoused by the UNWTO and others, the belief that all problems can be solved by exerting greater effort and demanding greater efficiencies within the status quo of continued tourism growth and consumption necessitates challenge'. Therefore, the following section now explores how tourism academics have been challenging the status quo, drawing ideas from degrowth as a possible framework for rethinking tourism and development. To contextualise the discussion on the 'real world', it commences with a brief example of when government-driven tourism growth is confronted by climate change and an environmentalist.

DEGROWTH FOR TOURISM

Introduction

In October 2022, the Canadian Minister of Tourism was in downtown Vancouver announcing CA\$1.2 million in new government funding for tourism. He commented on the waterfront view of the North Shore Mountains that served as a background to his press conference, stating that 'If a picture's worth a thousand words, the view today's a million'. During the subsequent question and answer part of the press conference, renowned environmentalist David Suzuki (who just happened to be passing by) took to the microphone and strongly contested this statement, arguing that the view of the mountain was in fact obscured by smoke from nearby forest fires. He then went on to offer harsh criticism of government officials for failing to act on climate change, observing that the warm dry weather in the region had caused drought conditions that, in turn, had extended the fire season, hence the obscured view. In a later interview about this confrontation, Suzuki argued that, on the one hand, the government was promoting tourism as a big economic opportunity for British Columbia with its natural scenery but, on the other hand, the environment which plays a big role in tourism is under threat from climate change (Weichel, 2022). This confrontation clearly illustrates that governmental support for further growth in tourism needs to be balanced with the mounting environmental crises to which tourism undoubtedly contributes. It also points to the question of whether, in this instance, degrowth might play a role in reducing the impacts of climate change in British Columbia while ensuring the benefits of tourism continue to support the local communities that rely heavily on the industry. The sections that now follow provide an overview of the small but growing body of literature on tourism degrowth, highlighting tourism policy before setting out a degrowth framework for rethinking tourism and development and identifying challenges and future research needs.

Overview of the Literature on Degrowth and Tourism

While elements of degrowth have been endorsed for many years (c.f., Georgescu-Roegen, 1971; Spieles, 2017 on the evolution of environmentalism), the degrowth literature in general gained prominence during the 2000s (see Table 2.3) whilst, as Lundmark et al. (2020) note, there was a significant increase in the number of publications on tourism degrowth in particular between 2018–2020 which has since continued. The early work on tourism and degrowth includes Bourdeau and Berthelot's (2008) presentation at the *First International Conference on Economic De-growth for Ecological Sustainability and Social Equity* in 2008 in Paris and the work of Hall (2009; 2011; 2013) and Andriotis (2014), the latter going on to release a book on the topic some years later (Andriotis, 2018). In his first publication on the topic, Hall (2009) argues that tourism's contribution to sustainable development should be understood within the context of degrowth as it presents an alternative to the economism paradigm that relies on growth in GDP. A decade later, the *Journal of Sustainable Tourism* published a special issue on tourism and degrowth in which the introductory article by Fletcher et al. (2019) sets out an emerging agenda for research and practice in tourism and degrowth. They also note that degrowth can be understood as both social theory and a social movement. This special issue was later published as a book in 2020 (Fletcher et al., 2020). In the same year Hall, Lundmark and Zhang (2020a) published an edited volume focusing on degrowth as a new perspective on tourism entrepreneurship, destinations and policy which includes a range of case studies illustrating how degrowth concepts may contribute to degrowth in tourism. In 2021, Andriotis (2021) followed up on his 2018 monograph with an edited volume containing a range of international case studies on tourism and degrowth and the following year Higgins-Desbiolles and Bigby (2022) published an edited volume on the 'local turn' in tourism which incorporates chapters on degrowth. However, despite this evident blossoming interest in the topic, degrowth discussions have yet to systematically engage with the tourism industry while, at the same time, tourism research more generally has largely neglected explicit discussion of degrowth (Fletcher et al., 2019).

Trends in the extant tourism degrowth literature are identified in a review by Lundmark et al. (2020) and their main findings can be summarised as follows. They note that the expansion of the degrowth literature in general can be explained in part by the increasing discourse on climate change and the Anthropocene and a greater awareness of the damage associated with the growth imperative. This, in turn, has led researchers to question the role of tourism in particular and whether it is contributing to a sustainable future or to a 'tragedy of the commons'. Through a bibliometric review, Lundmark et al. (2020) identify two main clusters of research on tourism degrowth, the first of which addresses economic development, tourism development and issues of overtourism while the second centres on issues related to sustainable tourism development and management. At the time of their literature review, the focus of the tourism degrowth literature was predominantly on urban areas and on Europe – especially the Mediterranean and coastal areas known for overtourism. Interestingly, while the European focus has tended to be on degrowth and tourism, North American studies incline towards a steady-state economy perspective. The work of Carver (2020) on Namibia and Cheung and Li (2019) on Hong Kong are noted as examples of studies outside Europe and this expansion in the scale and scope of the research has continued with, for example, more recent case studies on community-based tourism in Latin America (Cañada, 2021) and in Indonesia (Podlaszewska, 2021).

In Chapter 2 of this book, we explored the transformations in development theory and tourism (see Table 2.3) and identified degrowth emerging as a new (tourism) development paradigm. We explained how large-scale mass tourism development under modernisation was criticised as a form of neo-colonialism under dependency and, similarly, how economic neoliberalism which enabled the global expansion of multinational tourism enterprises was countered with calls for alternative and sustainable tourism. More recently, the growing concern over the contribution of tourism to carbon emissions and climate change has encouraged the expansion of the tourism degrowth literature and the increasing pressure on / criticism of the tourism growth model (Prideaux & Pabel, 2020). Furthermore, the impact of the Covid-19 pandemic on tourism raised questions about utilising tourism as a path to growth whilst the need to embrace new economic models has advanced research on tourism degrowth (Panzer-Krause, 2022; Sheldon, 2022; Dredge, 2022 on regenerative tourism). More generally, the back-and-forth arguments between proponents of tourism growth on the one side and critics of it on the other, with sustainable tourism being offered as a form of compromise, is emblematic of the tensions between modernisation and dependency and presents an opportunity to consider a trans-formation in development paradigms through degrowth.

In their review, Lundmark et al. (2020) note that while some components of degrowth, such as critiques of consumerism and commodification and a focus on responsibility, equality and well-being, are not new to tourism researchers, the explicit recognition of degrowth in tourism is relatively new. Likewise, Andriotis (2014) argues that while some elements of degrowth in tourism are implicit in long-discussed alternative forms of tourism such as sustainable tourism, green tourism, ecotourism, community-based tourism, slow tourism, pro-poor tourism and fair-trade tourism, these do not adopt the philosophical degrowth concepts of limits to growth, alternative lifestyles, voluntary simplic-ity and anti-materialism. It is also important to distinguish between a simple decline in visitor numbers due to economic crises, falling popularity or natural disasters and genuine degrowth in tourism which follows political-economic reorganisation (Fletcher et al., 2019). Hall (2009) examines the literature on sustainable consumption and degrowth in order to highlight the differences between, on the one hand, a 'green growth strategy' focused on efficiency and a commitment to growth and, on the other hand, a 'consumer-oriented sufficiency strategy' designed to slow consumption; he argues that both are required for degrowth in tourism.

Degrowth can be viewed as a large tent incorporating many perspectives in the pluriverse and so, before examining some of the more specific subtopics that are explored in the tourism degrowth literature, it is useful to consider briefly the work of two authors who summarise key aspects of the broader degrowth literature which they then map onto tourism. Butcher (2022) identifies three dimensions of degrowth in tourism. Under the economic dimension, degrowth is marked by a lower level of activity, including less international leisure travel and a decrease in leisure mobility; a contraction in commercial tourism and related industries; and greater equity in wealth distribution in tourism. The cultural dimension positions degrowth in opposition to consumerism and includes conviviality, whereby a slower and more authentic lifestyle is reflected in tourism. The cultural dimension also includes criticism of both the culture of mass tourism that is known to disregard the culture of others and of the disregard for the environment facilitated by a pro-growth consumer culture. Finally, the spatial dimension of degrowth, which is a relocalisation of economic activity on a smaller scale, includes staying local (staycation) with fewer and longer trips; tourism contributing to the relocalisation of other sectors such as agriculture; and tourism that has greater support for smaller, local businesses over global corporations (Butcher, 2022).

Similarly, Andriotis (2014) explores selected core themes of degrowth within the tourism context, some of which correspond with Butcher's (2022) ideas. For example, degrowth includes shifting away from a work-based model through a reduction in working hours along with policies to increase job satisfaction which, Andriotis (2014) suggests, would give people more time to travel and the ability to stay longer in destinations. Degrowth also emphasises the need to move towards low-impact modes of transportation which will result in a move from air travel towards trains, bicycles, hiking and walking. Slower modes of travel and low carbon consumption will encourage tourists to stay nearer to home, travelling shorter distances and staying longer which will increase the number of domestic tourists. Anti-materialism and sustainable consumption as elements of the degrowth philosophy recognise that increased production is generating waste and pollutants that are overwhelming the planet. Hence, Andriotis (2014) argues that in tourism, this would involve rejecting Western travel amenities and commoditised tourism products which have negative environmental impacts and waste resources. He also observes that degrowth calls for a re-examination of industrialisation; in the context of tourism, this would be reflected in less organised and industrialised vacations as well as a downscaling in tourism infrastructure. In addition, as travellers adopt an alternative (i.e., sustainable consumption) lifestyle and travel in a slower manner, they are able to engage more deeply with the destination and to participate in experiences which are not commodified, allowing a greater emphasis on the travel experience. The richness of the experience will be enhanced with the focus being on the locality and connections with local communities. Finally, degrowth focuses on increased benefits for the local population with community participation giving them increased control over resources, particularly amongst those excluded in the past from decision-making processes. A factor in increased participation is that some of degrowth's labour-intensive projects are more likely to be focused on a smaller scale rather than a capital-intensive industry (Andriotis, 2014). In tourism, this is reflected in community-based tourism, the contributions tourism can make in relocalisation and the enhancement of local tourism multipliers and networks such as strengthening the ties to local agriculture (for example, farm-to-table cuisine; see Telfer & Wall, 1996).

Many of these ideas of alternative, sustainable, responsible and regenerative tourism have much to offer to degrowth in tourism. Nitsch and Vogels (2022), for example, consider regenerative tourism in the context of boosting gender equality. Degrowth may offer a broader approach by reducing throughput and over consumption while protecting the environment and enhancing equity. Hall (2009: 57) argues that degrowth perspectives could be 'utilised to transition tourism to a "steady-state economy" which is qualitative development but not aggregate quantitative growth to the detriment of natural capital'.

Having examined these two broad overviews of the relationship between degrowth and tourism, the chapter now turns to more specific perspectives that make up the degrowth pluriverse being explored by tourism researchers. The structure of the sections below will in part follow Parrique's (2019, cited in Fitzpatrick et al., 2022) three dimensions of degrowth referred to earlier in this chapter, namely: (a) degrowth to reduce environmental pressures; (b) degrowth as emancipation from ideologies of neoliberalism, consumerism and extractivism; and (c), degrowth as a utopian destination where society is grounded in care, sufficiency and autonomy. While there is clearly overlap between all three of these sections, a selection of tourism degrowth conceptual papers and case studies will be highlighted. This will be followed by an analysis of degrowth policy for tourism and, collectively, these four sections will help establish an initial framework for rethinking tourism and development grounded in degrowth.

Tourism Degrowth to Reduce Environmental Pressures

Early contributions to the tourism degrowth literature emerged alongside heightened awareness of tourism's contributions to the environmental crises facing the planet (see Chapter 4). Attempts (albeit largely unsuccessful) to implement sustainable tourism policies have been driven by the desire to reduce the impacts of tourism, but tourism degrowth goes further by proposing an absolute reduction in throughput in the tourism economy to remain within environmental limits. In this context, it is not surprising that the phenomenon of so-called overtourism was one of the first issues to be addressed in tourism degrowth as many popular tourism destinations / environments were, prior to the Covid-19 pandemic, suffering from overcrowding. Implicitly relating the problem to the concept of degrowth, Milano et al. (2019) argue that over-tourism is a consequence of unregulated capital accumulation tied to growth strategies in an effort to sell cities as commodities. It is often attributed in part to the expansion of the sharing economy whereby the conversion of spare rooms (usually in private housing) into accommodation units has increased capacity, in so doing pushing tourism into residential neighbourhoods and squeezing locals out of the housing market through gentrification. In a similar vein, congested tourism attractions have exploited resources to their limits and has led to so-called creative destruction (Mitchell & de Waal, 2009). Some commentators therefore propose degrowth as a solution to some of the nega-tive environmental and social impacts associated with overtourism (Fonranari, Traskevich & Seraphin, 2021; Milano et al., 2019), with measures including moratoria on growth management plans, ecotaxes, tourism taxes and limiting both the capacity of tourism infrastructure such as airports or ports and of tourism activities including the use of marinas, ski slopes and golf courses (Fletcher et al., 2019). The challenge with these measures, however, is that they can result in a destination becoming more elitist and expensive, raising the issue of equity in tourism degrowth (Fletcher et al., 2019).

Cakar and Uzut (2020) investigate overtourism in the context of Istanbul, Turkey and identify demarketing and 'localhood' tourism activities as drivers for degrowth. Milano et al. (2019) also investigate degrowth as a social move-ment against overtourism driven by activist movements whilst Valdivielso and Moranta (2019) conclude that, in the context of overtourism in the Balearic Islands, degrowth has been used on the one hand as a platform for detouristification but, on the other hand, as greenwashing rhetoric to justify public policies aimed at the de-seasoning and decongestion of tourism while simultaneously promoting tourism expansion. Warnings have also been raised over the 'blue growth' imperative with Leposa (2020) examining the social and environmental injustices associated with marine tourism. Ertör and Hadjimichael (2022) call for blue degrowth and rethinking of the blue economy. Butcher (2021b), however, has criticised the degrowth advocacy promoted in light of the Covid-19 pandemic, questioning the claims made by proponents of tourism degrowth.

A second major trend in the tourism degrowth literature related to the environment is the concern over climate change and, in particular, the need to reduce carbon emissions generated by travel, in particular by aviation (Lundmark et al., 2020; Panzer-Krause, 2021; Prideaux & Pabel, 2020; Scott, Gössling & Hall, 2012). Seyfi, Hall and Saarinen (2022) consider substituting domestic for international tourism in light of the need to reduce carbon emissions and in the context of Covid-19, although drawing attention to the likely challenges involved in rescaling international mobilities to domestic mobilities and the need to consider changes to tourism provision and consumption behaviours. More generally, in a wide-ranging review of the research into tourism and climate change, Scott and Gössling (2022) reveal that more than three decades of research has not prepared the tourism sector for the net zero transition and that climate disruption will undoubtedly transform tourism over the next 30 years. Citing a recent Intergovernmental Panel on Climate Change report (IPCC, 2022c), they observe that concentrations of carbon dioxide in the atmosphere are rising at unprecedented levels and there are strategic 'knowledge gaps in terms of sector emissions, decarbonisation strategies, and the implications of deep decarbonisation pathways for tourism' (Scott & Gössling, 2022: 7). In addition, Gössling and Higham (2021) argue that new destination models are going to be required to shift tourism to a new paradigm which accounts for the carbon footprint of tourism revenue. Degrowth strategies have also been examined as a means of responding to declining tourism demand where key ecosystems in nature-based destinations have been threatened by significant climate change (Prideaux & Pabel, 2020). In the village of Saint-Firmin in the French Alps for example, the ski lift built in 1964 has recently been demolished as it had been inoperable for the last 15 years due to a lack of snow (Xu, 2022).

Tourism Degrowth as Freedom from Ideologies of Neoliberalism, Consumerism and Extractivism

The ecological crisis appears to be opening new ways of thinking about our relationship with the more-than-human world, empowering us to 'imagine a richer, more fertile future: a future free from the old dogmas of capitalism and rooted instead in reciprocity with the living world' (Hickel, 2020: 289). Capitalism has been the driver of modern tourism since its birth in the nineteenth century, even though the economic benefits of tourism have long been questioned with lower multiplier rates and high levels of leakage being closer to reality (Bryden, 1973). Hence, one of the fundamental philosophies of degrowth that is identified in the tourism degrowth literature in particular is the need to reject the ideologies of neoliberalism, consumerism and extractivism. Higgins-Desbiolles (2010), for example, argues that neoliberalism and its associated culture-ideology of consumerism is inherently unsustainable and that we need to move away from this value system. Likewise, Fletcher et al. (2019) suggest that the mounting critique of overtourism is a structural response to the ravages of capitalist development whilst, based on research in northern Finland, Kulusjärvi (2020) contends that tourism destinations need to diverge from growth-focused tourism strategies to make way for alternative economic pathways, agency and subjectivities that allow for a degrowth economy in destinations. In a similar vein, Mínguez, Blanco-Romero and Blázquez-Salom's (2022) study investigates the extent to which the Covid-19 pandemic presented an opportunity to change towards a degrowth approach in tourism. They conclude, however, that the neoliberal growth model still has a strong hold over tourism in Spain. In a detailed analysis of the media, they find that a degrowth approach has not been adopted by politicians, entrepreneurs or the media while news items transmitted a pro-regrowth economic and reactivation discourse which was defended by interest groups. Indeed, degrowth in tourism more generally is currently facing the challenge of governments and an industry seeking to regain what was lost during the Covid-19 pandemic. Consequently, Panzer-Krause (2019) emphasises that it is important that tourism degrowth strategists are represented as key actors in terms of communication and joint activities over the long-term to realise a shift away from 'business as usual'.

One of the criticisms of sustainable development is its concomitant link with neoliberalism. As noted earlier, the SDGs are still based upon a neoliberal mindset with continuing economic growth seen to be essential to their achievement. Saarinen (2020) adopts a critical approach towards sustainable development; acknowledging its connections to the neoliberalisation of tourism development thinking, he argues that in order to shift tourism towards a degrowth or post-growth economy, a radical reset in how the industry and its guiding policies understand and practise sustainability at a global scale is required. Suggestions to start the process include stepping away from the misleading sustainable growth rhetoric and focusing on a needs-based idea of sustainable development in tourism. Similarly, other commentators have indicated that, from a tourism degrowth perspective, the strategies associated with sustainable tourism do not go far enough. Notably, Boluk, Cavaliere and Higgins-Desbiolles (2019) have developed a conceptual framework of six themes to interrogate the SDGs in order to guide tourism towards more sustainable, equitable and just futures – and one of the themes is degrowth and the circular economy. Hall (2009: 53) was an early pioneer linking degrowth to sustainable tourism development, which he defined as 'tourism development without growth in throughput of matter and energy beyond regenerative and absorptive capacities'. Hall, Lundmark and Zhang (2020b) also ask whether the adoption of degrowth policies can facilitate tourism moving beyond BAU (Brundtland as usual).

Along with the conceptual explorations of the relationship between sustainable development and neoliberalism, tourism degrowth researchers have also considered the practical implications for the industry (see, for example, Margaryan, Fredman & Stensland, 2020). In particular, Corporate Social Responsibility (CSR) statements have been promoted as a means of demonstrating the tourism sector's commitment to sustainability, and these have been examined in the context of tour operations (Panzer-Krause, 2021). Addressing the important question of how to implant ideas of degrowth into the tourism industry, Panzer-Krause (2021) draws on Schumpeter's notion of 'creative destruction' to demonstrate that if innovative degrowth-inspired elements of travel, such as cooperation with local partners or indirect support for the community and environmental projects, are upscaled to a wider market, they may have the potential to force out traditional tourism offers. However, the opposite may occur if tour operators rely on practices such as utilising long-distance travel or visiting vulnerable places and communities. As a consequence, Panzer-Krause (2021) concludes that CSR certification schemes lack the necessary influence to generate a paradigm shift towards degrowth and that, more generally, degrowth-oriented policies and practices appear to be inapplicable to mainstream tourism. Indeed, shifting the tourism industry as a whole to operationalise degrowth strategies appears to be a major hurdle (not least its inherent capitalistic growth-profit orientation (McKercher, 1993)), and the industries' adoption of CSR and green technology so far has been criticised (Panzer-Krause, 2021).

More generally, Latouche (2009) argues that 'development' is toxic no matter what adjective is used, and that 'sustainable' development and its use of 'clean development mechanisms' (for example, energy and carbon saving technologies as being eco-efficient) is simply verbal diplomacy. The desirable advancements in these technologies still do not challenge the dangerous logic of development (Latouche, 2009). Again, and as will be explored later, shifting the tourism industry into a post-growth world will continue to be a major challenge. Fletcher (2019: 532) outlines post-capitalist tourism as '(1) forms of production not based on private appropriation of surplus value; and (2) forms of exchange not aimed at capital accumulation; that (3) fully internalise the environmental and social costs of production in a manner that does not promote commodification and (4) are grounded in common property regimes'. Fletcher et al. (2021a, 2021b) further explore pathways to post-capitalist tourism illustrating they can be operationalised in a variety of ways, from top-down state regulatory practices responding to the demands of social movements to bottom-up civil society initiatives. Degrowth policy will be examined later in this chapter.

To achieve degrowth in tourism, the second ideology that we need to move away from is consumerism. More simply stated, the need exists to change consumer attitudes. In an exploration of voluntary simplicity, Hall (2011) asked the question whether we really need to travel so much to be happy. A central question for tourism degrowth, then, is whether people will willingly adapt or, more precisely, reduce their consumption of tourism. Although Lundmark et al. (2020) suggest there has been little research conducted on tourists' mobility, there is increasing evidence, as discussed in the preceding chapter, that despite the publicity surrounding the environmental consequences of tourism, most if not all people continue to consume tourism 'as normal'. Indeed, research has revealed that it is common for tourists to make excuses for what they recognise to be unsustainable behaviour (Mkono & Hughes, 2020). Moreover, as we have observed elsewhere in the book, although travel has become democratised, tourism remains a privilege afforded to few yet these few are generating carbon emissions with global impact.

Within the tourism degrowth literature, a number of issues related to the consumption of tourism are discussed. For instance, the concept of freedom of movement is debated (Pranskūnienė & Perkumienė, 2021; Gascón, 2019), although reflecting the point made above, Hashimoto, Härkönen and Nkyi (2021: 214) argue that the UNWTO's efforts to promote the right to tourism and the liberty of tourist movement 'strongly favours a specific group of the worlds' populations – the wealthy'. The impact of Covid-19 on future travel behaviours is also addressed with some, such as Volger (2022), questioning whether post-pandemic tourism would be characterised by degrowth or so-called revenge or catch-up travel – at the time of writing, the latter would appear to be the case. Either way, Lundmark et al. 2020 suggest that it is important not just to focus simply on a reduction in tourism consumption for degrowth as this could lead to a recession, a central issue in discussions on the impact of the Covid-19 pandemic on tourism. Others question the benefits of encouraging tourists to make changes in their behaviour within a degrowth agenda. For example, Eimermann et al. (2020) discuss those they refer to as 'holistic simplifiers' and address some of the myths surrounding their sustainable lifestyles and practices; they suggest that even if tourists adopt lower-impact lifestyles there will still be challenges. Similarly, although Andriotis (2018) proposes that some types of tourist, such as backpackers, may potentially reduce their resource use by spending more time in the destination and minimising their consumption, portraying the consumption of certain types of travel as more in line with degrowth may be misleading. Indeed, Fletcher (2019) observes that ecotourism is now actually driving tourism growth as a form of Anthropocene tourism whereby tourists are visiting nature destinations before they are gone. In contrast, in response to climate change, Higgins-Desbiolles (2022) advocates tourism degrowth through the development of what she terms proximity travel. Touring closer to home (reducing travel distance) and on narrower travel circuits results in lower carbon emissions as well as generating benefits for local communities through localised tourism. Similarly, domestic tourism has been put forward as an important tourism degrowth strategy (Ballantine, 2020) while Renaud (2022) argues that there needs to be a reconsideration of global mobility with regards to the mass cruise tourism industry with mega-cruise ships being restricted or banned as part of a degrowth strategy.

The third ideology we need to turn away from is extractivism. The dominant neoliberal growth-based economy is often reliant on extractive industries which have negative impacts on the environment (see Chapter 4). The tourism industry, for example, relies heavily on the extraction of oil to fuel most modes of transport and for the development of infrastructure and many other products it uses, all of which contribute significantly to carbon emissions. In the case of Cotacachi County, Equador, Chassagne and Everingham (2019) argue that it is important to degrow socially and environmentally damaging extractive industries such as mining and instead to support community-based tourism initiatives based on Buen Vivir (see next section). Nevertheless, they note tourism as a whole can also be viewed as an extractive industry, especially where there is overtourism or the excessive exploitation of resources in the production and consumption of tourism. Carson and Carson (2020) argue that even in remote destinations in Australia, tourism can be driven by a boost-erist growth paradigm; they suggest that adopting a degrowth strategy may reposition resources amongst tourism markets and destinations (for example, between urban and rural).

Tourism Degrowth in Building a Society Grounded in Care, Sufficiency and Autonomy

Referring to the preamble to the UNWTO's (2001) *Global Code for Ethics for Tourism*, Higgins-Desbiolles et al. (2019) draw attention to the statement: 'The world tourism industry as a whole has much to gain by operating in an environment that favours the market economy, private enterprise and free trade that serves to optimize its beneficial effects on the creation of wealth and employment'. They point out that although the Code reflects the dis-course on sustainable development, it does not however address how issues of equity and inclusivity might be achieved (Higgins-Desbiolles et al., 2019). A critical element of degrowth in general is the need to build a society which emphasises equity, care, conviviality, autonomy, sufficiency, support for local communities and Indigenous voices and relocalisation, and many of these societal elements are also highlighted in the tourism degrowth literature. Higgins-Desbiolles (2020) argues that, in light of the Covid-19 pandemic, responsible tourism is not enough to reset tourism; rather, there needs to be a community-centred framework within tourism based on the rights and interests of local peoples and communities. The interests of local communities are also at the centre of Barkin's (2002) work which, drawing on examples from tourism, examines the many-faceted threats from globalisation to those in Latin America. He highlights how various community groups have taken control of their environment while rejecting a singular international economy by setting out on a different path of social and cultural diversity and environmental democracy for their own security and material well-being.

Higgins-Desbiolles et al. (2019) further emphasise the importance of social justice and equity and the need to redefine and redesign tourism so that it gives precedence to the rights of local communities over the rights of tourists and tourism businesses to make a profit. Their revised definition of tourism is 'the process of local communities inviting, receiving and hosting visitors in their local community for limited time durations, with the intention of receiving benefits from such actions' (Higgins-Desbiolles et al., 2019: 1936). These authors build on their work in Boluk et al. (2020) further developing their community-centred tourism framework which, they suggest, is a mechanism for degrowing tourism that, offering a reconciliatory approach to tourism stakeholders, moves towards a more equitable and sustainable tourism. Two examples from Ecuador further highlight the importance of community-based tourism in degrowth; Ruiz-Ballesteros (2020) reveals the importance of reciprocity, the commons and conviviality in Agua Blanca whilst Renkert (2019) similarly notes the potential of community-based tourism as a vehicle in creating a localised degrowth society in the Kichwa Anangu community.

Another key aspect of a degrowth society is the importance of the relocalisation. In their edited volume, Higgins-Desbiolles and Bigby (2022) embrace the 'local turn' in tourism as an approach to degrowth which places communities at the heart of tourism to safeguard community rights and benefits from tourism (see also Ingram, Slocum & Cavaliere, 2020 on neolocalism and tourism). This relocalisation reflects Cronin's (2012) concept of microspection, whereby a reduction in scale can lead to an expansion of insight and the unleashing of interpretive and imaginative possibilities. The 'local turn' or relocalisation provides economic support to local businesses and encourages tourists to travel locally. The potential of the sharing economy in local communities to increase social bonding and collaboration and to better allocate resources has been found to be aligned with degrowth principles; however, caution is needed if the sharing economy becomes too successful, as has happened in the case of Airbnb (Andreoni, 2020). Müller, Fletcher and Blázquez-Salom (2022) discuss convivial tourism as a form of proximity (local) tourism related to convivial conservation. Büscher and Fletcher (2019: 283) previously proposed convivial conservation as a 'post-capitalist approach to conservation that promotes radical equity, structural transformation and environmental justice and contributes to an overarching movement to create a more equal and sustainable world'.

Tourism degrowth scholars have also explored tourism within the Latin America concept of Buen Vivir that originated within Indigenous communities and espouses equity, social cohesion, empowerment (including decolonisation and culture), livelihood and capabilities, all of which are characteristics of degrowth (Chassagne & Everingham, 2019; Everingham & Chassagne, 2020). Chassagne and Everingham (2019) consider various tourism practices according to selected principles of Buen Vivir. Under the principles of decolonisation and culture, they find that tourism practices include cultural and knowledge exchange, promotion of traditional handicrafts and volunteer tourism. Under reciprocity, nature and community, tourism practices included eco- and agri-tourism initiatives and community stays. Finally, under plurality, well-being and contextuality, they highlight tourism practices related to participatory local government initiatives.

Resistance to tourism development as a form of activism is also explored in relation to tourism degrowth (Milano et al., 2019; Navarro-Jurado et al., 2019; Wegerer & Nadegger, 2020). Hughes and Mansilla (2021), for example, focus on degrowth social movement actors in Spanish cities and their efforts to reduce the flow and negative impacts of tourists while Otto (2017) investigates the synergies between degrowth and environmental justice movements with regards to protests over a mega-highway project designed to enhance tourism and agribusinesses in Chiapas, Mexico. The rise of these community resistance movements highlights the role of civil society in promoting tourism degrowth and giving a voice to those who are often not heard (Gürsoy, 2020).

Having examined the tourism degrowth literature in terms of the three themes of protecting the environment, the need to shift away from neoliberalism, consumerism and extractivism and the need to build a society that is built on equity, care, conviviality, autonomy and sufficiency, the chapter now turns to exploring degrowth policy for tourism.

Degrowth Policy for Tourism

A critical challenge for tourism and degrowth is how to take the interdisciplinary theoretical perspectives on degrowth and implement them as policy for tourism. As noted in Chapter 2, some degrowth advocates focus on only replacing GDP as a measure of development while other authors, such as Kallis (2018: 127), propose a more detailed public policy degrowth package that includes:

- GDP being abolished and substituted with other indicators of human and ecological well-being;
- work being shared, with a reduction of working hours to create employment in the absence of growth;
- a universal income or guaranteed bundle of public services, ensuring that everyone has enough to get by without depending on money;

- redistributive taxation to increase equality and the establishment of maximum income to arrest competition for positional consumption;
- a redirection of public investments from the private sector to the public and from infrastructure and activities that increase productivity to expenditures that green the economy and reclaim the commons; and
- environmental limit and taxes to finance low-income groups.

There are, then, a range of broader degrowth policies that could be implemented by governments that would have important impacts on tourism, whilst there are also tourism-specific degrowth policies that could be implemented to degrow the industry. Broadly, Milano et al. (2019) call for greater public sector involvement in and control of tourism to support degrowth in tourism whilst various destinations, such as Spain (see Blázquez-Salom et al., 2019) have attempted to implement more specific policies to address the problem of overtourism. These have enjoyed varying degrees of success although simply reducing visitor numbers is, of course, but one facet of degrowth. Debates on degrowth policies also include whether they should be voluntary or mandated and be the same in developed and developing countries.

Degrowth has slowly been making its presence felt in the sphere of policy making in many disciplines, including tourism. In a very comprehensive review of the degrowth literature from 2005 to 2020, Fitzpatrick et al. (2022) identify 1,166 texts (books, chapters, articles and theses) referring to degrowth of which 446 include specific policy proposals. From this systematic review, they were able to identify 530 proposals which they divide into 13 policy themes, one of which was tourism. The full list of the themes includes food, culture and education, energy and environment, governance and geopolitics, indicators, inequality, finance, production and consumption, science and technology, tourism, trade, urban planning and work (Fitzpatrick et al., 2022). It is important to note that policies implemented in any of the other 12 themes can have an indirect impact on tourism and, similarly, some of the policies linked to tourism appear in the other themes. For, example the theme of inequality policy includes the imposition of taxes on luxury consumption and ensuring minimum living wages whilst policies under the theme of production and consumption include reducing flying, limiting advertising, relocalising activities and placing quotas on flying. Within the tourism theme specifically, two main goals are identified: (a) *limits to tourism* and (b) *reconceptualising tourism*, under each of which Fitzpatrick et al. (2022) generate objectives and some example instruments. These two main goals are considered in some detail below. It is essential to recognise that for the purposes of this book, these degrowth policy findings are not to be interpreted as essential or required; rather, they are presented to generate discussion and debate over possible measures that could be utilised to degrow tourism. In addition, each destination is unique and degrowth policies if adapted will need to fit within local conditions. Those destinations highly reliant on tourism for their livelihood will need to approach degrowth differently than those with a much more diverse economy.

Under the goal *limits to tourism*, objectives include policies focused on targeting fossil fuel travel (especially high carbon and long-distance travel), promoting slow tourism and a moratorium on tourism developments. Example instruments under fossil fuels include; reducing travel levels (especially in sensitive areas); tax as well as regulate the full environmental costs of travel (especially for aviation) and tourism developments; implement and increase tourism taxes; switch faster aviation to boats which are slower; restrict or ban mega-ships and incorporate progressive taxes on ships based on their size and the number of passengers; and develop locally based cruise ship fleets and reduce overall shipping. Example instruments under promoting slow tourism include: unlearning travel consumption behaviours and changing the mentality of the consumer class in terms of the desire for speed, social privilege and elitism; incorporate lifecycle analysis; relocalisation; ethical consumption; create international Cittaslow networks; restrict platform capitalism such as Airbnb; and create decentralised platform cooperative models (Fitzpatrick et al., 2022).

Under the goal *rethinking tourism*, objectives include: local cooperative ownership; detailed spatial planning; prioritising the right to live over the right to travel; and tourism education. Under the objective local cooperative ownership, example instruments include community-based tourism; pro-poor tourism; ecotourism; dignified working conditions, not-for-profit social enterprises; staycations; and slow tourism. The detailed spatial planning objective involves regulating land use and land cover, and coherent management of destinations and heritage. Under the objective of prioritising the 'right to live' over the 'right to travel' which favours residents' rights and the environment over the short-term wants of wealthy tourists, example objectives include: resisting the UNWTO proposal to make tourism a human right; redefining the definition of tourism; revising or eliminating the Office of International Migration and the UNWTO so they favour justice, equity, residents, refugees and the environment; and creating penalties for excessive consumption or in other words promoting tourism sufficiency (Fitzpatrick et al., 2022).

Important observations are made across all degrowth policies in the literature review (Fitzpatrick et al., 2022) that have important lessons for tourism. While there has been a diversification in the disciplines embracing degrowth (tourism is specifically noted as a new area), a lack of precision is identified in many proposals and some policies are mentioned more frequently than others. The authors note that frequently mentioned proposals (for example, addressing inequality through wealth taxes) are not fully explored in terms of the complexity of implementation and of the numerous other policies that would need to be realised before the more frequently mentioned policy could be achieved. In tourism, for example, a frequently mentioned degrowth policy is targeting fossil fuel travel, especially air travel. To implement this, however, there would have to be a range of other related detailed policies such as improving electric train and bus routes, the taxation of jet fuel and restrictions on frequent flyers, to name just a few. There would also need to be coordination across sectors and across countries. In other words, simply stating a degrowth policy is much easier than implementing it. Finally, many degrowth policies are studied independently with few studying the positive or negative synergies between different proposals; the more synergies, the more complex is the transition to degrowth. Change can be bottom-up, slow, popular and have limited risks while other changes are top-down, fast, unpopular and are riskier (Fitzpatrick et al., 2022). What is evident is that there has been very limited implementation of degrowth policy for tourism which speaks to both the newness of degrowth as well as to the difficulties in challenging the current model of tourism development.

A DEGROWTH FRAMEWORK FOR RETHINKING TOURISM AND DEVELOPMENT

Table 7.1 presents a framework for rethinking tourism and development based on the review of the literature on tourism, development and degrowth. It applies the three elements of degrowth noted by Parrique (2019, cited in Fitzpatrick et al., 2022) and examines them in terms of tourism degrowth for (a) governments and destinations; (b) tourism industry actors (incorporating a range of actors – individual entrepreneurs, small and medium sized tourism businesses, community-based tourism organisations, multinational tourism organisations and related businesses); and (c) tourists. There are also elements in the framework that build on the concepts of sustainable, responsible and regenerative tourism although, as noted previously, these measures do not go far enough to 'rightsize' tourism (Hall, 2009) in the context of the current environmental crises. A transition to tourism degrowth can incorporate both top-down and bottom-up elements, systematic structural change at the global and societal levels as well as individual practices of downsizing (Fletcher et al., 2019). This initial framework is not meant to be comprehensive or prescriptive; rather, it sets out to investigate what degrowth would mean across tourism in the hope that it will generate further discussion and research. A key question to be addressed into the future is if degrowth were to be implemented (which, as we have suggested throughout this book, is unavoidable), how might governments and destinations, tourism industry actors and tourists themselves take steps to move away from the current growth model of tourism. In addition, a critical consideration for this framework is how to maintain tourism's developmental role in a degrowth context – there are clearly many countries, particularly those with mature, diverse economies, which could absorb degrowth in their tourism sectors, whereas for other countries this is not an option, at least in the shorter-term. Hence, questions surround the manner in which tourism might be 'shared' internationally within a global degrowth agenda.

The important point is that there is no one definitive model for degrowth and tourism; it will look different in different destinations guided by a range of diverse government policies. This lack of a set of prescribed steps can be seen as both a weakness and a strength in tourism degrowth. Tourism industry actors of differing scales and sizes will face both challenges and opportunities in implementing degrowth. Similarly, amongst tourists, many eager to return to travel after the Covid-19 pandemic restrictions, there will be supporters and detractors. The potential implications of the framework in Table 7.1 for both supply (Chapter 5) and demand (Chapter 6) will be investigated in the following two sections.

DEGROWTH IMPLICATIONS FOR THE SUPPLY OF TOURISM

Before focusing on the elements presented in Table 7.1, it is important to note that for degrowth to gain traction on a global scale there needs to be greater collaboration amongst international organisations with a responsibility for tourism, such as the UNWTO, to embrace and adapt to degrowth (see Chapter 5). In the Great Unsettling, the foundations of global governance are under threat. However, if we are to tackle international issues such as climate change and inequality, to both of which tourism contributes, global governance institutions and systems have a vital role to play in degrowth in general and for tourism degrowth in particular. Such global collaboration is possible; in the face of significant disagreements, for example, equity came to the forefront at COP27 in 2022 in Egypt with the creation of a 'loss and damage fund' for countries vulnerable to climate change. Although agreement regarding the specifics of the fund and how the money will be dispersed may not be achieved for some time, the important principle was established that the developed countries which contribute most to climate change will have to assist poor countries in mitigating its impacts (Volcovici, Evans & James, 2022). Similarly, international tourism organisations long committed to the growth of tourism will need to come together and recognise the limits of tourism growth in a finite world and be open to degrowth as a way forward so the developmental role of tourism can be shared more equitably.

Table 7.1 highlights selected policies and operational strategies for tourism supply for governments and destinations as well as for tourism industry actors.

Table 7.1   *A degrowth framework for rethinking tourism and development*

	Governments/Destinations	Tourism Industry Actors	Tourists
Decrease throughput to reduce environmental pressure	Shift from fossil fuels; Stay within ecological limits; Enhance low impact, low carbon modes of travel (e.g., train and cycle networks); Land use planning; Incorporate carbon footprint in destination tourism revenue; Adaptation, mitigation and resilience to climate change; Protect commons; Overtourism regulations	Shift from fossil fuels; Energy efficiency; Tourism products incorporate carbon footprint costs; Downscaling of tourism infrastructure	Travel less frequently and less far; Avoid carbon-intensive travel; Demand environmentally friendly tourism products; Purchase carbon offsets; Slow tourism; Domestic travel; Appreciate tourism experience more; Avoid destinations under stress
Shift from ideologies of neoliberalism, consumerism and extractivism	Shift away from GDP; Avoid commodification; Demarketing; Regulations on tourism advertising; Taxation on tourism overconsumption; Focus on domestic tourism; Reduction in tourism where appropriate	CSR statements aimed at degrowth; Avoid greenwashing; Cooperation over competition; Consolidation and downsizing; Links to local communities; Operate within ecological limits; Avoid planned obsolescence	Voluntary simplicity; Antimaterialism; Avoid overconsumption and conspicuous consumption; Authentic lifestyle; Avoid overly commodified tourism products
Vision of society as one of care, equity sufficiency, and autonomy	Wealth redistribution; Living wage in tourism; Reduce working hours; Localism; Support local tourism industry needs; Encourage domestic tourism; Encourage local participation	Pay living wages; Fair work policies; Policies of diversity, equity and inclusion; Pro-poor and fair-trade approaches; Utilise local supply chain; Contribute to relocalisation	Support local tourism providers; Conviviality in tourism; Contribute to relocalisation

Source: After Andriotis (2014); Panzer-Krause (2017); Gössling & Higham (2021); Lundmark, Zhang and Hall (2020); Parrique (2019 in Fitzpatrick, Parrique & Cosme, 2022); Banerjee et al. (2021); Butcher (2022); Collingridge (2022); Scott & Gössling (2022).

If governments and destinations are to implement degrowth policies, they would need to decide on a range of mandatory and voluntary measures. This could involve incentives and policies to try and nudge companies and people to alter their behaviour but, in the end, some mandatory measures may inevitably need to be put in place. The key point will be implementing tourism degrowth in different settings while maintaining tourism's developmental role. As mentioned above, those destinations dependent on tourism will still need to rely on it for their livelihood, whereas those with a more diverse economy may not need continued growth in arrivals (or may better handle a reduction in arrivals) and may be better able to implement tourism degrowth which would shift tourism employees to other sectors (as occurred after the Covid-19 pandemic). For economies heavily reliant on tourism, strong degrowth could be disastrous; in those destinations, further growth in tourism may in fact be necessary. If this were to occur, there are still policy options in Table 7.1 that could be applied to tourism to mitigate some of the negative aspects of tourism growth at the destination level. But the point is that, just as with consumption more generally, some countries must, in the interests of equitable development, be able to maintain or grow their tourism sector whilst others implement degrowth policies to contribute to overall degrowth in tourism on the global scale.

Supply policies and strategies should stress the importance of the low carbon imperative in terms of the climate crisis (Gössling & Higham, 2021). Hence, governments and destinations need to support low carbon forms of transportation, adopt policies to reduce tourism volumes where appropriate, such as demarketing or taxation on overconsumption, and focus on domestic tourism while implementing policies that promote equity, living wages and local communities. The challenge then becomes how to encourage governments, typically elected on a platform of growth, to implement such policies. It may mean a national government with a well-established tourism brand identity adopting a strategy of demarketing to align with calls for regulations on advertising in degrowth. Some elements of these policies have already been put in place, such as in Sao Paulo, Brazil, where all forms of outdoor advertising have been banned and in Amsterdam where outdoor advertisements for petrol and diesel cars and for air travel have been banned (Bearne, 2022). Hall and Wood (2021) argue that demarketing can make an important contribution to degrowth tourism at both local and regional scales, though acknowledge its limitations at other scales.

One example is the Faroe Islands which operate a policy of closing the islands to regular visitors for a few days each year but keeping them open for volunteer tourists to help maintain the natural environment. However, reducing numbers for a few days a year is only a very small step towards degrowth. Nevertheless, in an analysis of gross national happiness in two villages in Fiji, it was found the village with less tourism dependence had higher levels of well-being (Pratt, McCabe & Monvono, 2016). Could policies directed at less tourism in some destinations lead to greater happiness? Alternatively, one of the concepts associated with degrowth is a reduction in the length of the working week. In Britain, most of the 73 companies participating in a four-day working week experiment saw no loss in productivity and some significant improvements at the halfway point of the six-month trial (Gross, 2022). Could a reduced working week be applied in tourism degrowth? At the same time, the elements of fair work identified as fair pay, fair conditions, fair contracts, fair management and fair representation (Hadjisolomou et al., 2022) need to be incorporated in tourism degrowth. Extreme poverty has been measured as those living on less than US\$1.90 a day while many argue that US\$5.00 a day is a more honest version of poverty. In the Niagara Region in Ontario, Canada, one of the main tourism destinations in the country, the Ontario Living Wage Network argues that workers in Niagara need to earn CA\$19.80 to meet basic needs. This is up 4.8 percent from 2021 (Benner, 2022). Governments need to make sure those in tourism can earn a living wage, especially in light of challenges of rising inflation.

A sample of degrowth strategies for industry actors is also presented in Table 7.1. Based on an analysis of the tourism literature, it is this sector that has received the least attention in comparison to ideas for government degrowth policy and on how tourists should change their travel behaviour. This reflects both the newness of the area of study and the need for future research, but it also gets to the heart of the challenge facing degrowth; how to ask businesses that have been founded in the global economic model of growth to take a step back and follow the principles of degrowth. As observed by Banerjee et al. (2021), theorising post-growth imaginaries at a macro-economic level is difficult but is even more so when considering these concepts at an organisational level.

In the context of tourism degrowth, Panzer-Krause (2017) categorises businesses with regards to their ideological orientation towards sustainability. The four categories include strict modernists as 'rigid green growth strategists', semi-modernists, semi-conservatives and strict conservatives as 'resolute degrowth strategists'. From these categories, three sets of tensions at the business level are considered: '(1) egocentrism versus altruism; (2) a focus on expansion versus a willingness for consolidation and downsizing; and (3) an openness to collective efforts with regard to economic aspects versus an openness to collective efforts with regards to socio-environmental aspects' (Panzer-Krause, 2019: 929). Subsequently, Panzer-Krause (2019) has applied this scale in a study on rural tourism in Ireland, revealing a heterogeneity of entrepreneurs ranging from those focused on strict green growth to rigid degrowth. The challenge becomes how to encourage tourism suppliers who are mainly committed to growth to shift their policies towards degrowth, particularly at a time when they are trying to recover from the Covid-19 pandemic. Selected suggestions in Table 7.1 include developing a CSR statement guided by degrowth, moving away from fossil fuels, incorporating the cost of carbon in pricing, building stronger connections to local communities (relocalisation) and paying a living wage. The adoption of diversity, equity and inclusion policies (Im, Chung & Qin, 2023) will also move companies towards the kind of society advocated in degrowth. Inevitably, if degrowth is pursued, tourism industry actors will be facing a degrowth policy framework delivered by destination governments and changing numbers of tourists.

One of the commonalities across Table 7.1 is the need to reduce travel carbon emissions. Specifically in terms of aviation, Nunes (2022) raises the question of whether companies should abolish air miles loyalty programs for the sake of climate change. Interestingly, Safe Landing (2022), an organisation of aviation workers (including some former pilots) campaigning for long-term employment, is challenging industry leaders to follow the climate science and to reject dangerous levels of growth (also see Mayer 2022). They argue that brakes need to be put on the 'business as usual growth trajectory' emerging out of the pandemic otherwise higher levels of aviation will run into a climate crash (drastic decline), with flying dropping to levels even below those of the Covid-19 pandemic crash. Safe Landing claims it is better to introduce policies immediately to reduce aviation along a safe trajectory rather than waiting and trying to recover from the predicted climate crash in aviation. They also predict, as do many others, that flying will in any event become more expensive because of policies including aviation emissions pricing, frequent flyer levies, an increase in jet fuel (fossil fuel) costs as well as mandates for more expensive alternative fuels in the future. In addition, there will be a need to limit airline and airport capacity especially in higher income countries. In the end, they argue, overall air miles travelled must decrease and we will need to travel less frequently, less fast and less far (Safe Landing, 2022). Small, shorter-range electric and hydrogen airplanes may be what we fly in the future, but they still need to be created – hydrogen powered jet engines are 'still a long way off' (Leggett, 2022) – and airports and airlines will need to transform to accommodate these aircraft (Safe Landing, 2022).

DEGROWTH IMPLICATIONS FOR THE CONSUMPTION OF TOURISM

The tale of the Windigo, a mythical monster driven by excessive consumption, serves as an important warning from North American Indigenous cultures against overconsumption (Kimmerer, 2013). Yet despite the environmental and social consequences of excessive consumption, evidence of a return to overtourism and revenge travel after the Covid-19 pandemic demonstrates that tourism demand will in all likelihood continue to grow into the future. Conspicuous consumption is a function of the neoliberal growth model (see Chapter 6) and without continuous growth in the consumption of tourism, growth measured by GDP goes down.

A further reflection on the recent evolution of degrowth is that even though there are calls to degrow travel, tourists have largely been ignored in studies on tourism degrowth (Lundmark et al., 2020). One exception is Andriotis (2018) who considers the potential for tourists to travel using fewer resources, such as backpackers travelling slower, consuming less and staying longer. He also distinguishes between 'tourists' and 'travellers', suggesting that degrowth-inspired 'travellers' adopt anti-tourist practices and wish to be disassociated from the masses. While there may be those that align with this definition of a degrowth traveller, it will not be enough just to cater to these so-called 'travellers'; moreover, backpackers and other forms of 'traveller' have long existed – backpacking significantly predates the notion of degrowth – and in some respects are indistinguishable from mainstream tourists (Sharpley, 2018). Hence, degrowth will need to be promoted to all 'tourists' across the spectrum if it is to have any effect. Moreover, although degrowth for tourists aligns with other campaigns that seek to reduce the impacts of travel such as slow, responsible, pro-poor and justice tourism, degrowth goes beyond these forms of tourism and asks tourists to limit their travel (Fletcher et al., 2019), just as levels of consumption more generally should be reduced.

The main challenge facing tourism demand, as with consumption as a whole, is to change the behaviour of tourists, the key question being whether tourists will accept degrowth. Hall (2013) suggests three approaches to changing tourist behaviour, including the neoliberal utilitarian approach which utilises government regulations, such as tax incentives or carbon trading, social/psychological approaches, such as social marketing and nudging, and structural approaches that focus on systems of supply and production such as localism, voluntary simplicity and short-supply chains. These three approaches need to be combined with the process of policy learning, which includes the steps of focusing on individual decision making, strategies to effect individual behaviours and practices and, finally, a policy paradigm shift with a new goal hierarchy (Hall, 2013). Table 7.1 incorporates degrowth guidelines for tourists which would have tourists travelling less often, closer to home and using carbon friendly forms of transportation. All tourists (including the authors of this book) need to reconsider their future travel plans taking degrowth into account. This, in turn, means that we as tourists need to adapt our mindset to be less driven by conspicuous consumption and to step away from the influences of consumer culture.

More specifically, tourists will need to be encouraged to seek out less commodified and more environmentally friendly travel products. By travelling closer to home, tourists could also further contribute to relocalisation and support local providers. Tourists also need to consider staying away from destinations under stress, as the Fodor travel guide has recently proposed in their 'No List' which consists of destinations that should be avoided for now until they can recover (Collingridge, 2022). The list for 2023 includes: (i) natural attractions that need to regenerate (for example, Antarctica; France's coastline such as Étretat and Calanques National Park in Marseille); (ii) cultural hotspots without the resources to support crowds (for example, Venice, the Amalfi Coast, Cornwall, Amsterdam); and (iii) destinations suffering a water crisis (for example, Maui, the Southern European watershed including the Rhine and Danube River areas, the American west – Arizona and Nevada). Alternatively, tourists could travel virtually as a means of further degrowing tourism, especially to environmentally sensitive locations (for example, see Lekgau, Harilia & Feni, 2021), though of course this would remove the most fundamental element of the tourist experience: physical travel. Indeed, it should be emphasised that degrowth seeks to neither stop travel nor to diminish the importance of the spirit of travel; rather, it asks tourists to reassess their choices in response to the global environmental crisis. This, however, will be a big 'ask', especially if tourists are focused on 'what's in it for me if I do change my travel behaviour', whilst younger generations of tourists may well question having to make sacrifices that their parents did not.

Tourists' travel decisions might also be affected by degrowth policies implemented by governments and the industry. For example, international air travel is likely to become more costly, especially if carbon and frequent flyer taxes are added, potentially reducing demand. Conversely, the development of domestic and regional train routes might make rail travel more attractive and perhaps less expensive, particularly if subsidised, whilst innovative policies might also promote rail travel over flying. In France, for example, short haul domestic flights are to be banned (for an initial 3-year trial period) between cities that can be reached in two and a half hours or less by train (Reid, 2022). Tourists may also be purchasing other tourism products, such as hotel rooms and visitor attraction tickets, with a carbon footprint built into the prices. If tourists stay local and purchase local souvenirs, they would also be contributing more to local tourism suppliers and supporting local economies. If governments were to reduce the working week, tourists may have more time to travel, although some critics argue that if people have more time off, they will use it for energy-intensive activities such as long haul travel. However, research suggests the opposite; those with less leisure time consume more intensively, relying on high-speed travel, impulsive purchases, meal deliveries and retail therapy while those with more time off focus more on lower-impact activities such as exercise, volunteering, learning and socialising (Hickel, 2020).

CHALLENGES TO DEGROWTH FOR TOURISM

Many of the difficulties facing tourism degrowth in particular stem from the challenges associated with degrowth in general – specifically, that it represents a significant shift from the dominant neoliberal growth agenda (see Chapter 3 for criticisms on degrowth in general). Certainly, in the context of tourism, Fletcher et al. (2019: 1753) acknowledge that to implement degrowth is to question tourism development, which 'is tantamount to challenging the current capitalist productive model and its growth imperative'. At the same time, the diversity of perspectives and proposals falling under the banner of degrowth can make the paradigm seem unfocused (Videira et al., 2014). It can also be difficult to identify the causal chain of effects of complementary proposals and their resulting consequences if implemented (Videira et al., 2014). For example, tourism degrowth proposals implemented at an international or national level will have varying repercussions at the regional, local or firm level. This suggests that although Table 7.1 contains a range of possible policies and strategies for exploring tourism degrowth, translating theory into practice can become extremely difficult. Volger (2022), for example, observes that advocates of degrowth are not necessarily connected to the business realities at work in the tourism industry, whilst similar concerns were raised over the merits of tourism degrowth and its impact on the industry in the debate between Butcher (2021a) and Higgins-Desbiolles and Everingham (2022) presented in Chapter 3.

Lundmark et al. (2020) also identify several challenges associated with tourism degrowth. Degrowth policies will be very different across different geographic contexts and attempting to implement particular concepts, such as Buen Vivir, in different settings is a reflection of the wider challenges of implementing degrowth in tourism. They note that much of the research in degrowth has been linked to demarketing and social marketing, both designed to achieve more sustainable levels of tourism in particular situations, such as in destinations suffering from overtourism, rather than a comprehensive rethinking of the nature of tourism growth and development. Nor is history on the side of degrowth; since the late 1980s, alternative forms of tourism have failed to transform the dominant growth orientation of tourism, suggesting that tourism degrowth may be no more successful in doing so. As previously mentioned, Lundmark et al. (2020) also highlight that minimal work has been done on the relationship between mobility and degrowth except in relation to travel emissions and, finally, they stress the importance of considering the positionality of tourism researchers in degrowth theory, as ontological and activist positioning will have implications for tourism degrowth and policy making.

From a practical perspective, the implementation of tourism degrowth needs to be carefully managed. For example, Scheyvens, Movono and Auckram (2023) explored the multiple well-beings of Pacific peoples in tourism-dependent communities during the Covid-19 pandemic. They found that many people were able to draw on traditional skills, cultural systems, social capital and access to customary land to maintain their well-being even as household income significantly decreased. There were, however, others who were more vulnerable and suffered from mental health issues and increases in household conflict. Canavan (2021) also draws attention to the disadvantages of degrowth on small islands, such as the Isle of Man which has long been dependant on tourism. Conversely and ironically, degrowth itself has become the attraction in the declining village of Nagaro, Japan, where scarecrows are placed throughout the village re-enacting scenes from daily life, such as waiting at the bus stop, farming, fishing and so on, representing people who have left the village for life in the city or who have passed away (Hashimoto, Telfer & Telfer, 2021). However, while the scarecrows have become an attraction, falling numbers of residents and a lack of government funding have become serious issues for this village in decline.

A final challenge to consider for tourism degrowth is that of time. Every few years during election campaigns, for example, governments highlight tourism's contribution to economic growth. It will be very difficult for politicians to advocate a reduction in the number of tourists in an election cycle when increases in tourism are being built into national tourism development plans. Similarly, tourism businesses need to report quarterly or annual profits and so it would be equally problematic for a CEO of a tourism company to present a strategy of planned reductions. Yet it is these short time frames that are partly responsible for driving over-production and the overconsumption of tourism. In his book, Attenborough (2020) details the significant environmental damage humans have caused during his own lifetime. Sustainable tourism development requires us to protect resources for future generations, to think about a more distant future. Governments and some tourism businesses are setting net zero emission targets for 2050, but is this fast enough? Moreover, as discussed in Chapter 4, green growth (arguably the objective of net zero) is still growth. Are we willing to degrow tourism and deny the opportunities for the consumption of holidays and their related supply chains for our grandchildren's grandchildren and beyond?

In documenting the existential risks to humanity, Ord (2020: 218) asks us to contemplate time in a much broader scale than most of us consider. The 'universe we inhabit is thousands of times older than humanity itself. There were billions of years before us; there will be billions to come. In our universe, time is not a scarce commodity' (Ord, 2020: 218). By drawing attention to these humbling timescales, he not only considers human history, how much we have accomplished over time and how we continue to struggle with self-created existential threats; he also argues that by acting together to safeguard humanity, there is no reason why we could not live to see the 'grand themes of the universe unfold across the eons, … when we consider the potential they hold for what we might become, they inspire'. Yet many would argue that immediate action is required if humanity is to be safeguarded into the far future. When Covid-19 emerged, many countries demonstrated (some better than others) that rapid change to deal with threats is possible. The contemporary environmental crisis is, we would argue, such a threat, but how much more time will pass before tourism degrowth policies (and, indeed, degrowth more generally) are considered on a wider perspective before they are forced upon us by circumstances? Contrasting voices across time and space illustrate the challenges facing tourism degrowth; as Kallis (2018: 115) notes 'even if degrowth is socially and environmentally desirable, this does not make it politically feasible'.

FUTURE RESEARCH IN TOURISM DEGROWTH

The challenges facing tourism degrowth outlined above reflect, in part, a lack of knowledge and understanding of the concept. Indeed, research on tourism degrowth remains in its infancy and much work needs to be done in terms of both theory and practice, whilst the broader idea of degrowth itself is still under construction. This is perhaps unsurprising; degrowth is not just about economics and the environment, but about moving to a post-growth world that involves a re-enchantment of the world (Latouche, 2009).

With regards to tourism degrowth in particular, there has been limited research not only by tourism scholars but also on tourism within the broader degrowth literature. Hence, a number of potential strands of research can be proposed. From a theoretical perspective, research is needed on how the pluriverse of perspectives from both the Global North and the Global South can influence the direction of tourism degrowth and contribute to solutions to the crises facing the planet. Degrowth is not an alternative but, rather, a matrix of alternatives which, as Demaria and Latouche (2019: 149) note, can re-open human adventure to 'a plurality of destinies and spaces of creativity by throwing off the blanket of economic totalitarianism'. Nevertheless, developing alternative visions of a society based on something other than growth and *laissez-faire* economics is, according to Banerjee et al. (2021), a profound challenge for both theorists and society. They argue for a new political economy and postulate four categories with shifts from: (i) accumulation to distribution; (ii) extraction to restoration; (iii) competition to cooperation; and (iv) consumerism to sufficiency. Further research on tourism degrowth is needed in all four of these areas.

Creating a coherent and desirable model of degrowth includes not only a move beyond a theoretical exercise but also taking steps towards political implementation and creating concrete proposals. Latouche (2009) identifies the 8R's of degrowth (see Chapter 2): re-evaluate, reconceptualise, restructure, relocate, redistribute, reduce, re-use and recycle, all of which could be evaluated in detail in the context of tourism degrowth (see Higgins-Desbiolles et al., 2019 for initial work). Chapter 2 explored transformations in tourism and development theories and considered the tourism development dilemma. If degrowth is proposed as an alternative to the neoliberal growth model, future research is needed on how tourism's developmental role can be maintained in the context of different countries. There is no one methodology or set of policies to implement degrowth, so studies will be needed in a range of tourism locations and scales to determine alternative paths towards degrowth.

Table 7.1 presents a range of policies and strategies to facilitate governments, tourism industry actors and tourists contributing to degrowth, but these proposals all need much further investigation. Future research on governments and destinations might involve, for example, an evaluation of the strengths and weaknesses of various government degrowth policies (both voluntary and mandatory), an analysis of how governments can transition societies to low carbon forms of transportation, such as the further development of rail networks, and an investigation of the resistance that governments are likely to face in implementing degrowth. Other authors (Banerjee et al., 2021; Lundmark et al. 2020) have also developed a list of future research questions for degrowth in which they suggest investigating the institutional arrangements of the state and civil society in the transition to degrowth, noting that businesses may resist change and therefore states may have to play a greater role with help from civil society. Finally, Gonzaler and Espelt (2021) suggest that in the context of destinations, additional research is needed on the degrowth values of local residents towards tourism and tourists.

The second category in Table 7.1 comprises actors in the tourism industry. Selected future research questions include the extent to which tourism business will be receptive to degrowth, what the challenges are for tourism businesses in making stronger connections with local communities and businesses, and how tourism businesses can afford higher wages in inflationary times. Degrowth would mean businesses founded on a growth model having to reorient their business operations, a fundamental shift that would undoubtedly meet with strong opposition. The final category in Table 7.1 is tourists. Potential future research questions include whether tourists are willing to change their behaviours rooted in excessive consumption, what range of 'carrots' (for example, staycation tax credits) or 'sticks' (for example, taxes on frequent flyers) would be most effective in altering tourist behaviour, whether tourists will avoid international tourism hotspots and travel primarily locally, and how this will vary with age and the number of international trips taken in the past.

CONCLUSION: RETHINKING TOURISM AND DEVELOPMENT

The purpose of this book has been to rethink the relationship between tourism and development. Developmentalism, of which tourism is a part, is being driven by economic neoliberalism and the myth of eternal growth resulting in increasing inequality, the rise of the new global super-rich (Freeland, 2012) and environmental crises. Through the lens of degrowth, defined as a 'planned and democratic reduction of production and consumption as a solution to the social-ecological crises' (Fitzpatrick et al., 2022), this book has sought to develop a degrowth framework for rethinking tourism and development (see Table 7.1). In so doing, it is hoped that it has been provocative, generating discussion and stimulating others to explore further the questions raised. In other words, our approach has not been to be prescriptive but, rather, to engage the reader in debates, issues and questions to which we do not yet have the answers. There remain many unknowns with regards to degrowth and, in terms of tourism, it is about much more than simply a reduction in visitor numbers. Certainly, the global Covid-19 pandemic clearly demonstrated the disastrous economic impacts when the world did indeed stop travelling (see Hall, Scott & Gössling, 2020); as Jackson (2021: xv) observes, we have been 'given a history lesson of what economics looks like when growth disappears completely … and it looks nothing like the modern world has seen before'. Yet, this book is not suggesting that we should stop travelling. Rather, it has set out to argue that there needs to be a revaluation of the relationship between tourism and development through degrowth, to investigate the best way to maintain tourism's developmental role in destinations in the context of reducing global consumption levels in response to the broader crises facing the planet.

Readers of this book may feel that we have adopted an overly negative perspective on tourism, that we have engaged in 'tourism bashing'. Certainly, we have focused on many of the negative aspects of tourism. Where we have done so, however, has been for the purposes of generating discussion and exploring other options for tourism development, not least because it appears to be stuck within the broader framework of sustainable development, a concept which, as we have pointed out, remains based on the growth imperative. Tourism evidently plays a vital role in the development process for many destinations, communities, companies and individuals around the world, and this role must be maintained in areas that are highly dependent on it for their livelihoods. As is widely acknowledged, tourism generates income, employment, taxes and foreign exchange as well as contributing to environmental conservation through the establishment of parks and protected areas. Equally, tourism is part of human nature; perhaps the need to travel has always existed. People need to keep travelling, to explore, to learn about other cultures and see what is over the horizon. In short, there are many benefits for those who are wealthy enough to be able to participate in tourism, yet it needs to be recognised that only a small percentage of the world's population enjoy the privilege of participating in tourism, but their actions are contributing to the global environmental crisis that impacts most keenly on less developed nations and peoples.

At the COP27 summit in Sharm El Sheikh, Egypt, UN Secretary-General Antonio Guterres (2022) argued that '[we] are in the fight of our lives, and we are losing. Greenhouse gas emissions keep growing, global temperatures keep rising, and our planet is fast approaching tipping points that will make climate chaos irreversible. We are on a highway to climate hell with our foot still on the accelerator'. David Attenborough (2020) makes a similar plea for us to change course along the lines of the planetary boundaries model developed by a team of Earth scientists led by Johan Rockström and Will Steffen at the Stockholm Resilience Centre. In other words, to live sustainably we need to remain within specific planetary boundaries and we need to consider tourism's contribution to stressing these boundaries; as we have emphasised throughout this book, tourism is part of global consumption and cannot be viewed in isolation from it. These boundaries are biodiversity loss, land conversion, fertiliser use, climate change, chemical pollution, air pollution, ozone depletion, fresh water withdrawals and ocean acidification and, when this book was first envisioned, we had already broken through the first four boundaries in this list.

Attenborough (2020: 129) argues that 'we have arrived at this moment of desperation as a result of our desire for *preputial growth* in the world economy. But in a finite world, nothing can increase forever'. In 2022, during the writing of this book, two additional barriers have been exceeded: chemical pollution in January, and fresh water in April (Bonpote, 2022). Yet despite these critical and constant warnings, there is a danger that people are becoming immune to them, especially if climate change is not seen as an immediate direct threat. However, the developed world and its travellers have long been contributing to climate change, often at the expense of developed nations, and so degrowth asks travellers to re-evaluate their travel decisions – travel less often, less far, stay closer to home and travel by environmentally friendly means of transportation.

Degrowth represents a pluriverse of worldviews and practices and while it draws strength from diversity, it does not aspire to colonise or give meaning to every struggle or experience (Kallis, 2018). Degrowth is a process designed to facilitate the move towards to a 'post-growth' world that is no longer focused on acquisition and competition but on developing meaningful lives. It is the pursuit of a post-capitalist economy that is fairer, more just and more caring

(Hickel, 2020). Degrowth stresses equality both within and between nations and in a finite world, it asks those who are overconsuming to take steps to reduce consumption so that the most vulnerable have access to more resources. If degrowth is to be considered as an alternative to developmentalism, meaningful steps will have to be taken at the global level if degrowth is to occur at national, community, industry or individual levels.

However, while suggesting degrowth as a possible way forward, it is important to recognise the progress being made in many societies, economies and environments towards achieving some, if not all, of the SDGs – and these important strides need to continue. Moreover, although sustainable tourism development remains elusive, steps in this regard have been made towards finding a 'better' form of tourism and these efforts also need to continue and be enhanced. Arguably, tourism does have a role to play in contributing towards the SDGs but, at the same time, it must be acknowledged that they are still grounded within the (unsustainable) growth paradigm. In the end, sustainable tourism development is not enough to address the challenge of climate change and other environmental crises. In contrast, degrowth offers an additional perspective by reducing both production and consumption to protect the environment and develop a more equitable society. Nevertheless, as Latouche (2009) reasons, although on the one hand few would disagree that exponential growth is incompatible with a finite world and consumption must not exceed the biosphere's capacity for regeneration, it is on the other hand much more difficult to accept a reduction in production and consumption; the logic of systematic and dramatic growth must be called into question, along with our way of life built around this growth imaginary. Technological advances continue to be made; in December 2022, for example, a US lab achieved the first successful fusion reaction, an exciting development that could lead to abundant clean energy on Earth (Greshko, 2022). Yet, as Hickel (2020) notes, even with clean energy, a society obsessed with growth may still end up facing ecological disaster.

For now, degrowth remains primarily a thought-world. However, it presents us with a possible context for considering how to live in a world that is not dominated by the incessant growth in production and consumption that is driving the crises we now face. Degrowth is an idealistic ambition and there are tremendous barriers facing the implementation of degrowth in a global society locked into growth. Asking governments and destinations, tourism industry actors and tourists to reduce both the production and consumption of tourism will face stiff opposition. Yet, given its diversity, degrowth is not a standard platform of policies that can be applied uniformly and, as such, tourism degrowth will look different in different destinations. Some developed, diversified economies may see a reduction in tourism with employees taking positions in other sectors but there also may be managed increases in tourism in tourism-dependent destinations. Considering how those decisions will be made is a reflection on how difficult implementing degrowth may be, but there are glimmers of hope. For instance, protests against overtourism and new regulations to control it suggest that some components of degrowth are starting to gain attention. Similarly, so-called *flygskam*, or flight-shaming, is encouraging people to reconsider their travel carbon footprint and to fly less often or not at all. These actions are a beginning. However, as an editorial in *The Guardian* (2020) argues, individual efforts will not avert disaster; the answer lies in collective action by entire countries led by governments to push economies into a clean era. At the individual level, flight-shaming and other efforts to restrict carbon-intensive forms of consumption do not seek to suggest that one person is better than another or to displace anxiety from the public to the private realm. Rather, they demonstrate to leaders in both business and politics that 'we get it: life must change'.

Perhaps by proposing a tourism degrowth framework for rethinking tourism and development (Table 7.1), this book will encourage people to think about another way forward, not only for tourism but for their lifestyles as a whole. In their analysis of degrowth, Vandeventer and Lloveras (2020) draw on the work of Latour (2004: 246) who states: '[the] critic is not the one who debunks, but the one who assembles. The critic is not the one who lifts the rugs from under the feet of the naïve believers, but the one who offers the participants arenas in which to gather'. We hope that this book has provided such an area for people to gather, to debate, to question and rethink the relationship between development and tourism and to consider a path for tourism to a post-growth world.

References

Aamir, S. and Atsan, N. (2020) The trend of multisided platforms (MSPs) in the travel industry: Reintermediation of travel agencies (TAs) and global distribution systems (GDSs). *Journal of Tourism Futures*, 6(3), 271–279.

Abdullah, M. (2021) Revenge tourism: Trend or impact post-pandemic Covid-19? In A. Hudaiby, G. Kuamah, C. U. Abdullah, D. Turgarini, M. Ruhimat, O. Ridwanudin and Y. Yuniawati (Eds), *Promoting Creative Tourism: Current Issues in Tourism Research*. Abingdon: Routledge, pp. 623–627.

Abuhjeeleh, M. (2019) Rethinking tourism in Saudi Arabia: Royal vision 2030 perspective. *African Journal of Hospitality, Tourism and Leisure*, 8(5), 1–16.

ADB (2022a) *Regional: South Asia Tourism Infrastructure Development Project (Bangladesh, India, Nepal) – India*. Asian Development Bank. Available at: https://www.adb.org/projects/39399–013/main (Accessed 17 August 2022).

ADB (2022b) *ADB, Fiji Sign $3 Million Grant to Prepare for Tourism Upswing*. Asian Development Bank. Available at: https://www.adb.org/news/adb-fiji-sign-3-million-grant-prepare-tourism-upswing#:~:text=NADI%2C%20FIJI%20(23%20May%202022,much%2Danticipated%20upswing%20in%20tourist (Accessed 19 August 2022).

Adelman, S. (2017) The sustainable development goals: Anthropocentrism and neo-liberalism. In D. French and L. Kotze (Eds), *Sustainable Development Goals: Law, Theory and Implementation*. Cheltenham, UK and Northampton, MA, USA: Edward Elgar Publishing, pp. 15–40.

Aikau, H. and Gonzalez, V. (2019) Introduction. In H. Aikau and V. Gonzalez (Eds), *Detours: A Decolonial Guide to Hawai'i*. Durham: Duke University Press, pp. 1–13.

Alvord, K. (2000) *Divorce your Car! Ending the Loved Affair with the Automobile*. Gabriola Island, BC: New Society Publishers.

Anderson, E. (2020) *Reconstructing the Global Political Economy: An Analytical Guide*. Bristol: Bristol University Press.

Anderson, W. (2013) Leakages in the tourism systems: Case of Zanzibar. *Tourism Review*, 68(1), 62–76.

Andreoni, V. (2020). The trap of success: A paradox of scale for sharing economy and degrowth. *Sustainability*, 12(8). https//:doi:10.3390/SU12083153

Andriotis, A. (2014) Tourism development and the degrowth paradigm. *Turističko Poslovanje*, 13, 37–45.

Andriotis, A. (2018) *Degrowth in Tourism: Conceptual, Theoretical and Philosophical Issues*. Wallingford: CABI.

Andriotis, A. (Ed.) (2021) *Issues and Cases of Degrowth in Tourism*. Wallingford: CABI.

AQR (n.d.) Consumer culture. Association for Qualitative Research. Available at: https://www.aqr.org.uk/glossary/consumer-culture#:~:text=Consumer%20culture%20suggests%20that%20consumption,by%20practical%20or%20economic%20factors.

Arabadzhyan, A., Figini, P., García, C., González, M.M., Lam-González, Y.E. and León, C.J. (2021) Climate change, coastal tourism, and impact chains: A literature review. *Current Issues in Tourism*, 24(16), 2233–2268.

Arnould, E. J. (2011) Global consumer culture. In S. Jagdish and N. Malhotra (Eds), *Encyclopedia of International Marketing*. Hoboken: Wiley-Blackwell.

Arnould, E. and Thompson, C. (Eds) (2018) *Consumer Culture Theory*. London: Sage Publications.

Attenborough, D. (2020) *A Life on Our Planet: My Witness Statement and Vision for the Future*. London: Witness Books.

Australian Government (2022) THRIVE 2030: The Re-imagined Visitor Economy. A national strategy for Australia's visitor economy recovery and a return to sustainable growth, 2022 to 2030. Available at: https://www.austrade.gov.au/news/publications/thrive-2030-strategy (Accessed 22 August 2022).

Badcock, J. (2017) Spain's hotel chambermaids 'Las Kelly' fight for fair pay. *BBC News*, 18 October. Available at: http://www.bbc.com/news/world-europe-41650252

Baker, T. (2022) Trends show reversal of Chinese investment in Western hotels. CoStar, 14 March. Available at: https://www.costar.com/article/926134775/trends-show-reversal-of-chinese-investment-in-western-hotels

Ballantine, P. (2020) Don't leave town till you've seen the country: Domestic tourism as a degrowth strategy. In C. M. Hall, L. Lundmark and J. Zhang (Eds), *Degrowth and Tourism New Perspectives on Tourism Entrepreneurship, Destinations and Policy*. Abingdon: Routledge, pp. 187–201.

Bandura, A. (2007) Impeding ecological sustainability through selective moral disengagement. *International Journal of Innovation and Sustainable Development*, 2(1), 8–35.

Banerjee, S., Jermier, J., Perey, R. and Reichel, A. (2021) Theoretical perspectives on organizations and organizing in a post-growth era. *Organization*, 28(3), 337–357.

Baratti, L. (2022) As overtourism returns: Barcelona seeks to curb cruise ship traffic. *TravelPulse*, 20 June. Available at: https://www.travelpulse.com/news/cruise/as-overtourism-returns-barcelona-seeks-to-curb-cruise-ship-traffic.html (Accessed 18 August 2022).

Baretje, R. (1982) Tourism's external account and the balance of payments. *Annals of Tourism Research*, 9(1), 57–67.

Barkin, D. (2002) Globalization: Love it or leave it. *Latin American Perspectives*, 127, 29(6), 132–135.

Bastakis, C., Buhalis, D. and Butler, R. (2004) The perception of small and medium sized tourism accommodation providers on the impacts of the tour operator's power in Eastern Mediterranean. *Tourism Management*, 25(2), 151–170.

Bastin, J. F., Finegold, Y., Garcia, C., Mollicone, D., Rezende, M., Routh, D., Zohner, C. M. and Crowther, T. W. (2019) The global tree restoration potential. *Science*, 365(6448), 76–79.

Bastin, R. (1984) Small island tourism: Development or dependency? *Development Policy Review*, 2(1), 79–90.

Batarags, L. (2021) China's middle class is starting to look a lot like America's, and that's not a good thing. *Business Insider*, 7 December. Available at: https://www.businessinsider.com/china-middle-class-starting-to-look-like-americas-2021-12?r=US&IR=T (Accessed 5 July 2022).

Bauman, Z. (2005) *Liquid Life*. Cambridge: Polity Press.

Bearne, S. (2022) Should billboard advertising be banned? *BBC News*. Available at: https://www.bbc.co.uk/news/business-62806697 (Accessed 12 December 2022).

Beaudet, P. (2021) Globalization and development. In P. Haslam, J. Schafer and P. Beaudet (Eds), *Introduction to International Development.* Don Mills, ON: Oxford University Press, pp. 112–130.

Becken, S. (2013) A review of tourism and climate change as an evolving knowledge domain. *Tourism Management Perspectives*, 6, 53–62.

Becken, S. (2014) Water equity: Contrasting tourism water use with that of the local community. *Water Resources and Industry*, 7, 9–22.

Becken, S. (2019) Decarbonising tourism: Mission impossible? *Tourism Recreation Research*, 44(4), 419–433.

Becker, E. (2013) *Overbooked: The Exploding Business of Travel and Tourism.* London: Simon & Schuster.

Benckendorff, P., Sheldon, P. and Fesenmaier, D. (2014) *Tourism Information Technology*, 2nd Edn. Wallingford: CABI.

Benner, A. (2022) Niagara's living wage now nearly $20 an hour: Ontario Living Wage Network. *The St. Catharines Standard.* Available at: https://www.stca-tharinesstandard.ca/news/niagara-region/2022/11/14/niagaras-living-wage-no w-nearly-20-an-hour.html (Accessed 15 November 2022).

Berno, T. and Bricker, K. (2001) Sustainable tourism development: The long road from theory to practice. *International Journal of Economic Development*, 3(3), 1–18.

Bianchi, R. (2009) The 'critical turn' in tourism studies: A radical critique. *Tourism Geographies*, 11(4), 484–504.

Bianchi, R. (2015) Towards a new political economy of global tourism revisited. In R. Sharpley and D. J. Telfer (Eds) *Tourism and Development Concepts and Issues 2nd Edition*. Bristol: Channel View Publications, pp. 287–311.

Bianchi, R. (2018) The political economy of tourism development: A critical review. *Annals of Tourism Research*, 70(2018), 88–102.

Bianchi, R. V. and de Man, F. (2021) Tourism, inclusive growth and decent work: A political economy critique. *Journal of Sustainable Tourism*, 29(2–3), 353–371.

Biddle, P. (2021) *Ours to Explore: Privilege, Power and the Paradox of Voluntourism.* Lincoln: University of Nebraska Press.

Blázquez-Salom, M., Blamco-Romero, A., Vera-Rebollo, F. and Ivars-Baisal, J. (2019) Territorial tourism planning in Spain: From boosterism to tourism degrowth? *Journal of Sustainable Tourism*, 27(12), 1764–1785.

Boluk, K., Cavaliere, C. and Higgins-Desbiolles, F. (2019) A critical framework for interrogating the United Nations Sustainable Development Goals 2030 Agenda in tourism. *Journal of Sustainable Tourism*, 27(7), 847–864.

Boluk, K., Krolikowski, C., Higgins-Desbiolles, F., Carnicelli, S. and Wijesinghe, G. (2020) Rethinking tourism: Degrowth and equity rights in developing community-centric tourism. In C. M. Hall, L. Lundmark and J. Zhang (Eds), *Degrowth and Tourism New Perspectives on Tourism Entrepreneurship, Destinations and Policy*. Abingdon: Routledge, pp. 152–169.

Bond, M. and Ladman, J. (1980) International tourism: An instrument for third world development. In I. Vogeler and A. de Souza (Eds), *Dialectics of Third World Development*. New Jersey: Allanheld, Osmun & Co, pp. 231–240.

Boneham, I. (2022) Winter Olympics 2022: The environmental impact of fake snow, how it's made and why it poses a risk to athletes. *NationalWorld*, 16 February. Available at: https://www.nationalworld.com/news/environment/winter-olympics-th e-damaging-impact-of-fake-snow-on-the-environment-3569222

Bonpote (2022) The 6th planetary boundary is crossed: The freshwater cycle. Available at: https://bonpote.com/en/the-6th-planetary-boundary-is-crossed-the-freshwater-cycle/ (Accessed 15 December 2022).

Booking.com (2018) Where sustainable travel is headed in 2018. *Booking.com.* Available at: https://globalnews.booking.com/where-sustainable-travel-is-headed-in-2018/ (Accessed 27 September 2022).

Boorstin, D. (1964) *The Image: A Guide to Pseudo-Events in America.* New York: Harper & Row.

Boretti, A. and Rosa, L. (2019) Reassessing the projections of the World Water Development Report. *npj Clean Water*, 2(15). https://doi.org/10.1038/s41545-019-0039-9

Bourdeau, P. and Berthelot, L. (2008) Tourisme et décroissance: De la critique à l'utopie? In F. Flipo and F. Schneider (Eds), *Proceedings of the First International Conference on Economic De-Growth for Ecological Sustainability and Social Equity*, Paris, 18–19 April. Paris: Research & Degrowth, pp. 78–85.

Bourdieu, P. (1991) *Language and Symbolic Power.* Cambridge: Polity Press.

Bowen, J. (2019) *Low-cost Carriers in Emerging Countries.* Cambridge, MA: Elsevier.

Bramwell, B., Higham, J., Lane, B. and Miller, G. (2017) Twenty-five years of sustainable tourism and the *Journal of Sustainable Tourism*: Looking back and moving forward. *Journal of Sustainable Tourism*, 25(1), 1–9.

Bramwell, B. and Lane, B. (1993) Sustainable tourism: An evolving global approach. *Journal of Sustainable Tourism*, 1(1), 1–5.

Briassoulis, H. and van der Straaten, J. (Eds) (1992) *Tourism and the Environment: Regional, Economic and Policy Issues.* Amsterdam: Kluwer Academic Publishers.

British Airways (2022) *Planet: Protecting our Natural Environment.* Available at: https://www.britishairways.com/en-gb/information/about-ba/ba-better-world/planet

Britton, S. (1982) The political economy of tourism in the Third World. *Annals of Tourism Research*, 9(3), 331–358.

Britton, S. (1991) Tourism, capital, and place: Towards a critical geography of tourism. *Environment and Planning D: Society and Space*, 9, 451–278.

Brohman, J. (1996) New directions in tourism for third world development. *Annals of Tourism Research*, 23(1), 48–70.

Brooks, E. (2021) Lithium extraction environmental impact. *Eco-jungle*, 31 December. Available at: https://ecojungle.net/post/lithium-extraction-environmental-impact/ (Accessed 8 July 2022).

Brown, F. (1998) *Tourism Reassessed: Blight or Blessing?* Oxford: Butterworth Heinemann.

Bryden, J. (1973) *Tourism and Development: A Case Study of the Commonwealth Caribbean.* London: Cambridge University Press.

Büchs, M. and Koch, M. (2017) *Postgrowth and Wellbeing Challenges to Sustainable Welfare.* Cham: Palgrave Macmillan.

Büchs, M. and Koch, M. (2019) Challenges for the degrowth transition: The debate about wellbeing. *Futures*, 105(2019), 155–165.

Buckley, R. (2012) Sustainable tourism: Research and reality. *Annals of Tourism Research*, 39(2), 528–546.

Buhalis, D. and Law, R. (2008) Progress in information technology and tourism management: 20 years on and 10 years after the Internet – The state of eTourism research. *Progress in Tourism Management*, 29(2008), 609–623.

Buhalis, D. and Sinarta, Y. (2019) Real-time co-creation and nowness service: Lessons from tourism and hospitality. *Journal of Travel & Tourism Marketing*, 36(5), 536–582.

Burns, P. (1999) Paradoxes in planning tourism: Elitism or brutalism? *Annals of Tourism Research*, 26(2), 329–348.

Büscher, B. and Fletcher, R. (2017) Destructive creation: Capital accumulation and the structural violence of tourism. *Journal of Sustainable Tourism*, 25(5), 651–667.

Büscher, B. and Fletcher, R. (2019) Towards convivial conservation. *Conservation and Society*, 17(3), 283–296.

Business Research Company (2022) Ecotourism global market sees growth rate of 18% through 2022. *Business Research Company, Press Release*, 11 August. Available at: https://www.thebusinessresearchcompany.com/press-release/ecotourism-market-2022

Butcher, J. (2003) *The Moralisation of Tourism Sun, Sand... and Saving the World?* London: Routledge.

Butcher, J. (2021a) Debating tourism degrowth post COVID-19. *Annals of Tourism Research*, 89, 103250. https://doi.org/10.1016/j.annals.2021.103250

Butcher, J. (2021b) Covid-19, tourism and the advocacy of degrowth. *Tourism Recreation Research*. https://doi.org/10.1080/02508281.2021.1953306

Butcher, J. (2022) Degrowth. In D. Buhalis (Ed.), *Encyclopaedia of Tourism Management and Marketing*. ElgarOnline, pp. 809–811. https://doi.org/10.4337/9781800377486.degrowth

Butler, R. (1980) The concept of a tourist area cycle of evolution. *Canadian Geographer*, 24(1), 5–12.

Butler, R. (1990) Alternative tourism: Pious hope or Trojan horse? *Journal of Travel Research*, 28(3), 40–45.

Butler, R. (2018) Sustainable tourism in sensitive environments: A wolf in sheep's clothing? *Sustainability*, 10(6). https://doi.org/10.3390/su10061789

Butler, R. (2020) How much rainforest is being destroyed? *Mongabay,* 10 June. Available at: https://news.mongabay.com/2020/06/how-much-rainforest-is-being-destroyed/ (Accessed 18 July 2022).

CABI (2022) Growth in ecotourism may harm wildlife. CABI News Article. Available at: https://www.cabi.org/leisuretourism/news/5438

Cakar, K. and Uzut, I. (2020) Exploring the stakeholder's role in sustainable degrowth within the context of tourist destination governance: The case of Istanbul, Turkey. *Journal of Travel and Tourism Marketing*, 37(8–9), 917–932.

Campos, A., Mendes, J., Valle, P. and Scott, N. (2018) Co-creation of tourist experiences: A literature review. *Current Issues in Tourism*, 21(4), 369–400.

Cañada, E. (2021) Community-based tourism in a degrowth perspective. In K. Andriotis (Ed.), *Issues and Cases of Degrowth in Tourism*. Wallingford: CABI, pp. 42–64.

Canavan, B. (2021) Pushed over the periphery: Downsides of degrowth on a small island – experiences of tourism degrowth on the Isle of Man. In K. Andriotis (Ed.), *Issues and Cases of Degrowth in Tourism*. Wallingford: CABI, pp. 145–159.

Canon, G. (2022) Record Death Valley flooding 'a once-in-1,000-year event'. *The Guardian*, 10 August. Available at: https://www.theguardian.com/us-news/2022/aug/10/death-valley-floods-climate-crisis

CarbonBrief (2018) Tourism responsible for 8% of global greenhouse gas emissions, study finds. Available at: https://www.carbonbrief.org/tourism-responsible-for-8-of-global-greenhouse-gas-emissions-study-finds/ (Accessed 9 June 2022).

Cardoso, J. and Lange, C. (2007) A framework for assessing strategies and technologies for dynamic packaging applications in e-tourism. *Information Technology & Tourism*, 9(1), 27–44.

Caribbean Tourism Organisation (2022) Home. https://www.onecaribbean.org/

Carnival (2022) *Carnival Corporation & PLC Sustainable from Ship to Shore 2021, Sustainability Report*. Available at: https://carnival-sustainability-2022.nyc3.digitaloceanspaces.com/assets/content/pdf/FY-2021-Sustainability-Report_Carnival-Corporation-and-plc.pdf (Accessed 23 August 2022).

Carrascosa-López, C., Carvache-Franco, M., Mondéjar-Jiménez, J. and Carvache-Franco, W. (2021) Understanding motivations and segmentation in ecotourism destinations. Application to natural parks in Spanish Mediterranean area. *Sustainability*, 13(9). https://doi.org/10.3390/su13094802

Carrillo-Hidalgo, I. and Pulido-Fernández, J. (2019) The role of the World Bank in the inclusive financing of tourism as an instrument of sustainable development. *Sustainability*, 12(1). https://doi.org/10.3390/su12010285

Carson, D. A. and Carson, D. B. (2020) Opportunities and barriers for degrowth in remote tourism destinations: Overcoming regional inequalities. In C. M. Hall, L. Lundmark and J. Zhang (Eds), *Degrowth and Tourism: New Perspectives on Tourism Entrepreneurship, Destinations and Policy*. Abingdon: Routledge, pp. 100–115.

Carson, R. (1962) *Silent Spring*. New York: Houghton Mifflin.

Caruana, R. and Crane, A. (2011) Getting away from it all: Exploring freedom in tourism. *Annals of Tourism Research*, 38(4), 1495–1515.

Carvao, S. (2021) *Destination Management and Operations for Increased Domestic Tourism*. Keynote Presentation. Available at: https://webunwto.s3.eu-west-1.amazonaws.com/s3fs-public/2021-10/Keynote%20Presentation_Sandra%20Carvao_UNWTO_Domestic%20tourism_Executive_training%20programme_reduced%20size_0.pdf?YEvLysdYfaHq2H9g1Y4vb2Pko8eeR7fA=#:~:text=An%20estimated%209%20billion%20domestic,in%20number%20of%20tourist%20trips. (Accessed 26 September 2022).

Carver, R. (2020) Lessons for blue degrowth from Namibia's emerging blue economy. *Sustainability Science*, 15(1), 131–143.

CASSE (2021) *Definition of Steady State Economy*. Center for the Advancement of Steady State Economy. Available at: https://steadystate.org/discover/definition-of-steady-state-economy/ (Accessed 1 March 2022).

Cassey, D. (2022) Greenland eyes tourists from North America and Europe. *Routes*, 18 January, Available at: https://www.routesonline.com/news/29/breaking-news/297388/greenland-eyes-tourists-from-north-america-and-europe-/#:~:text=In%20addition%2C%20a%20new%20airport,a%20new%201%2C500%2Dm%20runway (Accessed 17 August 2022).

Cater, E. (2006) Ecotourism as a western construct. *Journal of Ecotourism*, 5(1–2), 23–39.

Ceballos, G., Ehrlich, P. and Raven, P. (2020) Vertebrates on the brink as indicators of biological annihilation and the sixth mass extinction. *Proceedings of the National Academy of Sciences*, 117(24), 13596–13602.

Celata, F. and Romano, A. (2022) Overtourism and online short-term rental platforms in Italian cities. *Journal of Sustainable Tourism*, 30(5), 1020–1039.

Chambers, R. (2006) What is poverty? Who asks? Who answers? International Poverty Centre Poverty in Focus, 3–4 December. Available at: https://opendocs.ids.ac.uk/

opendocs/bitstream/handle/20.500.12413/120/rc145.pdf?sequence=2 (Accessed 8 November 2022).

Chandler, N. (2020) What is the Butterfly Effect and how do we misunderstand it? *Howstuffworks*. Available at: https://science.howstuffworks.com/math-concepts/butterfly-effect.htm

Chassagne, N. and Everingham, P. (2019) Buen Vivir: Degrowing extractivism and growing wellbeing through tourism. *Journal of Sustainable Tourism*, 27(12), 1909–1925.

Chen, C., Su, C. and Chen, M. (2022) Are ES-committed hotels financially resilient to the COVID-19 pandemic? An autoregressive jump intensity model. *Tourism Management*, 93(2022). https://doi.org/10.1016/j.tourman.2022.104581

Cheung, K. S. and Li, L. H. (2019) Understanding visitor–resident relations in overtourism: Developing resilience for sustainable tourism. *Journal of Sustainable Tourism*, 27(8), 1197–1216.

Chon, K. (2019) *Hospitality in Asia: A New Paradigm*. Abingdon: Routledge.

Chon, K., Park, E. and Zoltan, J. (2020) The Asian paradigm in hospitality and tourism. *Journal of Hospitality & Tourism Research*, 44(8), 1183–1202.

Christou, P. (2022) *The History and Evolution of Tourism*. Wallingford: CABI.

Clancy, M. (1999) Tourism and development: Evidence from Mexico. *Annals of Tourism Research,* 26(1), 1–20.

Clancy, M. (2001) *Exporting Paradise: Tourism Development in Mexico*. Bingley: Emerald Group Publishing Limited.

Clancy, M. (2019) Overtourism and resistance: Today's anti-tourist movement in context. In H. Pechlaner, E. Innerhofer and G. Erschbamer (Eds), *Overtourism: Tourism Management and Solutions.* Abingdon: Routledge, pp. 14–24.

CoastAdapt (2017) Ocean acidification and its effects. *CoastAdapt,* 27 April. Available at: https://coastadapt.com.au/ocean-acidification-and-its-effects

Cohen, E. (1972) Towards a sociology of international tourism. *Social Research*, 39(1), 64–82.

Cohen, E. (1979) A phenomenology of tourist experiences. *Sociology*, 13, 179–201.

Cohen, E. (1987) Alternative tourism – A critique. *Tourism Recreation Research*, 12(2), 13–18.

Coles, T., Fenclova, E. and Dinan, C. (2013) Tourism and corporate social responsibility: A critical review and research agenda. *Tourism Management Perspectives*, 6 (2013), 122–141.

Collingridge, N. (2022) 10 destinations you should not visit in 2023, according to travel experts. *Travel off Path*, 5 November. Available at: https://www.traveloffpath.com/10-destinations-you-should-not-visit-in-2023-according-to-travel-experts/ (Accessed 13 December 2022).

Crick, M. (1989) Representations of international tourism in the social sciences. *Annual Review of Anthropology*, 18, 307–344.

Croall, J. (1995) *Preserve or Destroy: Tourism and the Environment*. London: Calouste Gulbenkian Foundation.

Cronin, L. (1990) A strategy for tourism and sustainable developments. *World Leisure and Recreation*, 32(3), 12–18.

Cronin, M. (2012) *The Expanding World Towards a Politics of Microspection*. Winchester: Zero Books.

Cruise Industry News (2022a) 32 new ships set to cruise in 2022. *Cruise Industry News*, 3 January, Available at: https://www.cruiseindustrynews.com/cruise-news/26487-32-new-ships-set-to-cruise-in-2022.html (Accessed 24 August 2022).

Cruise Industry News (2022b) *Cruise Industry News 2022 Market Report: Fastest Growing Market Segments.* Available at: https://www.cruiseindustrynews. com/cruise-news/27484-cruise-industry-news-2022-market-report-fastest-gro wing-market-segments.html (Accessed 24 August 2022).

Cruise Lines International (2021) *2021 State of the Cruise Industry Outlook.* Available at: https://cruising.org/-/media/research-updates/research/2021-state-o f-the-cruise-industry_optimized.ashx (Accessed 24 August 2022).

Cukier, J. (2002) Tourism employment issues in developing countries: Examples from Indonesia. In R. Sharpley and D. J. Telfer (Eds), *Tourism and Development: Concepts and Issues.* Clevedon: Channel View Publications, pp. 165–201.

Culler, J. (1981) Semiotics of tourism. *American Journal of Semiotics,* 1(1–2), 127–140.

Daldeniz, B. and Hampton, M. (2010) *Charity-based Voluntourism versus Lifestyle Voluntourism: Evidence from Nicaragua and Malaysia* (Working paper 211). University of Kent: Kent Business School.

Daly, H. (1972) In defense of a steady-state economy. *American Journal of Agricultural Economics,* 54(5), 945–954.

Daly, H. (1990) Sustainable growth: A bad oxymoron. *Journal of Environmental Science & Health Part C,* 8(2), 401–407.

Daly, H. (1991) *Steady-State Economics,* 2nd Edn. Washington, DC: Island Press.

Daly, H. (1996) *Beyond Growth: The Economics of Sustainable Development.* Boston, MA: Beacon Press.

Dann, G. (1977) Anomie, ego-enhancement and tourism. *Annals of Tourism Research,* 4(4), 184–194.

Dann, G. (1981) Tourist motivation: An appraisal. *Annals of Tourism Research,* 8(2), 187–219.

Dann, G. and Parrinello, G. (2007) Setting the scene. In G. Dann and G. Parrinello (Eds), *The Sociology of Tourism: European Origins and Developments.* Bingley: Emerald, pp. 1–63.

Davis, H. (1968) Potentials for tourism in developing countries. *Finance & Development,* 5(4), 34–39.

Davis, D. (1978) Development and the tourist industry in third world countries. *Society and Leisure,* 1, 301–322.

de Kadt, E. (1979) *Tourism: Passport to Development?* New York: Oxford University Press.

de la Dehesa, G. (2007) *Winners and Losers in Globalization.* Oxford: Blackwell Publishing.

Demaria, F. and Latouche, S. (2019) Degrowth. In A. Kothari, A. Salleh, A. Escobar, F. Demaria and A. Acosta (Eds), *Pluriverse: A Post-Development Dictionary.* New Delhi: Tulika Books, pp. 148–151.

Demaria, F., Schneider, F., Sekulova, F. and Martinez-Alier, J. (2013) What is degrowth? From an activist slogan to a social movement. *Environmental Values,* 22(2), 191–215.

Denchak, M. (2022) Water Pollution: Everything You Need to Know. Natural Resources Defense Council. Available at: https://www.nrdc.org/stories/wate r-pollution-everything-you-need-know

Dernbach, J. C. and Cheever, F. (2015) Sustainable development and its discontents. *Transnational Environmental Law,* 4(2), 247–287.

Desai, V. and Potter, R. (2002) The nature of development and development studies. In V. Desai and R. Potter (Eds), *The Companion to Development Studies*. New York: Oxford University Press, pp. 45–49.

Desai, V. and Potter, R. (2013) *The Companion to Development Studies*, 2nd Edn. Abingdon: Routledge.

Deutch, J. (2020) Is net zero carbon 2025 possible? *Joule*, 4, 2237–2243.

DoT (2014) Public experiences of and attitudes towards air travel: 2014. Department of Transport. Available at: https://www.gov.uk/government/statistics/public-experiences-of-and-attitudes-towards-air-travel-2014 (Accessed 18 March 2022).

Dredge, D. (2017) Social entrepreneurship and tourism. In P. Sheldon and R. Daniele (Eds), *Social Entrepreneurship and Tourism: Philosophy and Practice*. Cham: Springer International Publishing, pp. 35–55.

Dredge, D. (2022) Regenerative tourism: Transforming mindsets, systems and practices. *Journal of Tourism Futures*, 8(3), 269–281.

Dresner, S. (2002) *The Principles of Sustainability*. London: Earthscan Publications.

Dube, K., Nhamo, G. and Chikodzi, D. (2020) Climate change-induced droughts and tourism: Impacts and responses of Western Cape province, South Africa. *Journal of Outdoor Recreation and Tourism*, 39. https://doi.org/10.1016/j.jort.2020.100319

Dunk, R., Gillespie, S. and MacLeod, D. (2016) Participation and retentions in a green tourism certification scheme. *Journal of Sustainable Tourism*, 24(12), 1585–1603.

Dunne, D. (2021) Cruise-goers unaware of 'harmful' impact of unregulated industry on marine life and human health. *The Independent*, 29 September. Available at: https://www.independent.co.uk/climate-change/news/cruise-ships-climate-health-impacts-b1928659.html (Accessed 6 September 2022).

Durán-Román, J., Cárdenas-García, P. and Pulido-Fernández, J. (2021) Tourists' willingness to pay to improve sustainability and experience at destination. *Journal of Destination Marketing & Management*, 19. https://doi.org/10.1016/j.jdmm.2020.100540

Dyke, J., Watson, R. and Knorr, W. (2021) Climate scientists: Concept of net zero is a dangerous trap. *The Conversation*, 22 April. Available at: https://theconversation.com/climate-scientists-concept-of-net-zero-is-a-dangerous-trap-157368 (Accessed 28 January 2022).

Eagleton, T. (1992) *The Illusion of Postmodernism*. Oxford: Wiley-Blackwell.

Earth.org (2022) *13 Biggest Environmental Problems of 2022*. Available at: https://earth.org/the-biggest-environmental-problems-of-our-lifetime/

Earth Overshoot Day (2022) How many Earths? How many countries? Available at: https://www.overshootday.org/how-many-earths-or-countries-do-we-need/ (Accessed 4 July 2022).

Ehrlich, P. (1968) *The Population Bomb*. New York: Ballantine Books.

Eimermann, M., Lindgren, U., Lundmark, L. and Zhang, J. (2020) Mobility transitions and rural restructuring in Sweden. In C. M. Hall, L. Lundmark and J. Zhang (Eds), *Degrowth and Tourism: New Perspectives on Tourism Entrepreneurship, Destinations and Policy*. Abingdon: Routledge, pp. 54–68.

Ekpo, A. (2016) Growth without development in West Africa: Is it a paradox? In D. Seck (Ed.), *Accelerated Economic Growth in West Africa. Advances in Economic, Social and Political Development*. Springer, pp. 37–51.

Emelike, O. (2020) Indigenous African hotel brands are truly taking centre stage, *Business Today*, 7 February. Available at: https://businessday.ng/arts-and-life/article/indigenous-african-hotel-brands-are-truly-taking-centre-stage/ (Accessed 19 August 2022).

Enzensberger, H. M. (1996) A theory of tourism. *New German Critique*, (68), 117–135.

EOD (2021) *How Many Earths; How Many Countries?* Earth Overshoot day. Available at: https://www.overshootday.org/how-many-earths-or-countries-do-we-need/ (Accessed 4 November 2021).

Erisman, H. (1983) Tourism and cultural dependency in the West Indies. *Annals of Tourism Research*, 10(3), 337-361.

Ertör, I. and Hadjimichael, M. (2022) Editorial: Blue degrowth and the politics of the sea: Rethinking the blue economy. *Sustainability Science*, 15(2020), 1–10.

Escobar, A. (2015) Degrowth, postdevelopment and transitions: A preliminary conversation. *Sustainability Science*, 10(3), 451–462.

Escobar, A. (2018) *Designs for the Pluriverse: Radical Interdependence, Autonomy, and the Making of Worlds*. Durham: Duke University Press.

EU (2020) *Transition Pathway for Tourism. Brussels: European Union*. Available at: https://op.europa.eu/en/publication-detail/-/publication/404a8144–8892–11ec-8c40–01aa75ed71a1 (Accessed 25 August 2022).

Eugenio-Martin, J. and Perez-Granja, U. (2021) Have low-cost carrriers crowded out full service and charter carriers in tourism destinations? A Trivariate structural time series. *Journal of Travel Research*, 60(4), 810–832.

European Commission (n.d.) *Developments and Forecasts of Growing Consumerism*. Competence Centre on Foresight. Available at: https://knowledge4policy.ec.europa.eu/foresight/topic/growing-consumerism/more-developments-relevant-growing-consumerism_en (Accessed 2 November 2021).

Eurostat (2018) *Tourism Industries – Employment*. Available at: https://ec.europa.eu/eurostat/statistics-explained/index.php?title=Tourism_industries_-_employment (Accessed 21 April 2022).

Everingham, P. and Chassagne, N. (2020) Post COVID-19 ecological and social reset: Moving away from capitalist growth models towards tourism as Buen Vivir. *Tourism Geographies*. https//:doi:10.1080/14616688.2020.1762119

FAO (2017) *The State of Food Security and Nutrition in the World*. UN Food and Agriculture Organisation. Available at: https://www.fao.org/3/I7695e/I7695e.pdf

FAO, IFAD, UNICEF, WFP and WHO (2022) *The State of Food Security and Nutrition in the World: Repurposing food and agriculture policies to make healthy diets more affordable*. Rome: FAO. https://doi.org/10.4060/cc0639en

Featherstone, M. (1991) *Consumer Culture and Postmodernism*. London: Sage Publications.

Feifer, M. (1985) *Going Places*. London: Macmillan.

Fennell, D. (2007) *Ecotourism*, 3rd Edn. London: Routledge.

Feola, G. and Jaworska, S. (2019) One transition, many transitions? A corpus-based study of societal sustainability transition discourses in four civil society's proposals. *Sustainability Science*, 14(2019), 1643–1656.

Fitchett, J., Lindberg, F. and Martin, D. (2021) Accumulation by symbolic dispossession: Tourism development in advanced capitalism. *Annals of Tourism Research*, 86(2021). https://doi.org/10.1016/j.annals.2020.103072

Fitzpatrick, N., Parrique, T. and Cosme, I. (2022) Exploring degrowth policy proposals: A systematic mapping with thematic synthesis. *Journal of Cleaner Production*, 365(10), 132764. https://doi.org/10.1016/j.jclepro.2022.132764

Fletcher, R. (2011) Sustaining tourism, sustaining capitalism? The tourism industry's role in global capitalist expansion. *Tourism Geographies,* 13(3), 443–461.

Fletcher, R. (2019) Ecotourism after nature: Anthropocene tourism as a new capitalist 'fix', *Journal of Sustainable Tourism*, 27(4), 522–535.

Fletcher, R., Blanco-Romero, A., Blázquez-Salom, M., Murray Mas, I. and Sekulova, F. (2021a) Pathways to post-capitalist tourism. *Tourism Geographies*. https//:doi/org /10.1080/14616688.2021.1965202

Fletcher, R., Blanco-Romero, A., Blázquez-Salom, M., Cañada, E., Murray Mas, I. and Sekulova, F. (2021b) Post-capitalist tourism in a post-COVID-19 world. In F. Higgins-Desbiolles, A. Doering and B. Chewy (Eds), *Socialising Tourism: Rethinking Tourism for Social and Ecological Justice*. New York: Routledge, pp. 229–243.

Fletcher, R., Murray Mas, I., Blanco-Romero, A. and Blázquez-Salom, M. (2019) Tourism and degrowth: An emerging agenda for research and praxis. *Journal of Sustainable Tourism*, 27(12), 1745–1763.

Fletcher, R., Murray Mas, I., Blanco-Romero, A. and Blázquez-Salom, M. (Eds) (2020) *Tourism and Degrowth: Towards a Truly Sustainable Tourism*. Abingdon: Routledge.

Flightradar24 (2022) Flightradar24's 2019 by the numbers. Available at: https:// www.flightradar24.com/blog/flightradar24s-2019-by-the-numbers/#:~:- text=2019%20flight%20tracking%20by%20the%20numbers&text=Averag- ing%20188%2C901%20flights%20per%20day,when%20we%20tracked%20 230%2C409%20flights (Accessed 22 August 2022).

Fonranari, M., Traskevich, A. and Seraphin, H. (2021) (De)growth imperative: The importance of destination resilience in the context of overtoursim. In K. Andriotis (Ed.), *Issues and Cases of Degrowth in Tourism*. Wallingford: CABI, pp. 22–41.

Fox, J. (2019) 3 reasons why hotels are adding LEDs to lighting designs. *Hotel Management,* 9 September. Available at: https://www.hotelmanagement.net/desi gn/3-reasons-why-hotels-are-adding-leds-to-lighting-design (Accessed 23 August 2022).

Frank, A. (1966) The development of underdevelopment. *Monthly Review*, 18(4). Reprinted In C. Wilber (Ed.) (1988) *The Political Economy of Development and Underdevelopment*, 4th Edn. Toronto: McGraw-Hill Publishing Company, pp. 109–120.

Free Dictionary (n.d.) Paradigm. Available at: https://www.thefreedictionary.com/ paradigm (Accessed 6 May 2022).

Freeland, C. (2012) *Plutocrats: The Rise of the New Global Super-Rich and the Fall of Everyone Else*. Toronto: Anchor Canada.

Friedman, T. (2005) *The World is Flat. A Brief History of the Twenty-first Century*. New York: Farrar, Straus and Giroux.

Fukuyama, F. (1992) *The End of History and the Last Man*. London: Free Press.

Fukuyama, F. (2022) *Liberalism and its Discontents*. New York: Farrar, Straus and Giroux.

Galbraith, J. K. (1958) *The Affluent Society*. New York: Houghton Mifflin.

Galtung, J. (1986) Towards a new economics: On the theory and practice of self-reliance. In P. Ekins (Ed.), *The Living Economy: A New Economy in the Making*. London: Routledge, pp. 97–109.

Garay, E. (2022) How short-haul flight bans are transforming European travel. *Condé Nast Traveler*, 6 January. Available at: https://www.cntraveler.com/story/how-shor t-haul-flight-bans-are-transforming-european-travel (Accessed 23 August 2022).

Garcia, C., Deyà-Tortella, B., Lorenzo-Lacruz, J., Morán-Tejeda, E., Rodríguez-Lozano, P and Tirado, D. (2022) Zero tourism due to COVID-19: An opportunity to assess water consumption associated to tourism. *Journal of Sustainable Tourism*, DOI: 10.1080/09669582.2022.2079652

Gascón, J. (2019) Tourism as a right: A 'frivolous claim' against degrowth? *Journal of Sustainable Tourism*. 27(12), 1825–1838.

Georgescu-Roegen, N. (1971) *The Entropy Law and the Economic Process*. Cambridge, MA: Harvard University Press.

Georgescu-Roegen, N. (1994) *La Décroissance: entropie, écologie, économie*. (I. Rens & J. Grinevald (Eds) Paris: Sang de la Terre.

Gerszon, D., Yonzan, N., Hill, R., Lakner, C. Wu, H. and Yoshida, N. (2022) Pandemic, prices and poverty. World Bank Blogs. Available at: https://blogs.worldbank.org/opendata/pandemic-prices-and-poverty

GFN (2021a) *Ecological Footprint*. Global Footprint Network. Available at: https://www.footprintnetwork.org/our-work/ecological-footprint/ (Accessed 4 November 2021).

GFN (2021b) *Press Releases*. Global Footprint Network. Available at: https://www.footprintnetwork.org/category/press-releases/ (Accessed 4 November 2021).

Ghemawat, P. (2017) Globalization in the age of Trump. *Harvard Business Review* (July/August). https://hbr.org/2017/07/globalization-in-the-age-of-trump

Ghemawat, P. (2018) *The New Global Road Map: Enduring Strategies for Turbulent Times*. Boston: Harvard Business Review.

Ghilarducci, T. (2022) Money-losing Airbnb hosts have three options. *Washington Post*, 28 October. Available at: https://www.washingtonpost.com/business/money-losing-airbnb-hosts-have-three-options/2022/10/28/9fe9bd18-56c9-11ed-ac8b-08bbfab1c5a5_story.html (Accessed 26 October 2022).

Ghosh, B. (Ed.) (2001) *Dependency Theory Revisited*. London: Routledge.

Gilchrist, K. (2021) Travelers care deeply about sustainability – until it inconveniences them. *CNBC*, 18 June. Available at: https://www.cnbc.com/2021/06/18/sustainable-travel-travelers-care-but-few-want-to-pay-for-it-.html (Accessed 26 August 2022).

Gill, A. (2000) From growth machine to growth management: The dynamics of resort development in Whistler, British Columbia. *Environment and Planning A: Economy and Space*, 32(6), 1083–1130.

GlobalData Thematic Research (2021) *Personalisation in Travel and Tourism: Company Trends*. 21 May. Available at: https://www.hotelmanagement-network.com/comment/personalisation-travel-tourism-company-trends/ (Accessed 17 August 2022).

Goldsworthy, D. (1988) Thinking politically about development. *Development and Change*, 19(3), 505–530.

Gonzaler, V. and Espelt, N. (2021) How do degrowth values in tourism influence the host–guest exchange? An exploratory analysis in small towns in the rurality. *Journal of Tourism and Cultural Change*, 19(6), 884–903.

Goodwin, H. (2016) *Responsible Tourism: Using Tourism for Sustainable Development*, 2nd Edn. Oxford: Goodfellow Publishers.

Gorz, A. (1977) *Ecology as Politics*. Montréal: Black Rosa Books.

Gorz, A. (1991) (2012) *Capitalism, Socialism, Ecology*. London: Verso.

Gössling, S. (2002) Global environmental consequences of tourism. *Global Environmental Change*, 12(4), 283–302.

Gössling, S. (2006) Tourism and water. In S. Gössling and C.M. Hall (Eds), *Tourism and Global Environmental Change*. London: Routledge, pp. 180–194.

Gössling, S. (2013) National emissions from tourism: An overlooked policy challenge? *Energy Policy*, 59, 433–442.

Gössling, S., Hall, C. M. and Scott, D. (2015) *Tourism and Water*. Bristol: Channel View Publications.

Gössling, S. and Higham, J. (2021) The low-carbon imperative: Destination management under urgent climate change. *Journal of Travel Research*, 60(6), 1167–1179.

Gössling, S. and Humpe, A. (2020) The global scale, distribution and growth of aviation: Implications for climate change. *Global Environmental Change*, 65. https://doi.
org/10.1016/j.gloenvcha.2020.102194

Gössling, S. and Peeters, P. (2015) Assessing tourism's global environmental impact
1900–2050. *Journal of Sustainable Tourism*, 23(5), 639–659.

Gössling, S., Peeters, P., Hall, C. M., Ceron, J. P., Dubois, G. and Scott, D. (2012)
Tourism and water use: Supply, demand, and security. An international review.
Tourism Management, 33(1), 1–15.

Gottlieb, A. (1982) Americans' vacations. *Annals of Tourism Research*, 9(2), 165–187.

Government of Canada (2019) *Creating Middle Class Jobs: A Federal Tourism Growth
Strategy*. Ottawa: Government of Canada. Available at: https://ised-isde.canada.ca/
site/canadian-tourism-sector/sites/default/files/attachments/Tourism_Strategy_eng_
v8.pdf (Accessed 25 August 2022).

Graburn, N. (2001) Secular ritual: A general theory of tourism. In V. Smith and M.
Brent (Eds), *Hosts and Guests Revisited: Tourism Issues of the 21st Century*. New
York: Cognizant Communication Corporation, pp. 42–43.

Gravari-Barbas, M. (2020) Heritage and tourism: From opposition to coproduction. In
M. Gravari-Barbas (Ed.), *A Research Agenda for Heritage Tourism*. Cheltenham,
UK and Northampton, MA, USA: Edward Elgar Publishing. pp. 1–14.

Greenpeace (2021) *Get on Track: Train Alternatives to Short-Haul Flights in
Europe*. Greenpeace European Unit. Available at: https://www.greenpeace.org/
static/planet4-eu-unit-stateless/2021/10/135ec803-getontrack-gp-briefing-en-final.
pdf (Accessed 22 August 2022).

Grefe, G. and Peyrat-Guillard, D. (Eds) (2020) *Shapes of Tourism Employment: HRM
in the Worlds of Hotels and Air Transport, Volume 4*. Hoboken, NJ: Wiley.

Greshko, M. (2022) Scientists achieve a breakthrough in nuclear fusion. Here's what
it means. *National Geographic*, 13 December, Available at: https://www.nation-
algeographic.com/science/article/scientists-achieve-breakthrough-nuclear-fusion
(Accessed 15 December 2022).

Gretzel, U. and Fesenmaier, D. (2009) Information technology: Shaping the past,
present and future of tourism. In T. Jamal and M. Robinson (Eds), *The Sage
Handbook of Tourism Studies*. London: Sage Publications, pp. 558–580.

Gross, J. (2022) 4-Day workweek brings no loss of productivity in experiment. *The New York Times*, 22 September, Available at: https://www.nytimes.
com/2022/09/22/business/four-day-work-week-uk.html#:~:text=the%20
main%20story-,4%2DDay%20Workweek%20Brings%20No%20Loss%20of%20
Productivity%2C%20Companies%20in,companies%20say%20it's%20going%2-
0well (Accessed 21 November 2022).

Gullett, W. (2021) Virus-laden ships. In B. Stanford, S. Foster and C. Berdud (Eds),
Global Pandemic, Security and Human Rights. Abingdon: Routledge, pp. 194–211.

Gupta, A., Dash, S. and Mishra, A. (2019) All that glitters is not green: Creating
trustworthy ecofriendly services at green hotels. *Tourism Management*, 70(2019),
155–169.

Gürsoy, I. (2020) Old kids on the new block: Engaging civil society in tourism
degrowth. *Almatourism*, 11(21). https://doi.org/10.6092/issn.2036-5195/10109

Guterres, A. (2022) Speech Delivered at COP 27 Summit, Sharm El Sheikh, Egypt.

Guttentag, D. (2015) Airbnb: Disruptive innovation and the rise of an informal tourism
accommodation sector. *Current Issues in Tourism*, 18(12), 1192–1217.

Hadjisolomou, A., Booyens, I., Nickson, D., Cunningham, T. and Baum, T. (2022) *Fair Work for All? A Review of Employment Practices in the Scottish Hospitality Industry.* University of Strathclyde Business School. Available at: https://www.sbs.strath.ac.uk/download/misc/fair-work.pdf (Accessed 14 December 2022).

Hall, C. M. (2009) Degrowing tourism: Décroissance, sustainable consumption and steady-state tourism. *Anatolia*, 26(1), 46–61.

Hall, C. M. (2011) Consumerism, tourism and voluntary simplicity: We all consume but do we really have to travel so much to be happy? *Tourism Recreation Research*, 36(3), 298–303.

Hall, C. M. (2013) Framing behavioural approaches to understanding and governing sustainable tourism consumption: Beyond neoliberalism, 'nudging' and 'green growth'? *Journal of Sustainable Tourism*, 21(7), 1091–1109.

Hall, C. M. (2019) Constructing sustainable tourism development: The 2030 agenda and the managerial ecology of sustainable tourism. *Journal of Sustainable Tourism*, 27(7), 1044–1060.

Hall, C. M. (2022) Tourism and the capitalocene: From green growth to ecocide. *Tourism Planning & Development*, 19(1), 61–74.

Hall, C. M., Lundmark, L. and Zhang, J. (Eds), (2020a) *Degrowth and Tourism: New Perspectives on Tourism Entrepreneurship, Destinations and Policy.* Abingdon: Routledge.

Hall, C. M., Lundmark, L. and Zhang, J. (2020b) Conclusions – degrowing tourism: Can tourism move beyond BAU (Brundtland-as-Usual). In C. M. Hall, L. Lundmark and J. Zhang (Eds), *Degrowth and Tourism: New Perspectives on Tourism Entrepreneurship, Destinations and Policy.* Abingdon: Routledge, pp. 239–248.

Hall, C. M., Scott, D. and Gössling, S. (2020) Pandemics, transformations and tourism: Be careful what you wish for. *Tourism Geographies*, 22(3), 577–598.

Hall, C. M. and Wood, K. (2021) Demarketing tourism for sustainability: Degrowing tourism or moving the deckchairs on the Titanic. *Sustainability*, 13, 1585. https://doi.org/10.3390/su13031585

Harari, Y. (2018) *21 Lessons for the 21st Century.* Oxford: Signal McClelland & Stewart.

Harrigan, J. and Mosley, P. (1991) Evaluating the impact of World Bank structural adjustment lending. *Journal of Development Studies*, 27(3), 63–94.

Harrison, D. (1988) *The Sociology of Modernization and Development.* London: Routledge.

Harrison, D. (Ed.) (1992) *Tourism and the Less Developed Countries.* London: Belhaven Press.

Harrison, D. (2008) Pro-poor tourism: A critique. *Third World Quarterly*, 29(5), 851–868.

Harrison, D. (2015) Development theory and tourism in developing countries: What has theory ever done for us? *International Journal of Asia Pacific Studies*, 11(S1), 53–82.

Harvey, D. (1990) *The Condition of Postmodernity.* Oxford: Blackwell.

Harvey, D. (2005) *The New Imperialism.* Oxford: Oxford University Press.

Harvey, D. (2013) *Rebel Cities: From the Right to the City to the Urban Revolution.* London: Verso.

Hashimoto, A., Härkönen, E. and Nkyi, E. (2021) *Human Rights Issues in Tourism.* Abingdon: Routledge/Earthscan.

Hashimoto, A., Telfer, D. and Telfer, S. (2021) Life beyond growth? Rural depopulation becoming the attraction in Nagoro, Japan's scarecrow village. *Journal of Heritage Tourism*, 16(5), 493–512.

Hawkins, D. and Mann, S. (2007) The World Bank's role in tourism development. *Annals of Tourism Research*, 34(2), 348–369.

Heidrich, P., (2021) Theories of development economics. In P. Haslam, J. Schafer and P. Beaudet (Eds), *Introduction to International Development*. Don Mills, ON: Oxford University Press, pp. 41–59.

Held, D. (2010). *Cosmopolitanism: Ideals and Realities*. Malden: Polity Press.

Henning, G. (2012) The habit of tourism: Experiences and their ontological meaning. In R. Sharpley and P. Stone (Eds), *Contemporary Tourist Experience: Concepts and Consequences*. Abingdon: Routledge, pp. 25–37.

Hettne, B. (1995) *Development Theory and the Three Worlds*, 2nd Edn. New York: Longman.

Hettne, B. (2009) *Thinking About Development*. London: Zed Books.

Hettne, B. (2010) Development beyond market-led globalization. *Development*, 53(1), 37–41.

Hickel, J. (2017) *The Divide: A Brief Guide to Global Inequality and its Solutions*. London: Windmill Books.

Hickel, J. (2020) *Less is More: How Degrowth Will Save the World*. London: Windmill Books.

Hickel, J. (2021) What does degrowth mean? A few points of clarification. *Globalisations*, 18(7), 1105–1111.

Hickel, J. and Kallis, G. (2020) Is green growth possible? *New Political Economy*, 25 (4), 469–486.

Higgins-Desbiolles, F. (2010) The elusiveness of sustainability in tourism: The culture-ideology of consumerism and its implications. *Tourism and Hospitality Research*, 10(2), 116–129.

Higgins-Desbiolles, F. (2018) Sustainable tourism: Sustaining tourism or something more? *Tourism Management Perspectives*, 25(2018), 157–160.

Higgins-Desbiolles, F. (2020) Socialising tourism for social and ecological justice after COVID-19. *Tourism Geographies*, 22(3), 610–623.

Higgins-Desbiolles, F. (2022) Subsidiarity in tourism and travel circuits in the face of climate crisis. *Current Issues in Tourism*. https//:doi/org/10.1080/13683500.2022.2116306

Higgins-Desbiolles, F. and Bigby, B. (2022) Introduction: Embracing the local turn in tourism to empower communities. In F. Higgins-Desbiolles and B. Bigby (Eds), *The Local Turn in Tourism: Empowering Communities*. Bristol: Channel View Publications, pp. 1–27.

Higgins-Desbiolles, F., Carnicelli, S., Krolikowski, C., Wijesinghe, G. and Boluk, K. (2019) Degrowing tourism: Rethinking tourism. *Journal of Sustainable Tourism*, 27(12), 1926–1944.

Higgins-Desbiolles, F. and Everingham, P. (2022) Degrowth in tourism: Advocacy for thriving not diminishment. *Tourism Recreation Research*, 1–5. https://doi.org/10.10 80/02508281.2022.2079841

Higgins-Desbiolles, Scheyvens, R. and Bhatia, B. (2022) Decolonising tourism and development: From orphanage tourism to community empowerment in Cambodia. *Journal of Sustainable Tourism*, https://doi.org/10.1080/09669582.2022.2039678

Higuchi, Y. and Yamanaka, Y. (2017) Knowledge sharing between academic researchers and tourism practitioners: A Japanese study of the practical value of embedded-
ness, trust and co-creation. *Journal of Sustainable Tourism*, 25(10), 1456–1473.

Hilton (2019*) Light-Stay – A Decade of Managing our Environmental and Social
Impact*. 26 August. Available at: https://stories.hilton.com/hilton-history/lightstay-
a-decade-of-managing-our-environmental-and-social-impact (Accessed 24 August
2022).

Hilton (2022) *Travel with Purpose*. Available at: https://esg.hilton.com/wp-content/
uploads/sites/3/2022/06/2021-ESG-Report-Highlights.pdf (Accessed 24 August
2022).

Hirsch, F. (1976) *Social Limits to Growth*. Cambridge, MA: Harvard University Press.

Hiss, T. (2021) Travel and the mind. In M. Niblett and K. Beuret (Eds), *Why Travel?
Understanding our Need to Move and How it Shapes our Lives*. Bristol: Bristol
University Press, pp. 33–54.

HNN Staff (2021) Hospitality workers march through Waikiki calling on hotels to
bring them back. *Hawaii News Now*, 29 October. Available at: https://www.hawaiin-
ewsnow.com/2021/10/29/hospitality-workers-march-through-waikiki-calling-hotels
-bring-them-back/ (Accessed 25 August 2022).

Holden, A. (2016) *Environment and Tourism,* 3rd Edn. Abingdon: Routledge.

Holden, A. and Fennell, D. (Eds) (2012) *Routledge Handbook of Tourism and the
Environment*. Abingdon: Routledge.

Honey, M. and Bray, S. (2019) Environmental 'footprint of the cruise industry. In
M. Honey (Ed.), *Cruise Tourism in the Caribbean Selling Sunshine*. Abingdon:
Routledge, pp. 32–51.

Hoskin, R. and McGrawth, M. (2022) Climate Change: World aviation agrees 'aspirational' net zero plan. *BBC News*, 7 October, Available at: https://www.bbc.com/
news/science-environment-63165607 (Accessed 29 August 2022).

Howie, F. (1990) Editorial: The conference and its theme: Sustainable tourism development. In F. Howie (Ed.), *Proceedings of the Sustainable Tourism Development
Conference*. Edinburgh: Queen Margaret College, pp. 3–4.

Høyer, K. (2000) Sustainable tourism or sustainable mobility? The Norwegian case.
Journal of Sustainable Tourism, 8(2), 147–160.

Huang, S. (2022) Tourist motivation: A critical review. In R. Sharpley (Ed.), *Routledge
Handbook of the Tourist Experience*. Abingdon: Routledge, pp. 200–211.

Hughes, N. (2018) 'Tourists go home': Anti-tourism industry protest in Barcelona.
Social Movement Studies, 17(4), 471–477.

Hughes, N. and Mansilla, J. (2021) Political discourse analysis of the degrowth challenge to dominant tourism narratives in Spain. In K. Andriotis (Ed.), *Issues and
Cases of Degrowth in Tourism*. Wallingford: CABI, pp. 86–103.

Hunter, C. (1995) On the need to re-conceptualise sustainable tourism development.
Journal of Sustainable Tourism, 3(3), 155–165.

IATA (2021) *Net-Zero Carbon Emissions by 2050*. Press Release No. 66, International
Air Transport Association, 4 October. Available at: https://www.iata.org/en/pressroo
m/2021-releases/2021-10-04-03/

IATA (2022) *Our Commitment to Fly Net Zero by 2050*. Available at: https://www.iata
.org/en/programs/environment/flynetzero/ (Accessed 29 August 2022).

ICAO (2022) *Effects of Novel Coronavirus (COVID-19) on Civil Aviation: Economic
Impact Analysis*. 12 August. Available at: https://www.icao.int/sustainability/
Documents/COVID-19/ICAO_Coronavirus_Econ_Impact.pdf (Accessed 29 August
2022).

IEA (2022) World air passenger traffic evolution, 1980–2020. *International Energy Agency*. Available at: https://www.iea.org/data-and-statistics/charts/world-air-passenger -traffic-evolution-1980-2020 (Accessed 9 June 2022).

IHG (2022) IHG Green Engage system. Available at: https://www.ihg.com/content/us/ en/about/green-engage (Accessed 24 August 2022).

Illich, I. (1973) *Tools for Conviviality*. London: Harper & Row Publishers.

Im, J., Chung, Y. and Qin, D. (2023) Exploring diversity, equity, and inclusion in hospitality and tourism firms through organizational justice and stakeholder theories. *Tourism Management*, 95(2023), 104662.

Inequality (2021) Global inequality. *Inequality.org*. Available at: https://inequality.org/ facts/global-inequality/#global-wealth-inequality (Accessed 26 November 2021).

Ingram, L., Slocum, S. and Cavaliere, C. (Eds) (2020) *Neolocalism and Tourism: Understanding a Global Movement*. Oxford: Goodfellow Publishers.

Inkson, C. and Minnaert, L. (2018) *Tourism Management: An Introduction*, 2nd Edn. London: Sage Publications.

International Finance Corporation (2021) IFC's Work in Tourism. Available at: https:// www.ifc.org/wps/wcm/connect/industry_ext_content/ifc_external_corporate_site/ trp/tourism/trp_priorities_tourism (Accessed 29 August 2022).

IPCC (2021) *Climate Change 2021: The Physical Science Basis*. International Panel on Climate Change. Available at: https://www.ipcc.ch/report/sixth-assessment-report -working-group-i/ (Accessed 1 March 2021).

IPCC (2022a) Sixth Assessment Report: Press Release, 28 February. *Intergovernmental Panel on Climate Change*. Available at: https://www.ipcc.ch/report/ar6/wg2/ resources/press/press-release/ (Accessed 1 March 2022).

IPCC (2022b) The evidence is clear: the time for action is now. We can halve emissions by 2030. *Intergovernmental Panel on Climate Change*, Press Release, 4 April. Available at: https://www.ipcc.ch/site/assets/uploads/2022/04/IPCC_AR6_WGIII _PressRelease_English.pdf (Accessed 13 July 2022).

IPCC (2022c) Summary for policymakers. Climate change 2022: Impacts, adaptation and vulnerability. *Intergovernmental Panel on Climate Change*. Available at: https://www.ipcc.ch/report/ar6/wg2/ (Accessed 21 December 2022).

Irannezhad, E. and Mahadevan, R. (2021) Is blockchain tourism's new hope? *Journal of Hospitality and Tourism Technology*, 12(1), 85–96.

IRENA (2021) *World Adds Record New Renewable Energy Capacity in 2020*. Press Release, International Renewable Energy Agency, 5 April. Available at: https://www.irena.org/newsroom/pressreleases/2021/Apr/World-Adds-Record-New -Renewable-Energy-Capacity-in-2020

Iso-Ahola, S. (1982) Toward a social psychological theory of tourism motivation: A rejoinder. *Annals of Tourism Research*, 9(2), 256–262.

ITAC (2020) *Forward Together: A Strategic Recovery Plan For The Indigenous Tourism Industry in Canada 2020–2024*. Available at: https://indigenoustourism .ca/wp-content/uploads/2020/06/ITAC-Strategic-Recovery-Plan-2020–24.pdf (Accessed 19 August 2022).

IUCN/UNEP/WWF ([1991] 2009) *Caring for the Earth: A Strategy for Sustainable Living*. London: Earthscan.

Ivan, O. (2017) 'We make more money now, but we don't talk to each other anymore': On new tourism and capitalism in the Danube Delta. *Journal of Tourism and Cultural Change*, 15(2), 122–135.

Jackson, T. (2008) *Prosperity Without Growth: Economics for a Finite Planet*. London: Earthscan.

Jackson, T. (2016) *Prosperity Without Growth: Foundations for the Economy of Tomorrow*, 2nd Edn. Abingdon: Routledge.

Jackson, T. (2021) *Post Growth: Life after Capitalism*. Cambridge: Polity Press.

Jacobs, H. (2018) *Dubai's Glittering, Futuristic Metropolis Came at the Cost of Hundreds of Thousands of Workers and Recommending it as a Tourist Destination Feels Wrong*. Insider 15 December. https://www.businessinsider.com/dubai-development-tourism-workers-problem-2018–12

Jafari, J. (1989) Sociocultural dimensions of tourism: An English language literature review. In J. Bystrzanowski (Ed.), *Tourism as a Factor of Change: A Sociocultural Study*. Vienna: Vienna Centre, pp. 17–60.

Jamal, T. (2019) *Justice and Ethics in Tourism*. Abingdon: Routledge.

Jary, D. and Jary, J. (1991) *Collins Dictionary of Sociology*. London: Harper Collins.

Jenkins, C. (1991) Tourism development strategies. In L. Lickorish (Ed.), *Developing Tourism Destinations*, Harlow: Longman, pp. 59–118.

Josephs, L. (2022) American Airlines regional carriers hike pilot pay more than 50% as shortage persists. *CNBC*, 13 June. Available at: https://www.cnbc.com/2022/06/13/american-airlines-regional-pilots-get-big-pay-hikes-as-competition-for-pilots-intensifies-.html

Jover, J. and Díaz-Parra, I. (2020) Gentrification, transnational gentrification and touristification in Seville, Spain. *Urban Studies*, 57(15), 3044–3059.

Jurado-Rivas, C. and Sánchez-Rivero, M. (2019) Willingness to pay for more sustainable tourism destinations in world heritage cities: The case of Caceres, Spain. *Sustainability*, 11(21), 5880. https://doi.org/10.3390/su11215880

Juvan, E. and Dolnicar, S. (2014a) Can tourists easily choose a low carbon footprint vacation? *Journal of Sustainable Tourism*, 22(2), 175–194.

Juvan, E. and Dolnicar, S. (2014b) The attitude–behaviour gap in sustainable tourism. *Annals of Tourism Research*, 48, 76–95.

Juvan, E., Grün, B. and Dolnicar, S. (2018) Biting off more than they can chew: Hotel waste at hotel breakfast buffets. *Journal of Travel Research*, 57(2), 232–242.

Kaján, E. and Saarinen, J. (2013) Tourism, climate change and adaptation: A review. *Current Issues in Tourism,* 16(2), 167–195.

Kallis, G. (2018) *Degrowth*. Newcastle-upon-Tyne: Agenda Publishing Limited.

Kalosh, A. (2016) Chinese love of shopping boon and bane for Japan's top cruise port. *Seatrade Cruise News*, 26 August. https://checkpoint.url-protection.com/v1/url?o=https%3A//www.seatrade-cruise.com/news-headlines/chinese-love-shopping-boon-and-bane-japans-top-cruise-port&g=ZT I4ZjM1M2Q1M2NkNTdkNA==&h=NjIyMDgyY2M0NTJkMGEwYjhiMT MyNzliMmIyYTk0NTEyNmY0NGUzOTQ2MDVjODkyYTMzMzRlOGFi MzI5YjM5Yg==&p=Y3AxZTp1Y2xhbmxpdmU6YzpvOjM0YTkwODM1YW VjNmIzMTExOGJmNTljZjJmM2NkNWU5OnYxOnQ6VA== (Accessed 17 November 2022).

Kaplan, J. and Hoff, M. (2022) A record-high 1 million restaurant and hotel workers quit in November – and it show the labor shortage might really be a wage shortage. *Insider*, 4 January. Available at: https://www.businessinsider.com/record-high-restaurant-hotel-workers-quit-in-november-labor-shortage-2022–1 (Accessed 30 August 2022).

Kapoor, A. and Debroy, B. (2019) GDP is not a measure of human well-being. *Harvard Business Review*. 4 October. https://hbr.org/2019/10/gdp-is-not-a-measure-of-human-well-being

Kenney, C. (2017) How climate change and water and food insecurity drive instability. *Centre for American Progress*, 30 November. Available at: https://www
.americanprogress.org/article/climate-change-water-food-insecurity-drive
-instability/

Kerschner, C. (2010) Economic de-growth vs. steady state economy. *Journal of
Cleaner Production*, 18(2010), 544–551.

Kimmerer, R. (2013) *Braiding Sweetgrass: Indigenous Wisdom, Scientific Knowledge,
and the Teachings of Plants*. Minneapolis: Milkweed Editions.

Klein, N. (2007) *The Shock Doctrine: The Rise of Disaster Capitalism*. Toronto: Knopf
Canada.

Klein, N. (2014) *This Changes Everything Capitalism vs. Climate Change*. New York:
Simon and Schuster.

Klein, N. (2018) *The Battle for Paradise: Puerto Rico Takes on the Disaster Capitalists*.
Chicago: Haymarket Books.

Klein, N. (2019) *On Fire: The Burning Case for Green New Deal*. Toronto: Knopf
Canada.

Koch, M. and Buch-Hansen, H. (2020) In search of a political economy of the post-
growth era. *Globalisations*, 18(21), 1219–1229. https://doi.org/10.1080/14747731
.2020.1807837

Kothari, A., Salleh, A., Escobar, A., Demaria, F. and Acosta, A. (Eds), (2019a)
Pluriverse: A Post-Development Dictionary. New Delhi: Tulika Books.

Kothari, A., Salleh, A., Escobar, A., Demaria, F. and Acosta, A. (2019b) Introduction:
Finding pluriversal paths. In A. Kothari, A. Salleh, A. Escobar, F. Demaria and
A. Acosta (Eds), *Pluriverse: A Post-Development Dictionary*. New Delhi: Tulika
Books, pp. xxi–xxix.

Kotler, P., Haider, D. and Rein, I. (2002) *Marketing Places: Attracting Investment,
Industry and Tourism to Cities, States and Nations*. New York: The Free Press.

Kovel, J. (2002) *The Enemy of Nature: The End of Capitalism or the End of the World?*
London: Zed Books.

Kretzman, S. (2021) Penguins in crisis as sardine populations plummet. *Daily Maverik*,
23 December. Available at: https://www.dailymaverick.co.za/article/2021-12-23
-penguins-in-crisis-as-sardine-populations-plummet/ (Accessed 14 July 2022).

Krippendorf, J. (1986) Tourism in the system of industrial society. *Annals of Tourism
Research*, 13(4), 517–532.

Krippendorf, J. (1987) *The Holiday Makers: Understanding the Impact of Leisure and
Travel*. Oxford: Heinemann.

Kulusjärvi, O. (2020) Diverse tourism: A poststructural view on tourism destination
degrowth transition. In C. M. Hall, L. Lundmark and J. Zhang (Eds), *Degrowth and
Tourism: New Perspectives on Tourism Entrepreneurship, Destinations and Policy*.
Abingdon: Routledge, pp. 71–84.

Kuvan, Y. (2010) Mass tourism development and deforestation in Turkey. *Anatolia*,
21(1), 155–168.

Lampert, A. and Singh, R. (2022) The New Jet Set: How the COVID-driven boom in
private jets is still flying high. Reuters, 2 May. Available at: https://www.reuters
.com/business/aerospace-defense/new-jet-set-how-covid-driven-boom-private-jets
-is-still-flying-high-2022–05–02/ (Accessed 17 August 2022).

Lane, B. (1990) Sustaining host areas, holiday makers and operators alike. Proceedings,
Sustainable Tourism Development Conference, November. Edinburgh: Queen
Margaret College.

Lash, S. (1990) *Sociology of Postmodernism*. London: Routledge.

Latouche, S. (1996) *The Westernizing of the World*. Cambridge: Polity Press.

Latouche, S. (2009) *Farewell to Growth*. Cambridge: Polity Press.

Latour, B. (2004) Why has critique run out of steam? From matters of fact to matters of concern. *Critical Inquiry*, 30(2), 225–248.

Lazarus, J. (2008) Participation in poverty reduction strategy papers: Reviewing the past, assessing the present and predicting the future. *Third World Quarterly*, 29(6), 1205–1221.

Lea, J. (1988) *Tourism and Development in the Third World*. London: Routledge.

Ledsom, A. (2022) France travel: Many short-haul flights outlawed from April. Forbes, 3. Available at: https://www.forbes.com/sites/alexledsom/2022/04/03/france-travel -many-short-haul-flights-outlawed-from-april/?sh=777550b76183April (Accessed 30 August 2022).

Leggett, T. (2022) Rolls-Royce tests a jet engine running on hydrogen. *BBC News*. Available at: https://www.bbc.co.uk/news/business-63758937 (Accessed 22 December 2022).

Lekgau, R., Harilia, V. and Feni, A. (2021) Reimaging tourism: COVID-19 and the potential of virtual tourism in South Africa. *African Journal of Hospitality, Tourism and Leisure*, 10(4), 1516–1532.

Lenzen, M., Sun, Y.Y., Faturay, F., Ting, Y. P., Geschke, A. and Malik, A. (2018) The carbon footprint of global tourism. *Nature Climate Change*, 8(6), 522–528.

Leposa, N. (2020) Problematic blue growth: A thematic synthesis of social sustaina-bility problems related to growth in the marine and coastal tourism. *Sustainability Science*, 15(4), 1233–1244.

Lett, J. (1983) Ludic and liminoid aspects of charter yacht tourism in the Caribbean. *Annals of Tourism Research*, 10(1), 35–56.

Leys, C. (2009) *The Rise and Fall of Development Theory*. Bloomington, IN: Indiana University Press.

Liegey, V. and Nelson, A. (2020) *Exploring Degrowth: A Critical Guide*. London: Pluto Press.

Lieper, N. (2004) *Tourism Management*, 3rd Edn. Sydney: Pearson Education Australia.

Liu, Z. (2003) Sustainable tourism development: A critique. *Journal of Sustainable Tourism*, 11(3), 459–475.

Lloret, J., Carreño, A., Carić, H., San, J. and Fleming, L. (2021) Environmental and human health impacts of cruise tourism: A review. *Marine Pollution Bulletin*, 173. https://doi.org/10.1016/j.marpolbul.2021.112979

Lock, S. (2022) Leading Hotel Companies worldwide as of September 2021, by number of properties. Statista, 26 July, https://www.statista.com/statistics/197869/ us-hotel-companies-by-number-of-properties-worldwide/

Lodziak, C. (2002) *The Myth of Consumerism*. London: Pluto Press.

Lorenzen, M. (2021) Rural gentrification, touristification, and displacement: Analysing evidence from Mexico. *Journal of Rural Studies*, 86(2021), 62–75.

Lozanski, K. and Baumgartner, K. (2022) Local gastronomy, transnational labour: Farm-to-table tourism and migrant agriculture workers in Niagara-on-the-Lake. *Tourism Geographies*, 24(1), 73–95.

Ludwig, D., Hilborn, R. and Walters, C. (1993) Uncertainty, resource exploitation, and conservation: Lessons from history. *Science*, 260(2), 17, 36.

Lundmark, L., Zhang, J. and Hall, C. M. (2020) Introduction: Degrowth and tourism – implications and challenges. In C. M. Hall, L. Lundmark and J. Zhang (Eds), *Degrowth and Tourism: New Perspectives on Tourism Entrepreneurship, Destinations and Policy*. Abingdon: Routledge, pp. 1–21.

Lupoli, C., Morse, W., Bailey, C. and Schelhas, J. (2014) Assessing the impacts of international volunteer tourism in host communities: A new approach to organizing and prioritizing indicators. *Journal of Sustainable Tourism,* 22(6), 898–921.

Lury, C. (2011) *Consumer Culture,* 2nd Edn. Cambridge: Polity Press.

Lyotard. J. (1984) *The Postmodern Condition: A Report on Knowledge.* Manchester: Manchester University Press.

Mabogunje, A. (1980) *The Development Process: A Spatial Perspective.* London: Hutchinson.

MacCannell, D. (1976) *The Tourist: A New Theory of the Leisure Class.* New York: Schocken Books.

MacCannell, D. (1989) *The Tourist: A New Theory of the Leisure Class,* 2nd Edn. New York: Shocken Books.

Macilree, J. and Duval, D. (2020) Aeropolitics in a post COVID-19 world. *Journal of Air Transport Management,* 88. https://doi.org/10.1016/j.jairtraman.2020.101864

MacKay, S. (2021) The global south, degrowth and The Simpler Way movement: The need for structural solutions at the global level. *Globalizations,* 19(5), 828–835.

MacKinnon, J. B. (2021) *The Day the World Stops Shopping: How Ending Consumerism Gives Us a Better Life and a Greener World.* London: The Bodley Head.

Macnaught, T. (1982) Mass tourism and the dilemmas of modernisation in Pacific Islands communities. *Annals of Tourism Research,* 9(3), 359–381.

macrotrends (2021a) World GDP, 1960–1921. Available at: https://www.macrotrends .net/countries/WLD/world/gdp-gross-domestic-product (Accessed 26 November 2021).

macrotrends (2021b) World GDP per capita, 1960–2021. Available at: https://www .macrotrends.net/countries/WLD/world/gdp-per-capita (Accessed 26 November 2021).

Macy, J. and Johnstone, C. (2012) *Active Hope: How to Face the Mess We're in Without Going Crazy.* Navato, CA: New World Library.

Mallorquin, C. (2020) *Southern Perspectives on Development Studies.* Santiago, Chile: Ariadna Ediciones. Open access: https://library.oapen.org/handle/20.500.12657/45773

Mannell, R. and Iso-Ahola, S. (1987) Psychological nature of leisure and tourism experience. *Annals of Tourism Research,* 14(3), 314–331.

Margaryan, L., Fredman, P. and Stensland, S. (2020) Lifestyle entrepreneurs as agents of degrowth: The case of nature-based tourism businesses in Scandinavia. In C. M. Hall, L. Lundmark and J. Zhang (Eds), *Degrowth and Tourism: New Perspectives on Tourism Entrepreneurship, Destinations and Policy.* Abingdon: Routledge, pp. 41–53.

Marzouki, M., Froger, G. and Ballet, J. (2012) Ecotourism versus mass tourism: A comparison of environmental impacts based on ecological footprint analysis. *Sustainability,* 4(1), 123–140.

Mastini, R. (2017) Degrowth: The case for a new economic paradigm. *openDemocracy,* 8 June. Available at https://www.opendemocracy.net/en/degrowth-case-for -constructing-new-economic-paradigm/

Mathews, J. (2002) *Dragon Multinational: A New Model for Global Growth.* Oxford: Oxford University Press.

Mayell, H. (2004) Earth suffers as consumerism spreads. *National Geographic,* 12 January. Available at: https://www.nationalgeographic.com/environment/article/consumerism-earth-suffers (Accessed 4 July 2022).

Mayer, A. (2022) This former pilot says people need to fly less for the sake of the environment. *CBC What on Earth*, 13 October, Available at: https://www.cbc.ca/ news/science/what-on-earth-former-pilot-aviation-emissions-1.6615428 (Accessed 2 November 2022).

McCabe, S. (2015) Are we all post-tourists now? Tourist categories, identities and post-modernity. In T. Singh (Ed.), *Challenges in Tourism Research*, Bristol: Channel View Publications, pp. 18–26.

McGehee, N. (2014) Volunteer tourism: Evolution, issues and futures. *Journal of Sustainable Tourism*, 22(6), 847–854.

McGillivary, R. (2021) Disney is still moving forward with the second private destination in the Bahamas. *Cruisehive*, 15 June. Available at: https://www.cruisehive.com/ disney-is-still-moving-forward-with-second-private-destination-in-the-bahamas/ 52041 (Accessed 23 August 2022).

McKercher, B. (1993) Some fundamental truths about tourism: Understanding tourism's social and environmental impacts. *Journal of Sustainable Tourism*, 1(1), 6–16.

Mdingi, K. and Ho, S. (2021) Literature review on income inequality and economic growth. MethodsX. 8. 101402. https://doi.org/10.1016/j.mex.2021.101402

Meadows, D. H., Meadows, D. L., Randers, J. and Behrens, W. (1972) *Limits to Growth*. New York: Universe Books.

Mehlman-Orozco, K. (2017) *Hidden in Plain Sight: America's Slaves of the New Millennium*. Santa Barbara: Praeger.

Merriam-Webster (2022) Definition of theory. Available at: https://www.merriam -webster.com/dictionary/theory (Accessed 6 May 2022).

Middlemiss, L. (2018) *Sustainable Consumption: Key Issues*. Abingdon: Routledge.

Mieczkowski, Z. (1995) *Environmental Issues of Tourism and Recreation*. Lanham, MD: University Press of America.

Mihalič, T. (2015) Tourism and economic development issues. In R. Sharpley and D. Telfer (Eds), *Tourism and Development: Concepts and Issues,* 2nd Edn. Bristol: Channel View Publications, pp. 77–117.

Milano, C., Cheer, J and Novelli, M. (2018) Overtourism is becoming a major issue for cities across the globe. *The Conversation*, 18 July. Available at: https:// theconversation.com/overtourism-a-growing-global-problem-100029 (Accessed 22 August 2022).

Milano, C., Cheer, J. M. and Novelli, M. (Eds) (2019) *Overtourism: Excesses, Discontents and Measures in Travel and Tourism*. Wallingford: CABI.

Miller, G., Rathouse, K., Scarles, C., Holmes, K. and Tribe, J. (2010) Public understanding of sustainable tourism. *Annals of Tourism Research*, 37(3), 627–645.

Milner, H. (2021) Is global capitalism compatible with democracy? Inequality, insecurity and interdependence. *International Studies Quarterly*, 65(4), 1097–1110.

Mínguez, C., Blanco-Romero, A. and Blázquez-Salom, M. (2022) COVID-19 as a stimulus for growth? The Spanish journalistic treatment of tourism during confinement. *Cogent Social Sciences*, 8(1), 2137274. https://doi.org/10.1080/23311886 .2022.2137274

Minnaert, L., Maitland, R. and Miller, G. (2009) Tourism and social policy: The value of social tourism. *Annals of Tourism Research*, 36(2), 316–334.

Mitchell, C. and de Waal, S. (2009) Revisiting the model of creative destruction: St. Jacobs, Ontario, a decade later. *Journal of Rural Studies*, 25(1), 156–167.

Mishan, E. (1969) *The Costs of Economic Growth*. Harmondsworth: Penguin.

Miyoshi, C. and Mason, K. (2009) The carbon emissions of selected airlines and aircraft types in three geographic markets. *Journal of Air Transport Management*, 15(3), 138–147.

Mkono, M. and Hughes, K. (2020) Eco-guilt and eco-shame in tourism consumption contexts: Understanding the triggers and responses. *Journal of Sustainable Tourism*, 28(8), 1223–1244.

Monbiot, G. (2017) *Out of the Wreckage: A New Politics for an Age of Crisis*. London: Verso.

Moraes, C., Carrigan, M. and Szmigin, I. (2012) The coherence of inconsistencies: Attitude–behaviour gaps and new consumption communities. *Journal of Marketing Management*, 28(1–2), 103–128.

Mosedale, J. (2011). Re-introducing tourism to political economy. In J. Mosedale (Ed.), *Political Economy of Tourism: A Critical Perspective*. London: Routledge, pp. 25–38.

Mosedale, J. (Ed.) (2016) *Neoliberalism and the Political Economy of Tourism*. Abingdon: Routledge.

Müller, N., Fletcher, R. and Blázquez-Salom, M. (2022) Convivial tourism in proximity. In F. Higgins-Desbiolles and B. Bigby (Eds), *The Local Turn in Tourism: Empowering Communities*. Bristol: Channel View Publications.

Nash, D. (1989) Tourism as a form of imperialism. In V. Smith (Ed.), *Hosts and Guests: The Anthropology of Tourism*, 2nd Edn. Philadelphia: University of Pennsylvania Press, pp. 37–52.

National Geographic (n.d.). Effects of global warming. *National Geographic*. Available at: https://www.nationalgeographic.com/environment/article/global-warming-effects (Accessed 12 June 2022).

Navarro-Jurado, E., Romero-Padilla, Y., Romero-Martínez, J. M., Serrano-Muñoz, E., Habegger, S. and Mora-Esteban, R. (2019) Growth machines and social movements in mature tourist destinations: Costa del Sol-Málaga. *Journal of Sustainable Tourism*, 27(12), 1786–1803.

Navío-Marco, J., Ruiz-Gómez, L and Sevilla-Sevilla, C. (2018) Progress in information technology and tourism management: 30 years on and 20 years after the internet – Revisiting Buhalis & Law's landmark study about eTourism. *Tourism Management*, 69(2018), 460–470.

Nawijn, J. and Strijbosch, W. (2022) Experiencing tourism: Experiencing happiness? In R. Sharpley (Ed.), *Routledge Handbook of the Tourist Experience*. Abingdon: Routledge, pp. 24–36.

Nederveen Pieterse, J. (2000) After post-development. *Third World Quarterly*, 21(2), 175–191.

Niblett, M. and Beuret, K. (2021) *Why Travel? Understanding our Need to Move and How it Shapes our Lives*. Bristol: Bristol University Press.

Nilson, P. (2022) Cruise in 2022: The state of the industry. *Ship Technology*, 21 February. Available at: https://www.ship-technology.com/analysis/cruise-in-2022-the-state-of-the-industry/ (Accessed 30 August 2022).

Niñerola, A., Sánchez-Rebull, M-V. and Hernández-Lara, A-B. (2019) Tourism research on sustainability: A bibliometric analysis. *Sustainability*, 11(5), 1377. https://doi.org/10.3390/su11051377

Nitsch, B. and Vogels, C. (2022) Gender quality boost for regenerative tourism: The case of Karenni village Huay Pu Keng. *Journal of Tourism Futures*, 8(3), 375–377.

NOAA (2020) Ocean pollution and marine debris. *National Oceanic and Atmospheric Administration.* Available at: https://www.noaa.gov/education/resource-collections/ocean-coasts/ocean-pollution

NOAA (2022) Carbon dioxide now more than 50% higher than pre-industrial levels. *National Oceanic and Atmospheric Administration.* Available at: https://www.noaa.gov/news-release/carbon-dioxide-now-more-than-50-higher-than-pre-industrial-levels#:~:text=Prior%20to%20the%20Industrial%20Revolution,atmosphere%20for%20thousands%20of%20years (Accessed 10 July 2022).

Nofre, J. (2021) The touristification of nightlife: Some theoretical notes. *Urban Geography,* 42(10), 1552–1561.

Novicio, T. (2021) 15 largest cruise companies in the World. *Yahoo Finance,* 3 March. Available at: https://finance.yahoo.com/news/15-largest-cruise-companies-world-085750509.html (Accessed 30 August 2022).

Nunes, A. (2022) Should we get rid of air miles for climate change? *BBC Future Planet.* Available at: https://www.bbc.com/future/article/20221122-should-we-get-rid-of-air-miles-for-climate-change (Accessed 13 December 2022).

Obama, B. (2017) *President Obama's farewell address* [Transcript]. Available at: www.whitehouse.gov/farewell

OBR (2022) Air passenger duty. Office for Budget Responsibility. Available at: https://obr.uk/forecasts-in-depth/tax-by-tax-spend-by-spend/air-passenger-duty/ (Accessed 21 April 2022).

O'Connell, J. and Bouquet, A. (2015) Dynamic packaging spells the end of European charter airlines. *Journal of Vacation Marketing,* 21(2), 175–189.

OECD (1981) *The Impact of Tourism on the Environment.* Paris: Organisation for Economic Co-Operation and Development.

Ojeda, A. and Kieffer, M. (2020) Touristification. Empty concept or element of analysis in tourism geography. *Geoforum,* 115(2020), 143–145.

Okumus, B., Taheri, B., Giritlioglu, I. and Gannon, M. J. (2020) Tackling food waste in all-inclusive resort hotels. *International Journal of Hospitality Management,* 88. https://doi.org/10.1016/j.ijhm.2020.102543

Olivia, M. (2020) *Minimal: How to Simplify Your Life and Live Sustainably.* London: Ebury Publishing.

O'Neil, K. (2022) Las Vegas strip venue demolition set, new project weeks away. *The Street,* 27 July. Available at: https://www.thestreet.com/investing/las-vegas-strip-venue-demolition-set-new-project-weeks-away (Accessed 24 August 2022).

O'Neil, S. (2022) India enjoys hotel development boom as room rates regain 2019 levels. *Skift Global Forum,* 20 May. Available at: https://skift.com/2022/05/20/india-enjoys-hotel-development-boom-as-room-rates-regain-2019-levels/ (Accessed 26 August 2022).

Oppermann, M. and Chon, K. (1997) *Tourism in Developing Countries.* London: International Thomson Business Press.

Ord, T. (2020) *The Precipice: Existential Risk and the Future of Humanity.* New York: Hachette Books.

Otto, J. (2017) Finding common ground: Exploring synergies between degrowth and environmental justice in Chiapas, Mexico. *Journal of Political Ecology,* 24(1), 491–503.

Overton, J. (2022) *Issue Brief: The Growth in Greenhouse Gas Emissions from Commercial Aviation* (2019, revised 2022). Environmental and Energy Study Institute, 9 June. Available at: https://www.eesi.org/papers/view/fact-sheet-the

-growth-in-greenhouse-gas-emissions-from-commercial-aviation (Accessed 30 August 2022).

Oxfam (2021) Five shocking facts about extreme global poverty and how to even it up. Oxfam International. Available at: https://www.oxfam.org/en/5-shocking-facts -about-extreme-global-inequality-and-how-even-it (Accessed 26 November 2021).

Pang, S. F., McKercher, B. and Prideaux, B. (2013) Climate change and tourism: An overview. *Asia Pacific Journal of Tourism Research*, 18(1–2), 4–20.

Panzer-Krause, S. (2017) Un-locking unsustainable tourism destination paths: The role of voluntary compliance of tourism businesses with sustainability certification on the island of Rügen. *Zeitschrift für Wirtschaftsgeographie*, 61(3–4), 174–190.

Panzer-Krause, S. (2019) Networking towards sustainable tourism: Innovations between green growth and degrowth strategies. *Regional Studies*, 53(7), 927–938.

Panzer-Krause, S. (2021). Growing degrowth-oriented tourism? CSR certified tour operators as change agents. In K. Andriotis (Ed.), *Issues and Cases of Degrowth in Tourism*. Wallingford: CABI, pp. 104–123.

Panzer-Krause, S. (2022) Rural tourism in and after the COVID-19 era: 'Revenge Travel' or a chance for a degrowth-oriented restart? Cases from Ireland and Germany. *Tourism and Hospitality*, 3(2), 399–415.

Parrique, T. (2019) *The Political Economy of Degrowth*. Doctoral Dissertation, Economics, Université Clermont Auvergne and Stockholm University. https://tel .archives-ouvertes.fr/tel-02499463

Pasternak, C. (2021) Biological perspectives on travel. In M. Niblett and K. Beuret (Eds), *Why Travel? Understanding our Need to Move and How it Shapes our Lives*. Bristol: Bristol University Press, pp. 13–32.

Paul, T. (2022) 'Buy now, pay later' can help you fund your next trip but here's what you need to know about these loans. *CNBC*, 9 June. Available at: https://www.cnbc .com/select/buy-now-pay-later-for-travel-what-to-know-/ (Accessed 30 August 2022).

Payne, A. and Phillips, N. (2010) *Development*. Cambridge: Polity Press.

Pearce, P. (2022) The Ulysses factor revisited: Consolidating the travel career pattern approach to tourist motivation. In R. Sharpley, (Ed.), *Routledge Handbook of the Tourist Experience*. Abingdon: Routledge, pp. 169–184.

Peeters, P., Higham, J., Kutzner, D., Cohen, S. and Gössling, S. (2016) Are technology myths stalling aviation climate policy? *Transportation Research Part D: Transport and Environment*, 44, 30–42.

Peeters, P. and Landré, M. (2012) The emerging global tourism geography: An environmental sustainability perspective. *Sustainability*, 4(1), 42–71.

Pentelow, L. and Scott, D. (2011) Aviation's inclusion in the international climate policy regimes: Implications for the Caribbean tourism industry. *Journal of Air Transport Management*, 17(3), 199–205.

Pigram, J. (1980) Environmental implications of tourism development. *Annals of Tourism Research*, 7(4), 554–583.

Pigram, J. (1990) Sustainable tourism: Policy considerations. *Journal of Tourism Studies*, 1(2), 2–9.

Pilling, D. (2019) It's time to redefine GDP to help save the planet. *Time*, 21 November. Available at: https://time.com/5735520/economic-growth-gdp/

Plastic Oceans (2022) *The Facts*. Available at: https://plasticoceans.org/the-facts/

Podlaszewska, A. (2021) Degrowing the commoditization process in community-based tourism and local entrepreneurship. In K. Andriotis (Ed.), *Issues and Cases of Degrowth in Tourism*. Wallingford: CABI, pp. 64–85.

Poon, A. (1993) *Tourism, Technology and Competitive Strategies.* Wallingford: CAB International.

Poore, J. and Nemecek, T. (2018) Reducing food's environmental impacts through producers and consumers. *Science*, 360(6392), 987–992.

Popescu, L. (2008) *The Good Tourist: An Ethical Traveller's Guide.* London: Arcadia Books.

Porritt, J. (2007) *Capitalism as if the World Matters.* London: Routledge.

Pranskūnienė, R. and Perkumienė, D. (2021) Freedom of movement and degrowth. In K. Andriotis (Ed.), *Issues and Cases of Degrowth in Tourism.* Wallingford: CABI, pp. 160–177.

Pratt, S., McCabe, S. and Monvono, A. (2016) Gross happiness of a 'tourism village' in Fiji. *Journal of Destination Marketing & Management*, 5(1), 26–35.

Prideaux, B. and Pabel, A. (2020) Degrowth as a strategy for adjusting to the adverse impacts of climate change in a nature-based destination. In C. M. Hall, L. Lundmark and J. Zhang (Eds), *Degrowth and Tourism: New Perspectives on Tourism Entrepreneurship, Destinations and Policy.* Abingdon: Routledge, pp. 116–131.

Prideaux, B. and Phelan, A. (2022) The circular economy. In D. Buhalis (Ed.). *Encyclopedia of Tourism Management and Marketing.* Cheltenham, UK and Northampton, MA, USA: Edward Elgar Publishing. pp. 488–491. https://doi.org/10 .4337/9781800377486.the.circular.economy

Pryce, A. (1998) The World Bank Group and tourism. *Travel and Tourism Analyst*, 5, 75–91.

Querejazu, A. (2016) Encountering the pluriverse: Looking for alternatives in other worlds. *Revista Brasileria de Política Internacional*, 59(2). https://doi.org/10.1590/ 0034–7329201600207

RAC (2021) Are electric cars really better for the environment? *RAC*, 18 March. Available at: https://www.rac.co.uk/drive/electric-cars/choosing/are-electric-cars -really-better-for-the-environment/ (Accessed 8 July 2022).

Reardon, S. (2011) Melting Antarctic causing penguins to starve. *Science.* Available at: https://www.science.org/content/article/melting-antarctic-ice-causing-penguins -starve (Accessed 11 November 2022).

Redclift, M. (1987) *Sustainable Development: Exploring the Contradictions.* London: Routledge.

Reid, C. (2022) France's plan to ban short-haul domestic flights wins approval from European Commission. Forbes, 3 December. Available at: https://www.forbes.com/ sites/carltonreid/2022/12/03/frances-plan-to-ban-short-haul-domestic-flights-wins -approval-from-european-commission/?sh=503146522385 (Accessed 23 December 2022).

Reiff, P. (2006) *Triumph of the Therapeutic: Uses of Faith After Freud.* Wilmington, DE: ISI Books.

Renaud, L. (2020) Reconsidering global mobility: Distancing from mass cruise tourism in the aftermath of COVID-19. *Tourism Geographies*, 22(3), 679–689.

Renaud, L. (2022) Reconsidering global mobility – distancing from mass cruise tourism in the aftermath of COVID-19. *Tourism Geographies*, 22(3), 679-689.

Renkert, S. R. (2019). Community-owned tourism and degrowth: A case study in the Kichwa Anangu community. *Journal of Sustainable Tourism*, 27(12), 1893–1908.

Rist, G. (2014) *The History of Development: From Western Origins to Global Faith*, 4th Edn. London: Zed Books.

Ritchie, H. (2019) Half of the world's land is used for agriculture. *Our World in Data*, 11 November. Available at: https://ourworldindata.org/global-land-for-agriculture (Accessed 19 July 2022).

Ritchie, H. and Roser, M. (2018) Now it is possible to take stock: Did the world achieve the Millennium Development Goals? *Our World in Data*, 28 September. Available at: https://ourworldindata.org/millennium-development-goals (Accessed 26 November 2021).

Robbins, T. (2008) Are you being green washed? *The Guardian*, 6 July. Available at: https://www.theguardian.com/travel/2008/jul/06/green.ethicalholidays (Accessed 31 August 2022).

Roe, D. and Urguhart, P. (2001) *Pro-Poor Tourism: Harnessing the World's Largest Industry for the World's Poor*. London: International Institute for Environment and Development. Available at: https://pubs.iied.org/sites/default/files/pdfs/migrate/11007IIED.pdfhttps://pubs.iied.org/sites/default/files/pdfs/migrate/11007IIED.pdf (Accessed 29 April 2022).

Rojek, C. (2007) *The Labour of Leisure: The Culture of Free Time*. Los Angeles: Sage Publications.

Rojek, C. (2010) *Cultural Studies*. Cambridge: Polity.

Romano, O. (2020) *Towards a Society of Degrowth*. Abingdon: Routledge.

Rosenow, J. and Pulsipher, G. (1979) *Tourism: The Good, The Bad, and The Ugly*. Lincoln, NE: Media Productions and Marketing.

Roser, M. (2021) Data Review: How many people die from air pollution? *Our World in Data*. Available at: https://ourworldindata.org/data-review-air-pollution-deaths (Accessed 15 July 2022).

Roser, M., Ritchie, H. and Ortiz-Espina, E. (2019) World Population Growth. *Our World in Data*. Available at: https://ourworldindata.org/world-population-growth (Accessed 1 July 2022).

Ross, M. (2019) Feeding the largest cruise ships in the world. *CNN Travel*, 30 September. Available at: https://www.cnn.com/travel/article/cruise-ships-food-supplies/index.html (Accessed 30 August 2022).

Rostow, W. (1967) *The Stages of Economic Growth: A Non-Communist Manifesto*, 2nd Edn. Cambridge: Cambridge University Press.

Rucinski, T. and Shivdas, S. (2021) United Airlines to outsource catering operations from October. *Reuters*, 29 July. Available at: https://www.reuters.com/business/aerospace-defense/united-airlines-outsource-catering-operations-october-2021-07-29/ (Accessed 31 August 2022).

Ruhanen, L., Weiler, B., Moyle, B. and McLennan, C. (2015) Trends and patterns in sustainable tourism research: A 25-year bibliometric analysis. *Journal of Sustainable Tourism*, 23(4), 517–535.

Ruiz-Ballesteros, E. (2020) Community-based tourism and degrowth. In C. M. Hall, L. Lundmark and J. Zhang (Eds), *Degrowth and Tourism: New Perspectives on Tourism Entrepreneurship, Destinations and Policy*. Abingdon: Routledge, pp. 170–186.

Ryan, C. (2002) *The Tourist Experience: A New Introduction*, 2nd Edn. London: Thomson Learning.

Ryan, C. (2010) Ways of conceptualizing the tourist experience: A review of literature. *Tourism Recreation Research*, 35(1), 37–46.

Saarinen, J. (2020) Sustainable growth in tourism? Rethinking and resetting sustainable tourism for development. In C. M. Hall, L. Lundmark and J. Zhang (Eds), *Degrowth and Tourism: New Perspectives on Tourism Entrepreneurship, Destinations and Policy.* Abingdon: Routledge, pp. 135–151.

Sachs, W. (1996) Introduction. In W. Sachs (Ed.), *The Development Dictionary: A Guide to Knowledge as Power.* London: Zed Books, pp. 1–6.

Sachs, W. (2017) The Sustainable Development Goals and Laudato si': Varieties of Post-development? *Third World Quarterly*, 38(12), 2573–2587.

Sachs, W. (2019) Foreword: The Development Dictionary revisited. In A. Kothari, A. Salleh, A. Escobar, F. Demaria and A. Acosta (Eds), *Pluriverse: A Post-Development Dictionary.* New Delhi: Tulika Books, pp. xi–xvi.

Sadiku, M., Okhiria, O and Musa, S. (2020) Essence of Globalization 3.0. *Journal of Scientific and Engineering Research*, 7(9), 35–40.

Safe Landing (2022) Why Safe Landing. Available at: https://safe-landing.org/why -safe-landing/ (Accessed 15 November 2022).

Saner, E. (2021) Lotion in the ocean: Is your sunscreen killing the sea? *The Guardian*, 6 August. Available at: https://www.theguardian.com/environment/2021/aug/06/ lotion-in-the-ocean-is-your-sunscreen-killing-the-sea

Sarantakou, E. and Terkenli, T. (2019) Non-institutionalized forms of tourism accommodation and overtourism impacts on the landscapes: The case of Santorini, Greece. *Tourism Planning and Development*, 16(4), 411–433.

Savage, M. (2022) Is Finland's Wood City the future of building? *BBC News*. Available at: https://www.bbc.co.uk/news/business-62798950 (Accessed 27 September 2022).

Schafer, J., Haslam, P. and Beaudet, P. (2021) What is development? From economic growth to the sustainable development goals. In P. Haslam, J. Schafer and P. Beaudet (Eds), *Introduction to International Development.* Don Mills, ON: Oxford University Press, pp. 3–23.

Scheyvens, R., Movono, A. and Auckram, S. (2023) Pacific peoples and the pandemic: Exploring multiple well-beings of people in tourism-dependent communities. *Journal of Sustainable Tourism*, 31, 111–130.

Schwartzman, D. (2012) A critique of degrowth and its politics. *Capitalism Nature Socialism*, 23(1), 119–125.

Scott, D. and Gössling, S. (2022) A review of research into tourism and climate change – Launching the *Annals of Tourism Research* curated collection on tourism and climate change. *Annals of Tourism Research*, 95. https://doi.org/10.1016/j.annals .2022.103409

Scott, D., Gössling, S. and Hall, C. M. (2012) International tourism and climate change. *Wiley Interdisciplinary Reviews: Climate Change*, 3(3), 213–232.

Segreto, L., Manera, C. and Pohl, M. (Eds) (2009) *Europe at the Seaside: The Economic History of Mass Tourism in the Mediterranean.* New York / Oxford: Berghahn Books.

Sen, A. (1985) *Commodities and Capabilities.* New Delhi: Oxford University Press.

Sen, A. (1999) *Development as Freedom.* Oxford: Oxford University Press.

Sen, A. (2011) *The Idea of Justice.* Cambridge, MA: Harvard University Press.

Séraphin, H. and Yallop, A. (2020) Introduction. In H. Séraphin and A. Yallop (Eds), *Overtourism and Education.* Abingdon: Routledge, pp. 1–4.

Seyfi, S., Hall, C. M. and Saarinen, J. (2022) Rethinking sustainable substitution between domestic and international tourism: A policy thought experiment. *Journal of Policy Research in Tourism Leisure and Events.* https://doi.org/10.1080/19407963 .2022.2100410

Shani, A. and Arad, B. (2014) Climate change and tourism: Time for environmental skepticism. *Tourism Management*, 44, 82–85.

Sharpley, R. (2000) Tourism and sustainable development: Exploring the theoretical divide. *Journal of Sustainable Tourism*, 8(1), 1–19.

Sharpley, R. (2004) The impacts of tourism in the Lake District. In D. Hind and J. Mitchell (Eds) *Sustainable Tourism in the English Lake District*. Sunderland: Business Education Publishers, pp. 208–242.

Sharpley, R. (2006) Ecotourism: A consumption perspective. *Journal of Ecotourism*, 5(1+2), 7–22.

Sharpley, R. (2018) *Tourism, Tourists and Society*, 5th Edn. Abingdon: Routledge.

Sharpley, R. (2003) Tourism, modernisation and development on the island of Cyprus: Challenges and policy responses, *Journal of Sustainable Tourism* 11(2+3), 246-265.

Sharpley, R. (2020) Tourism, sustainable development and the theoretical divide: 20 years on. *Journal of Sustainable Tourism*, 28(11), 1932–1946.

Sharpley, R. (Ed.) (2022a) *Routledge Handbook of the Tourist Experience*. Abingdon: Routledge.

Sharpley, R. (2022b) Tourist experiences: Liminal, liminoid or just doing something different? In R. Sharpley (Ed.), *Routledge Handbook of the Tourist Experience*. Abingdon: Routledge, pp. 89–100.

Sharpley, R. and Harrison, D. (2019) Introduction: Tourism and development: Towards a research agenda. In R. Sharpley and D. Harrison (Eds), *A Research Research Agenda for Tourism and Development*. Cheltenham, UK and Northampton, MA, USA: Edward Elgar Publishing, pp. 1–34.

Sharpley, R. and Kato, K. (2021) Introduction: Tourism in Japan – from the past to the present. In R. Sharpley and K. Kato (Eds), *Tourism Development in Japan: Themes, Issues and Challenges*. Abingdon: Routledge, pp. 1–18.

Sharpley, R. and Telfer, D. (Eds) (2015) *Tourism and Development: Concepts and Issues*, 2nd Edn. Bristol: Channel View Publications.

Shaw, G. and Williams, A. (1994) *Critical Issues in Tourism: A Geographical Perspective*. Oxford: Blackwell.

Sheldon, P. (2022) The coming of age of tourism: Embracing new economic models. *Journal of Tourism Futures*, 8(2), 200–207.

Shields, P. (2011) A case for wanderlust: Travel behaviors of college students. *Journal of Travel & Tourism Marketing*, 28(4), 369–387.

Simon, D. (2007) Beyond antidevelopment: Discourses, convergences, practices. *Singapore Journal of Tropical Geography*, 28(2007), 205–218.

Slade, G. (2007) *Made to Break: Technology and Obsolescence in America*. Cambridge: Harvard University Press.

Smith, K. (1990) Tourism and climate change. *Land Use Policy*, 7(2), 176–180.

Smith, V. and Eadington, W. (1992) *Tourism Alternatives: Potentials and Pitfalls in the Development of Tourism*. Philadelphia: University of Pennsylvania Press.

Solón, P. (2022) What are Systemic Alternatives? Available at: https://systemicalternatives.org/2019/03/26/what-are-systemic-alternatives/

Spenceley, A. (2022) Pro-poor tourism's evolution and implications arising from the Covid-19 pandemic. *Tourism Planning & Development*, 19(1), 13–25.

Spieles, D. (2017) *Environmentalism: An Evolutionary Approach*. Abingdon: Routledge.

Standing, G. (2014) *The Precariat: The New Dangerous Class*. London: Bloomsbury Academic.

Stankov, U., Filimonau, V. and Vujičić, M.D. (2020) A mindful shift: An opportunity for mindfulness-driven tourism in a post-pandemic world. *Tourism Geographies*, 22(3), 703–712.

Star Alliance (2022) Fly to more than 1300 destinations worldwide with the Star Alliance. Available at: https://flights.staralliance.com/en/ (Accessed 17 August 2022).

State of Hawaii (2022) June 2022 visitor count second highest since January 2020. Available at: https://dbedt.hawaii.gov/blog/22–35/#:~:text=HONOLULU%E2%80 %94According%20to%20preliminary%20visitor,percent%20recovery%20from %20June%202019 (Accessed 31 August 2022).

Statista (2022a) Average number of holidays abroad per person in the United Kingdom (UK) between 2011 and 2019. *Statista.* Available at: https://www.statista .com/statistics/480184/average-number-of-abroad-holidays-per-person-in-the-uk/ (Accessed 18 March 2022).

Statista (2022b) Low cost carriers' worldwide market share from 2007 to 2020. *Statista.* Available at: https://www.statista.com/statistics/586677/global-low-cost -carrier-market-capacity-share/

Steger, M. (2019) Globalization and the populist challenge. *Global-e* 12(52), 26 November. Available at: https://globalejournal.org/global-e/november-2019/ globalization-and-populist-challenge

Steger, M. and James, P. (2019) *Globalization Matters: Engaging the Global in Unsettled Times.* Cambridge: Cambridge University Press.

Steger, M. and James, P. (2020) Disjunctive globalization in the era of the Great Unsettling. *Theory, Culture & Society,* 37(7–8), 187–203.

Steiger, R., Scott, D., Abegg, B., Pons, M. and Aall, C. (2019) A critical review of climate change risk for ski tourism. *Current Issues in Tourism,* 22(11), 1343–1379.

Stevens, S. (2003) Tourism and deforestation in the Mt Everest region of Nepal. *Geographical Journal,* 169(3), 255–277.

Stiglitz, J. (2018) *Globalization and its Discontents Revisited.* London: W. W. Norton & Company.

Streeten, P. (n.d.) Ten years of human development. *UNDP Human Development Reports.* Available at: https://hdr.undp.org/en/content/ten-years-human-development -0#:~:text=The%20first%20Human%20Development%20Report,for%20balancing %20budgets%20and%20payments (Accessed 23 May 2022).

Sun, Y., Lin, P. and Higham, J. (2020) Managing tourism emissions through optimizing the tourism demand mix: Concept and analysis. *Tourism Management,* 81(2020). https://doi.org/10.1016/j.tourman.2020.104161

Sun, Y., Mengyu, L., Lenzen, M., Malik, A and Pomponi, F. (2022) Tourism, job vulnerability and income inequality during the COVID-19 pandemic. *Annals of Tourism Research Empirical Insights,* 3(1). https://doi.org/10.1016/j.annale.2022 .100046

Taloş, A. M., Lequeux-Dincă, A. I., Preda, M., Surugiu, C., Mareci, A. and Vijulie, I. (2021) Silver tourism and recreational activities as possible factors to support active ageing and the resilience of the tourism sector. *Journal of Settlements and Spatial Planning,* 8, 29–48.

Taylor, C. (2009) *A Secular Age.* Cambridge, MA: Harvard University Press.

TCC (2022) About the TCC. Travelers' Century Club. Available at: https:// travelerscenturyclub.org/about (Accessed 11 November 2022).

Telfer, D.J. and Wall, G. (1996) Linkages between tourism and food production. *Annals of Tourism Research,* 23(3), 635–653.

Telfer, D. J. (2009) Development studies and tourism. In T. Jamal and M. Robinson (Eds), *The Sage Handbook of Tourism Studies.* London: Sage, pp. 146–165.

Telfer, D. J. (2015) The evolution of development theory and tourism. In R. Sharpley and D. Telfer (Eds), *Tourism and Development: Concepts and Issues,* 2nd Edn. Bristol: Channel View Publications, pp. 3–73.

Telfer, D. J. (2019) Tourism and (re)development in the developed world. In R. Sharpley and D. Harrison (Eds), *A Research Agenda for Tourism and Development.* Cheltenham, UK and Northampton, MA, USA: Edward Elgar Publishing, pp. 206–232.

Telfer, D. J. and Sharpley, R. (2016) *Tourism and Development in the Developing World,* 2nd Edn. Abingdon: Routledge.

Telfer, D. and Wall, G. (2000). Strengthening backward economic linkages: Local food purchasing by three Indonesian hotels. *Tourism Geographies,* 2(4), 421–447.

Terry, W. (2017) Flags of Convenience and the global cruise labour market. In W. Terry, R. Dowling and C. Weeden (Eds), *Cruise Ship Tourism.* Wallingford, UK: CABI, pp. 72–78.

Tharoor, I. (2017) The man who declared the 'end of history' fears for democracy's future. *The Washington Post,* 9 February. Available at: https://www.washingtonpost .com/news/worldviews/wp/2017/02/09/the-man-who-declared-the-end-of-history -fears-for-democracys-future/

The Guardian (2020) The Guardian view on 'flight shame': Face it – life must change. *The Guardian,* 17 January, Available at: https://www.theguardian.com/ commentisfree/2020/jan/17/the-guardian-view-on-flight-shaming-face-it-life-must -change (Accessed 15 December 2022).

Thunberg, G. (2018) Speech Delivered at UN Climate Change COP 24 Conference.

Timothy, D. (2005) *Shopping Tourism, Retailing, and Leisure.* Clevedon: Channel View Publications.

Todaro, M. and Smith, S. (2020) *Economic Development,* 13th Edn. Toronto: Pearson.

Torkington, K., Stanford, D. and Guiver, J. (2020) Discourse(s) of growth and sustainability in national tourism policies. *Journal of Sustainable Tourism,* 28(7), 1041–1062.

Torres, R. (2003) Linkages between tourism and agriculture in Mexico. *Annals of Tourism Research,* 30(3), 546–566.

Tosun, C. (2000) Limits to community participation in the tourism development process in developing countries. *Tourism Management,* 21(6), 613–633.

Tourism Concern (2014) The Impact of All-Inclusive Hotels on Working Conditions and Labour Rights. London: Tourism Concern.

Tourism Review (2021) *Top 10 Largest Hotel Groups in the World,* 2 November. Available at: https://www.tourism-review.com/top-10-world-largest-hotel-groups -news1988 (Accessed 17 August 2022).

Towner, J. (1985) The Grand Tour: A key phase in the history of tourism. *Annals of Tourism Research,* 12(3), 297–333.

Towner, J., Barke, M. and Newton, M. (1996) *Tourism in Spain: Critical Issues.* Wallingford: CABI.

Trainer, T. (2021) What does Degrowth mean? Some comments on Jason Hickel's 'A few points of clarification.' *Globalizations,* 18(7), 1112–1116.

Trainer, T. (2022) A technical critique of the Green New Deal. *Ecological Economics,* 195. https://doi.org/10.1016/j.ecolecon.2022.107378

Transport & Environment (2019) Luxury cruise giant emits 10 times more air pollution (SOx) than all of Europe's cars – study. *Transport & Environment,* 4 June. Available at: https://www.transportenvironment.org/discover/luxury-cruise

-giant-emits-10-times-more-air-pollution-sox-all-europes-cars-study/?gclid= EAIaIQobChMIj4vG6o6A-gIVlO3tCh1xWgCHEAAYAiAAEgIUIvD_BwE

Trueman, R. (2020) *The Rise and Triumph of the Modern Self: Cultural Amnesia, Expressive Individualism and the Road to Sexual Evolution*. Wheaton, IL: Crossway.

Tuan, Y-F. (1986) *The Good Life*. Madison, WI: University of Wisconsin Press.

TUI (2020) TUI Sustainability Strategy. Available at: https://www.tuigroup.com/en -en/responsibility/sustainability/strategy# (Accessed 24 August 2022).

TUI (2022) About TUI Group. Available at: https://www.tuigroup.com/en-en/about-us/ about-tui-group (Accessed 24 August 2022).

Turner, G. (2008) A comparison of *The Limits to Growth* with 30 years of reality. *Global Environmental Change*, 18, 397–411.

Turner, L. and Ash, J. (1975) *The Golden Hordes: International Tourism and the Pleasure Periphery*. London: Constable & Robinson.

UN (n.d.) For a livable climate: Net-zero commitments must be backed by credible action. United Nations Net Zero Coalition. Available at: https://www.un.org/en/ climatechange/net-zero-coalition

UN (2015) *The Millennium Development Goals Report*. New York: United Nations. Available at: https://www.un.org/millenniumgoals/2015_MDG_Report/pdf/MDG %202015%20rev%20(July%201).pdf (Accessed 26 November 2021).

UN (2017) *World Population Prospects*. Volume II: Demographic Profiles. UN Department of Economic and Social Affairs, Population Division. New York: United Nations.

UN (2021) *Global Issues: Ending Poverty*. United Nations. Available at: https://www .un.org/en/global-issues/ending-poverty

UN (2022) Global indicator framework for the Sustainable Development Goals and targets for the 2030 Agenda for Sustainable Development. United Nations. Available at: https://unstats.un.org/sdgs/indicators/Global%20Indicator%20Framework%20after% 202022%20refinement_Eng.pdf (Accessed 19 August 2022).

UNDP (2011) *Human Development Report 2011. Sustainability and Equity: A Better Future for All*. New York: United Nations Development Programme. Available at: https://hdr.undp.org/system/files/documents/human-development-report-2011 -english.human-development-report-2011-english (Accessed 23 May 2022).

UNDP (2019) *Human Development Report 2019. Beyond Income, Beyond Averages, Beyond Today: Inequalities in Human Development in the 21st Century*. New York: United Nations Development Programme. Available at: https://hdr.undp.org/system/ files/documents/hdr2019pdf.pdf (Accessed 29 October 2021).

UNDP (2020) *Human Development Report 2020. The Next Frontier: Human Development and the Anthropocene*. New York: United Nations Development Programme. Available at: https://hdr.undp.org/system/files/documents/hdr20 20overviewenglishpdf_1.pdf (Accessed 29 October 2021).

UNDP (2020b) We have to push through this year to survive. United Nations Development Programme. Available at: https://stories.undp.org/we-have-to-push -through-this-year-to-survive (Accessed 19 August 2022).

UNDP and OPHI (2021) Global Multidimensional Poverty Index 2021: Unmasking Disparities by Ethnicity, Caste and Gender. https://hdr.undp.org/system/files/ documents//2021mpireportenpdf.pdf

UNEP (n.d.) Worldwide food waste. United Nations Environment Programme. Available at: https://www.unep.org/thinkeatsave/get-informed/worldwide-food -waste (Accessed 4 February 2022).

UNEP (2016) Microplastics: Trouble in the food chain. *UNEP Frontiers Report.* Available at: https://wesr.unep.org/media/docs/early_warning/microplastics.pdf (Accessed 15 July 2022).

UN-Water (2021) Summary Progress Update 2021: SDG 6 – Water and sanitation for all. UN-Water. Available at: https://www.unwater.org/publications/summary -progress-update-2021-sdg-6-water-and-sanitation-all

UNWTO (n.d., a) Tourism in the 2030 Agenda. UN World Tourism Organisation. Available at: https://www.unwto.org/tourism-in-2030-agenda (Accessed 4 February 2022).

UNWTO (n.d., b) *2020: A Year in Review.* Madrid: UN World Tourism Organization. Available at: https://www.unwto.org/covid-19-and-tourism-2020 (Accessed 25 March 2022).

UNWTO (2001) *Global Code of Ethics for Tourism.* UN World Tourism Organization. Available at https://webunwto.s3.eu-west-1.amazonaws.com/imported_images/37802/ gcetbrochureglobalcodeen.pdf

UNWTO (2011) *Tourism Towards 2030: Global Overview.* Madrid: UN World Tourism Organization. Available at: https://www.globalwellnesssummit.com/wp -content/uploads/Industry-Research/Global/2011_UNWTO_Tourism_Towards _2030.pdf (Accessed 18 March 2022).

UNWTO (2014) *Measuring Employment in the Tourism Industries – Guide with Best Practices.* Madrid: UN World Tourism Organization. Available at: https://www.e -unwto.org/doi/pdf/10.18111/9789284416158 (Accessed 21 April 2022).

UNWTO (2019) *International Tourism Highlights, 2019 Edition.* Madrid: UN World Tourism Organization. https://doi.org/10.18111/9789284421152

UNWTO (2020a) *Policy Brief: Covid-19 and Transforming Tourism.* Madrid: UN World Tourism Organization. Available at: https://www.unwto.org/news/un-policy -brief-on-tourism-and-covid-19 (Accessed 11 August 2022).

UNWTO (2020b) *One Planet Vision for A Responsible Recovery of The Tourism Sector.* Madrid: UN World Tourism Organization. Available at: https://webunwto .s3.eu-west-1.amazonaws.com/s3fs-public/2020-06/one-planet-vision-responsible -recovery-of-the-tourism-sector.pdf (Accessed 11 August 2022).

UNWTO (2021) *International Tourism Highlights, 2020 Edition.* Madrid: UN World Tourism Organization. https://doi.org/10.18111/9789284422456

UNWTO (2022) *About Us.* Madrid: UNWTO. Available at: https://www.unwto.org/ about-us (Accessed 19 August 2022)

UNWTO/UNEP (2008) *Climate Change and Tourism: Responding to Global Challenges.* Madrid / Milan: World Tourism Organization / United Nations Environment Programme.

Urry, J. (1990) *The Tourist Gaze.* London: Sage Publications.

Urry, J. (1994) Cultural change and contemporary tourism. *Leisure Studies*, 13(4), 233–238.

US Census (2020) Income and Poverty in the United States: 2020. Available at: https://www.census.gov/library/publications/2021/demo/p60-273.html (Accessed 4 February 2022).

Ussi, M. and Sharpley, R. (2012) Tourism and governance in Small Island Developing States (SIDS): The case of Zanzibar. *International Journal of Tourism Research*, 16(1), 87–96.

Uysal, M. and Sirgy, J. (2019) Quality-of-life indicators as performance measures. *Annals of Tourism Research*, 76(2019), 291–300.

Valdivielso, J. and Moranta, J. (2019). The social construction of the tourism degrowth discourse in the Balearic Islands. *Journal of Sustainable Tourism*, 27(12), 1876–1892.

Vandeventer, J. and Lloveras, J. (2020) Organising degrowth: The ontological politics of enacting degrowth in OMS. *Organization*, 28(3), 358–379.

Videira, N., Schneider, F., Sekulova, F. and Kallis, G. (2014) Improving understanding on degrowth pathways: An exploratory study using collaborative casuals models. *Futures*, 55, 58–77.

Virilio, P. (2009) *Le futurisme de L'instant: Stop-eject*. Paris: Galilée.

VNA (2022) Thailand unveils strategy for sustainable tourism development. *Vietnam New Agency*, 31 August. Available at: https://en.vietnamplus.vn/thailand-unveils-strategy-for-sustainable-tourism-development/230919.vnp (Accessed 23 August 2022).

Voase, R. (1995) *Tourism: The Human Perspective*. London: Hodder & Stoughton.

Volcovici, V., Evans, D. and James, W. (2022) COP27 delivers climate fund break-through at cost of progress on emissions. *Reuters*, 21 November, Available at: https://www.reuters.com/business/cop/countries-agree-loss-damage-fund-final-cop27-deal-elusive-2022–11–20/ (Accessed 28 November).

Volger, R. (2022) Revenge and catch-up travel or degrowth? Debating tourism and post COVID-19. *Annals of Tourism Research*, 93. https://doi.org/10.1016/j.annals.2021.103272

Wall, G. and Mathieson, A. (2006) *Tourism: Change, Impacts and Opportunities*. Harlow: Pearson Prentice Hall.

Wall-Reinius, S., Ioannides, D. and Zampoukos, K. (2019) Does geography matter in all-inclusive resort tourism? Marketing approaches of Scandinavian tour operators. *Tourism Geographies*, 21(5), 766–784.

Water Footprint Network (n.d.) Water footprint of crop and animal products: A comparison. Available at: https://waterfootprint.org/en/water-footprint/product-water-footprint/water-footprint-crop-and-animal-products/

WCED (1987) *Our Common Future*. Oxford: Oxford University Press.

Wearing, S. and McGehee, N. (2013) Volunteer tourism: A review. *Tourism Management*, 38, 120–130.

Weaver, D., Moyle, B., Casali, L. and McLennan, C. (2022) Pragmatic engagement with the wicked tourism problem of climate change through 'soft' transformative governance. *Tourism Management*, 93(2022). https://doi.org/10.1016/j.tourman.2022.104573

Weedon, C. (2013) *Responsible Tourist Behaviour*. Abingdon: Routledge.

Wegerer, P. and Nadegger, M. (2020) It's time to act! Understanding online resistance against tourism development. *Journal of Sustainable Tourism*. https://doi.org/10.1080/09669582.2020.1853761

Weichel, A. (2022) 'This is an emergency': David Suzuki addresses profanity-laden climate rant. *CTV News Vancouver*, 17 October. Available at: https://bc.ctvnews.ca/this-is-an-emergency-david-suzuki-addresses-profanity-laden-climate-rant-1.6113446 (Accessed 15 November 2022).

Wheeller, B. (1992) Eco or ego tourism: New wave tourism. *ETB Insights Vol III*. London: English Tourist Board, D41–44.

Wheeller, B. (1993) Sustaining the ego. *Journal of Sustainable Tourism*, 1(2), 121–129.

WHO (2022) Obesity and overweight. World Health Organisation. Available at: https://www.who.int/news-room/fact-sheets/detail/obesity-and-overweight Accessed 4 February 2022 (Accessed 4 February 2022).

222 Rethinking tourism and development

Wilkinson, F. (2019) Traffic jams are just one of the problems facing climbers on Everest. *National Geographic*, 29 May. Available at: https://www.nationalgeographic.com/adventure/article/everest-season-deaths-controversy-crowding-perpetual-planet (Accessed 24 August 2022).

Wilkinson, P. (2017) Cruise ship tourism in the Caribbean: The mess of mass tourism. In D. Harrison and R. Sharpley (Eds), *Mass Tourism in a Small World*. Wallingford: CABI, pp. 210–231.

Wilkinson, R. and Pickett, K. (2010) *The Spirit Level: Why Equality is Better for Everyone*. London: Penguin Books.

Williams, P. and Ponsford, I. (2009) Confronting tourism's environmental paradox: Transitioning for Sustainable Tourism. *Futures: The Journal of Policy, Planning and Future Studies*, 41(6), 396–404.

Wong-Parodi, G., Fischhoff, B. and Strauss, B. (2015) Resilience vs. Adaptation: Framing and action. *Climate Risk Management*, 10, 1–7.

Wood, J. (2019) Europe bucks global deforestation trend. *World Economic Forum*, 25 July. Available at: https://www.weforum.org/agenda/2019/07/forest-europe-environment/

Wood, K. and House, S. (1991) *The Good Tourist: A Worldwide Guide for the Green Traveller*. London: Mandarin.

Wood, R. (2004) Global currents: Cruise ships in the Caribbean. In D. Duval (Ed.), *Tourism in the Caribbean: Trends, Development, Prospects*. London: Routledge, pp. 152–171.

World Bank (2017) World Development Report 2017: Governance and the Law. Washington: World Bank. doi:10.1596/978-1-4648-0950-7

World Bank (2021) *Measuring Poverty*. Available at: https://www.worldbank.org/en/topic/measuringpoverty#1 (Accessed 4 February 2022).

World Bank (2022) World Bank Country and Lending Groups. https://datahelpdesk.worldbank.org/knowledgebase/articles/906519-world-bank-country-and-lending-groups

World Data Atlas (2018) *Contribution of Travel and Tourism to Total GDP*. Available at: https://knoema.com/atlas/topics/Tourism/Travel-and-Tourism-Total-Contribution-to-GDP/Contribution-of-travel-and-tourism-to-GDP-percent-of-GDP (Accessed 30 December 2018).

World Economic Forum (2022) *Travel & Tourism Development Index 2021: Rebuilding for a Sustainable and Resilient Future*, 24 May. Available at: https://www.weforum.org/reports/travel-and-tourism-development-index-2021/in-full/about-the-travel-tourism-development-index (Accessed 30 August 2022).

Wright, K., Kelman, I. and Dodds, R. (2021) Tourism development from disaster capitalism. *Annals of Tourism Research*, 89(2021). doi.org/10.1016/j.annals.2020.103070

WTO (1980) *Manila Declaration on World Tourism*. Madrid: World Tourism Organization.

WTTC (2020) *Travel & Tourism: Global Economic Impact & Trends 2020*. World Travel & Tourism Council. Available at: https://wttc.org/Portals/0/Documents/Reports/2020/Global%20Economic%20Impact%20Trends%202020.pdf?ver=2021-02-25-183118-360 (Accessed 16 March 2022).

WTTC (2021a) *Economic Impact Reports*. World Travel and Tourism Council. Available at: https://wttc.org/Research/Economic-Impact (Accessed 11 February 2022).

WTTC (2021b) *A Net Zero Roadmap for Travel & Tourism*. World Travel & Tourism Council. Available at: https://wttc.org/Portals/0/Documents/Reports/2021/WTTC _Net_Zero_Roadmap.pdf (Accessed 9 June 2022).

WTTC (2022) About Us. https://wttc.org/About/About-Us

WTTC and Wyman, O. (2020) *To Recovery and Beyond: The Future of Travel and Tourism in the Wake of COVID-19*. World Travel & Tourism Council. Available at: https://wttc.org/Portals/0/Documents/Reports/2020/To%20Recovery %20and%20Beyond-The%20Future%20of%20Travel%20Tourism%20in%20the% 20Wake%20of%20COVID-19.pdf?ver=2021–02–25–183120–543 (Accessed 30 August 2022).

WWF (2020a) *Living Planet Report 2020: Bending the Curve of Biodiversity Loss – Summary*. Gland, Switzerland: World Wide Fund for Nature.

WWF (2020b) Deforestation fronts. *World Wide Fund for Nature*. Available at: https:// wwf.panda.org/discover/our_focus/forests_practice/deforestation_fronts_/

Xu, F. and Buhalis, D. (2021) *Gamification for Tourism*. Bristol: Channel View Publications.

Xu, X. (2022) Village in the French Alps demolishes its ski lift because there's no snow left. *CNN Travel*, 21 November. Available at https://www.cnn.com/travel/article/ french-ski-resort-dismantled-ski-lift-scn/index.html (Accessed 24 November 2022).

Young, G. (1977) *Tourism: Blessing or Blight?* Harmondsworth: Penguin.

Yukon (2022) Find out about the Yukon Sustainable Tourism Framework. Available at: https://yukon.ca/en/sustainabletourism (Accessed 25 August 2022).

Yrigoy, I. (2021) Strengthening the political economy of tourism: profits, rents and finance. *Tourism Geographies*. (Ahead of print). https://doi.org/10.1080/14616688 .2021.1894227

Yunus, M. (2017) *A World of Three Zeros: The New Economics of Zero Poverty, Zero Unemployment and Zero Net Carbon Emissions*. New York: Public Affairs.

Zandt, F. (2021) The road to net zero. *Statista*, 17 November. Available at: https://www .statista.com/chart/26053/countries-with-laws-policy-documents-or-timed-pledges -for-carbon-neutrality/ (Accessed 13 September 2022).

Zascerinska, S., Sharpley, R. and Wright, D. (2022) Living life or denying death? Towards an understanding of the bucket list. *Tourism Recreation Research*. https:// doi.org/10.1080/02508281.2021.2015673

Ziai, A. (Ed.) (2007) *Exploring Post-development: Theory and Practice, Problems and Perspectives*. Abingdon: Routledge.

Zuelow, E. (2015) *A History of Modern Tourism*. London: Palgrave Macmillan.

Index

'Richard Sharpley and David Telfer have done it again! Building on their previous work, the theoretical potency and empirical strength of this book provides a deep foundation for rethinking development in all its forms. The excellent work herein is the most erudite and comprehensive treatise on tourism and development ever written.'
Dallen J. Timothy, Arizona State University, USA

'This excellent, thought-provoking book calls us to rethink the complex and often paradoxical relationships between tourism and development. Based on their extensive analysis, Sharpley and Telfer invite us to consider a path for tourism to a post-growth world. This is a timely and important book - essential reading for all those thinking about the future of tourism.'
Jarkko Saarinen, University of Oulu, Finland, and Uppsala University, Sweden

'There has never been a more critical moment to rethink tourism and its relationship to development. Sharpley and Telfer's book highlights key concerns, and most importantly, helps to steer us in the direction of a more equitable, inclusive, sustainable and just tourism system.'
Regina Scheyvens, Massey University, New Zealand

'Rethinking Tourism and Development provides a timely and thought-provoking contribution which contests current practices in large parts of the global tourism industry. By reviewing previous paradigms of development and today's consumerism, as well as the global environmental crisis, they uncover a toxic mixture in which tourism plays an important part. Hence, they call for a radical rethinking of growth-oriented pathways in tourism development and suggest degrowth as a remedy. Though not all will embrace such a prescription, the book makes students and scholars of tourism aware that business-as-usual is not an option and indeed a rather perilous way to go. Thus, this is an imperative read for those interested in sustaining tourism and destinations.'
Dieter K. Müller, Umeå University, Sweden